W9-AYY-830

SHADOW
WAR

THE UNTOLD STORY OF HOW BUSH
IS WINNING THE WAR ON TERROR

SHADOW
WAR

RICHARD MINITER

Since 1947
REGNERY
PUBLISHING, INC.
An Eagle Publishing Company • Washington, DC

Copyright © 2004 by Richard Miniter

All rights reserved. No part of this publication may be reproduced or transmitted in any form or by any means electronic or mechanical, including photocopy, recording, or any information storage and retrieval system now known or to be invented, without permission in writing from the publisher, except by a reviewer who wishes to quote brief passages in connection with a review written for inclusion in a magazine, newspaper, or broadcast.

Library of Congress Cataloging-in-Publication Data

Miniter, Richard.

Shadow war: the untold story of how Bush is winning the war on terror / Richard Miniter.
p. cm.
Includes bibliographical references and index.

ISBN 0-89526-052-2 (acid-free paper)

1. War on Terrorism, 2001– 2. Terrorism—Government policy—United States.
3. Intelligence service—United States. 4. Qaida (Organization) 5. Bin Laden, Osama, 1957– I. Title.
HV6432.M546 2004
973.931—dc22

                                                                    2004019763

Published in the United States by
Regnery Publishing, Inc.
An Eagle Publishing Company
One Massachusetts Avenue, NW
Washington, DC 20001

Visit us at www.regnery.com

Distributed to the trade by
National Book Network
4720-A Boston Way
Lanham, MD 20706

Printed on acid-free paper
Manufactured in the United States of America
10 9 8 7 6 5 4 3 2 1

Books are available in quantity for promotional or premium use. Write to Director of Special Sales, Regnery Publishing, Inc., One Massachusetts Avenue, NW, Washington, DC 20001, for information on discounts and terms, or call (202) 216-0600.

To the soldiers, sailors, airmen, Marines, special operatives, intelligence agents, and all others in harm's way in the great global fight against terrorism: May the world understand your sacrifice, even if it never learns your names.

CONTENTS

PROLOGUE

"Why should fear, killing, destruction, displacement, orphaning, and widowing continue to be our lot, while security, stability, and happiness be your lot?"

> —OSAMA BIN LADEN, ON AN AUDIOTAPE RELEASED
> NOVEMBER 12, 2002

"Our response involves far more than instant retaliation and isolated strikes. Americans should not expect one battle, but a lengthy campaign, unlike any other we have ever seen. It may include dramatic strikes, visible on TV, and covert operations, secret even in success."

> —PRESIDENT GEORGE W. BUSH, ADDRESS TO A JOINT SESSION
> OF CONGRESS AND THE AMERICAN PEOPLE, SEPTEMBER 20,
> 2001

THE THREE VITAL, UNANSWERED QUESTIONS of the War on Terror are: Where is Osama bin Laden? Why hasn't there been another terrorist strike inside the U.S. since September 11, 2001? Is President Bush winning the war?

This book is about answering those three questions. It unfolds during the first 911 days of President Bush's War on Terror, from the September 11, 2001, attacks on New York and Washington, D.C., to the March 11, 2004, bomb blasts in Madrid, Spain. It is a story of sleeper cells and patient plots, phone intercepts and covert operations, boldly triumphant captures and heartbreakingly close escapes. It illustrates the manifold difficulties of intelligence collection—the race against time, the false leads, the pieces of the puzzle that don't fit—and shows that intelligence failures can be turned into operational successes. It is a story of daring conspiracies to kill hundreds and desperate efforts to safeguard millions. It is a largely untold tale of a secret war that sprawls over four continents. On its outcome turns the future of the free world.

Where is bin Laden?

He is not buried on some Afghan battlefield. There is no evidence (no body, no intercepted call, no reliable eyewitness) that bin Laden is dead.

Indeed, there is a wealth of evidence that bin Laden is healthy and in command. Tactical intelligence teams picked up his voice giving battle orders in the rocky redoubts of Tora Bora, Afghanistan, in 2001. To hear the voice that ordered the deaths of three thousand innocents must have been an eerie experience. Until 2002, the National Security Agency was often able to listen in on the calls bin Laden made on his Thuraya satellite phone. This was one of the greatest intelligence coups of the war—and one of its best-kept secrets until an overseas intelligence service let it slip. And, until 2003, Western intelligence services heard bin Laden's key officers repeat his orders and discuss the terror master in the present tense. In addition, captured al Qaeda members, including bin Laden's personal doctor, insist that "the emir" is still alive.

Even the Internet provides evidence that bin Laden is alive. "If he were dead, the Islamist terror groups that work with him would be mourning," said Rohan Gunaratna, an expert on al Qaeda who often consults with intelligence services. But they are not. Instead, the al Qaeda websites that Gunaratna monitors "have been transmitting messages with the high style of Arabic [that is] characteristic of bin Laden."[1]

Perhaps the strongest evidence that bin Laden is vigorous enough to command is that al Qaeda functions as a global entity, meticulously assembling terror strikes. The group is organized along ethnic lines and is riven with factions. From al Qaeda members in custody we know that the Yemenis resent the Egyptians, who are paid more; the Saudis have ideological disputes with the Egyptians and Syrians; nearly everyone looks down on the Sudanese; and so on. It takes a lot of effort to hold this far-flung organization together, let alone keep its many misfits motivated and focused. Without the force of bin Laden's personality and the aura of invincibility that he radiates, al Qaeda would fly apart. Since al Qaeda seems to function as one entity, we can conclude that bin Laden is still alive and is still in charge.

But *where* is he?

A number of senior administration officials I interviewed, on condition of anonymity, have each agreed that they believe bin Laden is most likely in Pakistan.[2] Most of the press seems to agree.

Yet I have discovered sources who offer a dramatically different account—one that, if correct, has enormous implications for national security.

According to two Iranian intelligence operatives who told me they saw bin Laden in October 2003, bin Laden is constantly on the move, shuttling from Iranian safe houses controlled by the Iranian Revolutionary Guard to areas of Afghanistan controlled by the Iranian-backed warlord Gulbuddin Hekmatyar. In 2002, these Iranian operatives briefed key administration officials, who find the accounts "credible." Indeed, I have seen documents demonstrating that my Iranian sources "have already saved American lives." (See Chapter One: Bin Laden's Secret Refuge, for more information.)

The Iranian government, which denies that bin Laden is in the country, has publicly acknowledged that more than five hundred "low-level" al Qaeda operatives are there. Iran has rejected all attempts to extradite or even allow the U.S. or its allies to interview these allegedly "low-level" figures. That's because at least some of these al Qaeda members are not foot soldiers, but leaders.

Meanwhile, the hunt for bin Laden continues along the Afghanistan border. An elite unit composed of Delta Force, SEAL commandos, and CIA paramilitary troops, known as "Task Force 121," believes it is closing in.[3] We can only hope they are on the right track.

Why hasn't there been another terror strike on the American homeland?

Since September 11, 2001, al Qaeda has made many attempts to kill large numbers of Americans. So far, these attempts have failed—because they have been thwarted. "Somewhere in the world, we defeat something like a plot a day," one American intelligence source told me.[4]

These arrested attacks do not make the evening news—they are, as President Bush said, "secret even in success."[5] Some of these thwarted plots are revealed here for the first time.

Worldwide, al Qaeda has killed close to one thousand civilians since September 11, 2001—but the death toll could have been far higher. Bin Laden originally considered a larger version of the September 11 attacks, which included five targets on the East Coast and five on the West Coast. That plan was eventually vetoed because, as the September 11 mastermind Khalid Shaikh Mohammed told his American interrogators, "it would be too difficult to synchronize."[6]

Instead, al Qaeda envisioned a "second wave" of attacks on West Coast cities after September 11.[7] The targets included the Library Tower in Los Angeles (chosen partly because Mohammed had seen it "blown up" in the hit film *Independence Day*)[8] and the Sears Tower in Chicago. Zacarias Moussaoui, known to the media as the "twentieth hijacker," was most likely training for the second wave of attacks.[9]

These plots were stopped. How? "Afterwards, we never got time to catch our breath, we were immediately on the run," Mohammed explained. "Before September 11, we could dispatch operatives with the expectation of follow-up contact, but after October 7 [2001, when the U.S. and its allies began a massive bombardment of al Qaeda strongholds in Afghanistan], that changed 180 degrees. There was no longer a war room...."[10]

In sum, aggressive execution of the War on Terror—everything from aerial bombardment and covert operations to relentless counter-intelligence and patient police work—has kept the terrorists at bay. And, yes, luck played a part.

The attempted terror attacks on the American mainland are not limited to flying bombs, and not all terror leads are what they seem. Sudan helped unravel a feared plot to assassinate President Bush after September 11, 2001, according to Sudanese intelligence officials I interviewed. This plot has not been previously reported and appears, for the first time, in this book. (See Chapter Three: The 2002 Plot to Kill Bush.)

Other thwarted attacks include an assault on U.S. warships off the coast of Spain, an attempt to bomb the U.S. embassy in Paris, and another plot to explode a truck bomb at the U.S. embassy in Mali.

Outside the United States, al Qaeda has made some "successful" attacks—but American and allied intelligence efforts have made these "victories" Pyrrhic. After each attack, cell members have been killed or captured and forced to reveal the whereabouts of their confederates. So al Qaeda, at the margin, gets weaker with each attack.

Like bees, they can sting only once before they are dead. And, like bees, many are swatted before they sting. Our intelligence services and those of our allies have become surprisingly effective at the street level.

Consider each al Qaeda bombing since September 11:

■ In Djerba, a small city on an island off the coast of Tunisia, al Qaeda detonated a gasoline truck near a historic synagogue, killing twenty-one people, including fourteen German tourists, on April 11, 2002.[11] Tunisian security forces, working with French and American intelligence, rounded up the entire surviving cell.

- On October 12, 2002, the second anniversary of the bombing of the USS *Cole*, al Qaeda operatives and their local allies, Jemaah Islamiya, bombed two packed nightclubs in Bali, Indonesia. Two hundred and two people perished, mostly Australians.[12] The resulting investigation helped identify and eliminate al Qaeda cells in the United Kingdom, Italy, Spain, Germany, Yemen, the Netherlands, and the Philippines.[13]

- On May 12, 2003, following a jail break in Yemen, nineteen al Qaeda members staged a four-car bombing of a gated apartment complex in the Saudi Arabian capital, Riyadh. Thirty died, among them eight Americans. Another sixty lay wounded. A Saudi investigation led to the arrests and executions of more than a dozen al Qaeda members.

- Four days later, on May 16, five massive bombs exploded simultaneously in Casablanca, Morocco's run-down industrial capital. Another forty people perished, mainly Muslims. Again, more terror cells were "rolled up."

- On November 15, 2003, two synagogues in Istanbul, Turkey, were bombed. On November 20, 2003, the British consulate and the London-based HSBC bank in Istanbul were bombed, killing sixty-two people (counting four terrorists linked to al Qaeda.) This was the first time since September 11 that al Qaeda had been able to strike twice in the same country in quick succession. But the after-action pattern remained the same: Dozens of al Qaeda members were captured and two cells smashed.

- And then Europe was shocked on the morning of March 11, 2004. Four packed commuter trains in Madrid, Spain's picturesque capital, were simultaneously bombed, ultimately killing 202 people and wounding some 1,500. Within days, Spanish police began making arrests and uncovered a massive network. The cell leader of the Madrid bombings, Sarhane Ben Adbelmajid Fahket, met in Turkey with Amer Azizi, an al Qaeda commander who had recruited the head of al Qaeda's Spanish network and was tied to the September 11 attacks.[14] While Azizi is still at large, the Madrid ringleader is dead; he, along with six of his co-conspirators, blew themselves up on April 2 to avoid capture. Another seventeen suspects are behind bars, awaiting trial. As of August 2004, all but two members of his cell are either dead or incarcerated.[15]

In the 911 days from September 11, 2001, to March 11, 2004, dozens of al Qaeda plots have been foiled and each of its seven major attacks have cost it entire cells and key commanders. In addition, counter-terrorism operations have killed or captured more than two-thirds of the pre–September 11 al Qaeda leadership.

The terrorists will keep trying to mount attacks on America and its allies—but ongoing counter-intelligence operations will make "success" both difficult and costly.

It is harder to sneak up on a nation at war than on one at peace. Cofer Black, the head of CIA counter-terrorism operations on September 11, put it succinctly: "After September 11, the gloves came off."

The days of the velvet glove are indeed long gone, much to the surprise of some foreign leaders. In a series of private meetings at the White House, President Bush made it clear that he was fighting to win. Abdullah Saleh, the president of Yemen, a small, arid republic on the southwestern edge of the Arabian peninsula, met with Bush in the White House in December 2002. Almost a year and a half had passed since the September 11 attacks. Saleh hoped that Bush had softened. The Yemeni president tried to make him understand that Yemen could not risk being too helpful in the War on Terror and that invading Iraq would be a mistake. Investigative journalist Murray Weiss reported what happened next.[16] Citing an

Arab proverb, Saleh said, "If he were to put a cat in a cage, it could likely turn into a fierce lion."

Bush's response was stinging. "The cat has rabies and the only way to cure the cat is to cut off its head."

Saleh got the message. Yemen lifted its objections and allowed a Predator, a small, pilotless plane weighing fewer than nine hundred pounds, to roam its skies hunting for al Qaeda. Within a few months, the Predator focused in on a carload of terrorists speeding down a concrete highway. The Predator fired its missile. The vehicle exploded.

In the burning wreckage, investigators found the DNA of one of the al Qaeda leaders responsible for the attack on the USS *Cole*, which killed seventeen sailors, injured another forty-four, and, for the first time since World War II, almost cost the U.S. Navy a warship. We may never know what murderous plans were defeated by putting these terrorists on the road to a dusty death, but we can be grateful that their plans were not made manifest.

Meanwhile, U.S. Special Forces have trained a number of elite counter-terrorism troops in Yemen. They have engaged al Qaeda terrorists in firefights across northern Yemen, killing and wounding more than a dozen. It is one small front in a larger global war. The sum of these many small actions is not small.

Is President Bush winning the War on Terror?

From the September 11, 2001, attacks in New York and Washington, D.C., to the March 11, 2004, bomb blasts in Madrid, Spain, al Qaeda has been far more active than most readers realize—and so have the United States and its allies.

There have been many clandestine victories against al Qaeda. More than 3,000 al Qaeda operatives have been seized or slain in 102 countries since September 11, 2001.[17]

Even as firefighters dug out the living and the dead on September 11, President Bush ordered CIA paramilitary teams off to the wastes of Afghanistan. (The British special forces arrived six days later, due to defective helicopters.) Some began forging ties with the Northern Alliance, the main opposition to the Taliban, and with other warlords. Others began to interrogate the many al Qaeda prisoners the Alliance had been holding for years in its high-altitude camps. Soon valuable real-time intelligence began to flow back to Washington over secure frequency-hopping phones.

These clandestine efforts became the basis for planning the immense airstrikes of October 7, 2001. Within a month, U.S. and allied forces had swept the Taliban from the Afghan capital, Kabul, and had driven them from their stronghold, the city of Kandahar.

In November, a Predator drone found its prey in front of a small rough-stone house south of Kabul: Mohammed Atef, the head of al Qaeda's military wing. Atef had approved the September 11 strikes on America. Thousands of miles away, at the CIA head-quarters in Langley, Virginia, an analyst looked at the live black-and-white video feed from the Predator.

The Predator fired a "Hellfire" missile. Atef was killed in the fireball. He was the first major al Qaeda leader to die—and he wouldn't be the last.

"Some two-thirds of al Qaeda's key leaders have been captured or killed," President Bush said in March 2004. "The rest of them hear us breathing down their necks...."[18]

A note on sources and methods

Time

This book begins on September 11, 2001,[19] and ends on March 11, 2004.[20] We are now in the midst of the drama; we do not yet know which bit players will emerge as major characters. Did the pilotless Predator plane that killed Mohammed Atef in November 2001 change the course of the war? Was the capture of Atef's replacement, Khalid Shaikh Mohammed, a turning point to victory? We can only guess. We can't yet trace the chain of causes and effects to the end. As Laertes counseled his son Odysseus, it is how a thing ends that transforms our view of its life. Readers should note that the datelines beginning each section are there to set the scene; they are not meant to imply that I was present at each instance.

Terrain

Although the war ranges over seventy countries, my on-the-ground reporting is limited to less than a dozen. So reviewers are free to point out that I missed a key development in China's western Xinjiang province, essential intelligence from Uzbekistan, or even Canada's valuable arrests of al Qaeda suspects. Books are like suitcases; one can stuff only so much in.

I selected my sites carefully. In each, I am able to report major new developments—which have been mostly missed by the major media—based on solid sources, including intelligence chiefs, defense ministers, ambassadors, and eyewitnesses.

I traveled to Baghdad, Bangkok, Singapore, Manila, Hong Kong, Khartoum, Cairo, Paris, London, Frankfurt, Hamburg, New York, and Washington, D.C.

I also reviewed tens of thousands of pages of court documents and government reports, studied the growing academic literature (including papers from the U.S. Army War College and the Naval War College), reports from think tanks and research organizations (including the indispensable American Enterprise Institute and the Center for Strategic and International Studies in Washington, D.C.), and examined many unpublished private papers written by CIA officials and military officers.

Access to Sources

I have interviewed and re-interviewed dozens of participants and experts, including working and retired members of the intelligence services of the United States, Western Europe, East Africa, the Middle East, and Southeast Asia, many of whom were helpful in providing documents, recollections, and insights. Much of what they told me has never been reported and I am grateful for their time and trust.

In order to maintain a coherent, readable narrative, I have overlooked or passed lightly over a variety of contentious topics only tangentially related to America's shadow war, including the wars in Afghanistan and Iraq; the presence or absence of weapons of mass destruction in Iraq; President Bush's personal military record; the treatment of enemy combatants in America's base in Guantanamo Bay, Cuba, or Abu Ghraib prison, Iraq; the president's alleged links to the bin Laden clan;[21] the detention of aliens inside the United States and Western Europe; the USA Patriot Act; Bush's "unilateralism" of seventy countries versus his critics' "multilateralism" of France, Germany, Belgium, and the United Nation's Secretariat; and so on. Instead of the usual well-worn stories, the reader will find many fresh accounts of heretofore unreported covert operations and intelligence coups. I believe it is a fair trade.

This book is the result of lengthy investigation and many trips both to the front lines and into the halls of government. I've tried to be as thorough and accurate as possible, but necessarily there will be omissions, perhaps even essential ones. This is unavoidable for three reasons: Much of the information here is presented to the public for the first time and was designed to be kept secret; an investigation of this type is limited by the number of sources that will talk and the perspectives of those sources; and finally, neither the Bush administration nor the press has provided a framework to build on. Imagine putting together a puzzle without a picture of the finished work.

The reader will find that there are many unnamed sources in this book. This is unavoidable when interviewing intelligence sources, military officers, and government officials. I have granted anonymity to sources only when it was an absolute requirement. Most authors, working with similar sources, have made the same hard bargains.

When I have relied on translations that may be subject to multiple interpretations, I have given the reader the source of those translations. In cases where I have received foreign language documents from foreign governments, I have indicated which governments supplied them and I have had the documents independently translated.

Many of the details and descriptions are based on things I have seen or that have been described to me by reliable eyewitnesses. Others were culled from court records, government reports, and similar authoritative documents. Still others were carefully assembled from reams of congressional reports, news accounts, and other sources.[22]

The full story of President Bush's War on Terror has not yet been told. As far as I know, no author has attempted to authoritatively answer the war's three vital questions: Where is Osama bin Laden? Why hasn't there been another strike inside the United States? Is President Bush winning the war? No one has written anything like the book you hold in your hands—this is the first fresh account of how America and its allies are faring in the War on Terror.

CHAPTER ONE

BIN LADEN'S SECRET REFUGE

"I would like to assure the Muslims that Sheikh Osama bin Laden is in good health and all the rumors about Sheikh Osama's illness and being wounded in Tora Bora are devoid of any truth."

—SULEIMAN ABU GHAITH, SPOKESMAN FOR AL QAEDA[1]

TORA BORA, AFGHANISTAN—On December 10, 2001, a U.S. Special Forces team picked up the signal somewhere in the teeth of the rocky hills ringing Tora Bora.[2] It was weak, but clear enough. Osama bin Laden's voice, harsh and urgent, giving battle orders.

It was a low-power signal. He was seemingly close. Somewhere in the crags above or the ravines below.

Bin Laden was last seen by a villager in the hamlet of Gardez south of Tora Bora,[3] directing a row of pickups packed with armed men driving into the dry hills.[4]

Now he was just a disembodied voice. Then he was gone. It would be the closest U.S. forces would get to bin Laden in 2001.

There is no evidence that American or allied troops (including the motley crew of the Northern Alliance) "let bin Laden get away." The mountainous environment—especially in the winter when blanketed in deep snow and buffeted by strong winds that can ground helicopters—made encircling al Qaeda's forces at Tora Bora impossible. Where bin Laden would hide in the next few years would be a matter of intense debate in intelligence circles. My exclusive intelligence sources offered a surprising account of bin Laden's secret refuge.

WASHINGTON, D.C.—How did he get away? A few weeks after bin Laden disappeared, Deputy Secretary of Defense Paul Wolfowitz showed me and several others a map of Afghanistan superimposed over a map of the continental United States. On this giant five-by-three-foot map, Afghanistan stretched from Washington, D.C., to New Orleans and from Cincinnati to Atlanta. The implications were clear: Afghanistan is far bigger than most Americans realize and there remain many places for terrorists to hide. The land is a smuggler's paradise of deep ravines, caves, crevices, dry plains prone to visibility-destroying dust storms, and snow-capped peaks soaring high above the limits of American helicopters. Rough terrain is only part of the story. The inhabitants, hardened by more than three decades of revolution, civil war, and dictatorship, do not easily trust outsiders, especially ones with automatic weapons. They know that terrorists and other wanted men tend to retaliate against talkative farmers. U.S. Special Forces and regular troops have been digging wells and inoculating children in the hopes of winning "hearts and minds." So far, it has worked, with small gains of tactical intelligence. But anything short of garrisoning every village—an impossible feat—is unlikely to give these Afghans a sense of security strong enough to allow them to speak freely about al Qaeda's movements.

Where bin Laden went after leaving Tora Bora depends on which set of sources one believes. Each has individually been found credible by some American and British intelligence and military officials. Collectively, all cannot be correct. One set of sources says that bin Laden has forged a rough alliance with Iran and may have hidden there at times during 2002 and 2003. Another set of sources says he moves between Pakistan's wild tribal regions and Afghanistan's lawless border towns.

Like those of Elvis, false sightings of bin Laden abound. In my travels and conversations with government officials in Southeast Asia and sub-Saharan Africa, I have heard my share of bogus "scoops," supposed eyewitness accounts of spotting bin Laden in one place or another. A senior Sudanese intelligence official told me that both he and the CIA station chief in Khartoum have received a number of "eyewitness reports." One informant said that he saw bin Laden in western Sudan in the province of West Darfur, hard on the border with Chad. Another said bin Laden was in Juba, a war-torn city in the predominantly Christian south of Sudan.[5] Both of these Sudanese tipsters wanted money. Each report was investigated and found to be false. "In my eight years working in Sudan," said David Hoile, a British subject who is a consultant to the government of Sudan and to Western companies with investments in the area, "I have learned not to get too excited by initial reports."

Sometimes foreign officials themselves are duped by their sources. In March 2004, I went to a walled compound at Number Five V. Luna Road in Quezon City, the Philippines, to see the new national security advisor, Norberto B. Gonzalez. At his black-topped conference table with a commanding view of the city, with my tape recorder running, Gonzalez revealed that just the night before he had received "a very credible report" that bin Laden was in Mindanao, a majority Muslim region in the southern Philippines.[6]

"The report is pretty credible, that's why I am going to look into it," Gonzalez told me. "It's beyond my imagination, yeah, to think of bin Laden in the Philippines. Of course, there are ways, there are ways. But the implication for me is that, wow, if bin Laden thinks he can be safe in the Philippines, then it's really a reflection of how bad we are, with the net that we have here. It's a big insult."[7]

Were there any specifics?

"Just that. It's a teaser," he said.

Gonzalez did not want to appear too intrigued. "I don't want to be interested because it will cost me money. I'll wait," he told me. "I'll call you if I have something." Of course, he never called—and the story never panned out.

A senior official in a Philippine intelligence service laughed when I told him about Gonzalez's report of bin Laden in the Philippines. He suspected that a political rival was trying to embarrass Gonzalez, who was new to the job and to the intelligence field. Like the police and the press, spy masters should learn that sources have many hidden motives.

Accounts that bin Laden may have fled by sea, say via the Pakistani port of Karachi, to his ancestral homeland of Yemen or to Somalia also seem baseless. An Afghan intelligence official who works closely with the American team hunting for bin Laden bluntly dismissed the idea, saying, "We have no evidence to support that." A senior Bush administration official agreed.

So false sightings abound and sources often have ulterior motives. The reader would be wise to be wary. Virtually all of the accounts of bin Laden are cases of mistaken identity or fraud motivated by attention seekers, money grubbers, or anti-government zealots.

Bin Laden is cautious and disciplined. He has learned not to use his Thuraya satellite phone, to avoid even "trusted reporters" at al Jazeera, and to conceal his movements from America's satellites and Predator aircraft—all mistakes that led to the death or capture of his top operatives. He is unlikely to be caught in a café in Rawalpindi sipping his chai tea.

Yet he may be ultimately captured in Pakistan. "I'd bet on Pakistan," a senior Bush administration official told me in June 2004.

Citing Afghan premier Hamid Karzai, he added, "I wouldn't be surprised if we corner him in a villa in Quetta."[8]

Deputy Secretary of Defense Paul Wolfowitz also believes bin Laden is in Pakistan. "He is almost surely not in Afghanistan. He's probably in Pakistan."[9]

With a spirit of wary skepticism, let us now turn to a startling account about bin Laden's recent movements. While it cannot be completely confirmed—and indeed by its nature cannot be until bin Laden loses either his freedom or his life—I believe my sources are sincere and credible, as do those who have debriefed them. This is the best information available, yet, like so much intelligence matter, it might well prove to be wrong. The reader must be his own intelligence agent and sift and choose.

The Iran alliance

Here is an exclusive account based on the testimony of two Iranian intelligence officials. If true, this is the first recent eyewitness account of bin Laden ever reported. One official agreed to put his name on the record. The other has already been credited with saving American lives, according to Defense Department documents provided to the U.S. Senate.

If true, these accounts reveal a frightening new alliance between bin Laden and Iran, the largest state sponsor of terrorist organizations in the world.

BALUCHISTAN, PAKISTAN—Bin Laden fled Afghanistan following the battle of Tora Bora in December 2001. He briefly retreated into the Pakistan-controlled portion of Kashmir in January 2002.

By June 2002, bin Laden had reportedly moved south into Baluchistan, a mountainous, autonomous tribal region in western Pakistan. It was a sensible place for him to hide. The Baluch are a nation without a country; their ancestral homeland straddles

Pakistan, Afghanistan, and Iran. The men are tall, pale, often bearded, and known for their fearsome hostility to all central governments. Bin Laden could easily blend in. It is likely that his confederates have family and friends among the Baluch. A number of high-ranking al Qaeda operatives are ethnic Baluch, including Ramzi Yousef, the mastermind of the 1993 World Trade Center bombing, and Yousef's uncle, Khalid Shaikh Mohammed, the operational planner of the September 11 attacks.

The Baluch have a long history of harboring terrorists. Saddam Hussein financed Baluch terrorists against Pakistan as far back as 1969, Iraq expert Laurie Mylroie told me.[10]

In July 2002, Pakistani president Pervez Musharraf announced that he was sending commandos into the tribal areas of Pakistan to flush out bin Laden. If Pakistani troops were quick and thorough, bin Laden would find himself surrounded—and perhaps even betrayed for the $25 million price on his head. Relying on the goodwill of Baluch cutthroats, he must have known, was not a viable long-term strategy.

Seemingly desperate, bin Laden recorded an extraordinary audiotape and sent it via courier to Ali Khomenei, the grand ayatollah of Iran's Supreme Council.[11] On that tape, according to a former Iranian intelligence officer I interviewed in Europe, bin Laden asked for Iran's help. In exchange for safe harbor and funding, he pledged to put al Qaeda at the service of Iran to combat American forces in Afghanistan and in Iraq, where al Qaeda leaders believed American intervention was inevitable. Bin Laden reportedly pledged, "If I die, my followers will be told to follow you [Khomenei]."[12]

Apparently the taped appeal worked. Murtaza Rezai, the director for Ayatollah Khomenei's personal intelligence directorate, began secret negotiations with bin Laden. Under the agreement between the Iranian Revolutionary Guard and al Qaeda, several convoys transported bin Laden's four wives, as well as his eldest son and heir apparent, Saad bin Laden, into Iran. Saad reportedly remains there today.[13]

Then, on July 26, 2002, bin Laden himself crossed into Iran from the Afghanistan border near Zabol, traveling north to the Iranian city of Mashad.

Over the next year, bin Laden holed up in a series of safe houses controlled by the Iranian Revolutionary Guard between Qazvin and Karaj, two cities along a highway west of Teheran. He moved frequently to avoid detection or betrayal. He was not alone. Two intelligence sources told me bin Laden was "guarded by the Revolutionary Guard."

Bin Laden also traveled with al Qaeda's number two man, Dr. Ayman al-Zawahiri, who was wounded and required medical treatment, my sources said. They did not know the extent of al-Zawahiri's injuries or the type of treatment he received.

For a time, bin Laden moved freely with and crossed into Afghanistan at will, usually through an Iranian border checkpoint near Zabol. It was on one of these trips inside Iran that my two sources say they saw bin Laden alive and well.

NAJMABAD, IRAN—Najmabad is a small city on the dry flatlands of central Iran, less than a one-hour drive from Teheran, the Islamic republic's capital. At a walled compound of three concrete buildings, in a briefing room lined with fraying couches and chairs, a clutch of Iranian Revolutionary Guard officers were in the midst of a meeting on October 23, 2003. It seemed like just another hot afternoon.

Then an officer stepped in and asked the group to clear the room for important "foreign visitors."

In their hasty departure, two Iranian intelligence officers saw bin Laden and his deputy, al-Zawahiri, stepping out of a four-wheel-drive vehicle, flanked by a small contingent of bodyguards. They appeared to be traveling in a three-car convoy. Bin Laden was seen walking toward a guarded entrance to the complex.

According to these two sources, bin Laden no longer resembles the picture that the FBI has put on its wanted posters. He has trimmed his beard to fit the more traditional look of a Shi'ite cleric and he seemed to have put on weight, according to the intelligence officials.

Al-Zawahiri had also changed his appearance, the sources say. He wore dark glasses and had dyed his beard. He also seemed thinner and wore a black turban tied in the style of an Iranian cleric. The world's two most wanted men were trying to pass themselves off as Iranians.

Bin Laden's new appearance may explain why neither he nor his deputy has appeared on videotapes. They do not want to broadcast their disguises. Instead, they have distributed almost a dozen audiotapes, some of which seem to have been recorded over phone lines.

A parade of senior al Qaeda figures continued to march into Iran throughout 2003, my two sources later learned. Bin Laden's chief financial officer, Mustafa Ahmed Mohammed, crossed into Iran at Zabol on November 3, 2003, along with his wife and ten children. They made the six-hour journey to Mashad in two Soviet-era Zil limousines in the company of Iranian Revolutionary Guard officers.

Behind the limousines trailed a heavily loaded truck. The money man's cargo included ten metal-sided trunks said to contain some $20 million in cash and raw opiate products with a street value of $10 million. My sources did not see the truck or its contents—they are relying on what they heard from other Iranian intelligence officials.

Over the next few days, the Iranian Revolutionary Guard supplied Mohammed with a new passport, national identity card, and other documents. His new alias is "Abu Yazid." He arrived in Teheran on November 9, 2003. U.S. officials believe Mohammed himself funneled as much as $250,000 to the September 11 hijackers through a bank account in Dubai, in the United Arab Emirates.

At bin Laden's request, Mohammed was bringing in the money to finance an Iran-al Qaeda spring offensive in Afghanistan aimed at destabilizing the government of Afghan president Hamid Karzai and seizing control of Afghanistan's western provinces. As the snow melts on Afghanistan's peaks, the guerrillas usually follow the water down into the plains. War in Afghanistan has a season, too.

Mohammed traveled into Iran with the help of the infamous Afghan warlord Gulbuddin Hekmatyar and is believed to have returned to Afghanistan in the spring of 2004. Hekmatyar is a notorious warlord known both for his history of duplicitously switching sides and for his bloody massacres. A senior Bush administration official confirmed that the warlord has long been backed by Iran.[14]

Mohammed's steel trunks packed with cash and opium were intended as payment for men and materials that Iran supplied for the coming offensive. One source told me in November 2003 that the offensive could come as soon as March 2004. As it happened, the offensive began in late March—in both Iraq and Afghanistan.

My two Iranian sources independently said they had "no doubt" that they had seen bin Laden and al-Zawahiri. Both terrorists have been personally known to them over the last two decades. In their capacity as intelligence officers for the Iranian government, both sources say they were briefed on bin Laden's movements as well as his taped message to Iran's high command and the other elements of the story presented here.

The first source agreed to provide his real name for publication, an extraordinary move in intelligence circles. Malak Reza was an Iranian intelligence officer. He has recently left the Islamic republic's secret services and is living with his family in the West. He speaks only Farsi, the native language of Iran, and was introduced to me by the second source.

For his safety, the second source wishes to be identified in print as "Choopan," which means "shepherd" in Farsi. Choopan said he has been responsible for coordinating the activities of Ali Khomenei's personal intelligence directorate. Iran is known to have seventeen parallel intelligence organizations.

I went to elaborate lengths to test Choopan's credibility and identity. I have interviewed him four times, including a lengthy face-to-face interview in a European city. He told a consistent story over a two-month period without adding fresh details or making significant changes.

To prove that he is an active intelligence agent, I asked him for the names of secret Iranian operatives currently active in Europe. He gave me two names. British intelligence has confirmed that these two names—which have never been publicly connected to the Iranian intelligence network that honeycombs Europe—are indeed believed by that service to be those of active Iranian intelligence agents.

Choopan also showed me several photographs of himself with prominent anti-Israel terrorists who were backed by Iran in the 1980s. In the pictures, Choopan and the terrorists are embracing and mugging for the camera.

Senior Bush administration officials confirmed in official letters to the Senate Select Committee on Intelligence that they met with Choopan in 2001 and have found him to be reliable over the last few years. Those documents, which I have seen under the condition that I do not quote from them, reveal specific incidents in which Choopan's intelligence was used to thwart a pending attack on American troops in Afghanistan. An Iranian "hunter-killer" team had been dispatched to Afghanistan in 2001 to terminate U.S. Special Forces personnel. When the general in charge of those forces was given Choopan's information, the Americans were able to seize the initiative and defeat the Iranian threat. The information was not only timely and accurate but also saved American lives.

"The guy is credible," said Michael A. Ledeen, who has met with Choopan several times over the last three years in Rome and other locations.

Ledeen, a resident scholar of the American Enterprise Institute in Washington, D.C., is a former special advisor to the secretary of state and, during the Reagan years, was a consultant to the National Security Council. Widely described as a neoconservative, Ledeen is Washington's leading critic of the Iranian regime. "I have known him [Choopan] for many years, spoken with him on many subjects, and always found him to be reliable and credible. He doesn't exaggerate and he says 'I don't know' when he doesn't know. Information supplied by him was thoroughly vetted by American military intelligence and it was found be correct. In fact, his information helped save American lives in Afghanistan in 2001."

Time has also made Choopan's account appear more credible. In December 2003, he told me that Ahmed Chalabi, the head of the Iraqi National Congress and then a favorite among neoconservatives, was working with the Iranians and even receiving money from one of their intelligence agencies. I did not believe him at the time and at this writing I take no position on Chalabi. In May 2004, front-page stories in the *New York Times* and the *Washington Post* alleged that Chalabi had passed sensitive intelligence to Iran. Chalabi denies the charges. Whatever the merits of the case against Chalabi, Choopan has clearly had access to intelligence about Iran long before it became public. Second, in November 2003, Choopan predicted a massive "spring offensive" against U.S. forces in Iraq in March or April 2004. Moqtar al-Sadr, an Iranian-backed extremist, launched just such an offensive in March 2004.

Finally, this eyewitness testimony is the first credible and detailed account by multiple sources of a contemporary sighting of bin Laden. The *Financial Times* also believes Choopan to be credible. It provided a short version of Choopan's account of bin Laden's appearance, though without named sources or the wealth of detail cited here.

What about motivation? Both Choopan and Reza do not seem to have the usual ulterior motives. Neither has ever asked me or, as far as I have been able to determine, British or American officials for money. Choopan has been an intelligence source for several Western governments for years and has proved reliable.

Choopan says that he is speaking out because, like many Iranians, he has come to loathe the mullahs who have ruled his country since the 1979 fundamentalist revolution. He also says that he was tortured and imprisoned by the regime on false charges and that his life was spared only by the personal intervention of a high-ranking family member. Though his well-placed friends enabled him to return to duty, his belief in the regime never returned.

Seeing his fellow Shi'ite Muslims prosper in a liberated Iraq, Choopan said, inspired him to approach a Western intelligence service and, separately, to speak to me. He was introduced to me through two private sector executives based in Europe who are well connected with several intelligence services.

The government of Iran denies that bin Laden is or ever has been in the country. Iran also forcefully denies that al-Zawahiri, al Qaeda's money man Mohammed, or any senior al Qaeda leaders are within its borders or that it has any knowledge of bin Laden's future plans.

The public record of statements by key Iranian officials tells a different story.

Iran has publicly admitted that it holds upwards of five hundred al Qaeda operatives under house arrest, describing these terrorists as "low-level." In March 2003, some two dozen were transferred to the custody of Saudi Arabia. Negotiations to extradite the remaining al Qaeda members from Iran to the U.S. or Britain have failed as of August 2004.

A jailbreak of dozens of al Qaeda prisoners was reported in *Al Hayat*, a London-based Arabic newspaper, on December 14, 2003.[15] This jailbreak is believed by at least one American intelligence analyst to be an elaborate cover to permit the Iranians to release al Qaeda without taking any political heat.

Why would Iran harbor one of the world's most notorious terrorists and risk the wrath of the West? Choopan gives three reasons. First, the Iranians believe they can keep bin Laden's presence a secret and plausibly deny it if publicly accused.

Second, the mullahs are feeling increasingly threatened by the War on Terror. Iran sees allied armies and rough new democracies springing up on its borders with Afghanistan and Iraq.

Choopan added that Iran's leaders were horrified by the "velvet revolution" that toppled Georgia's president Edward Shevardnadze in December 2003. The Georgian premier lost his post after twelve years in power following popular anger over a questionable election. The Iranians, Choopan said, believe the CIA was behind the peaceful coup d'etat. (The press generally credits billionaire George Soros, who funded opposition groups, and a well-organized reform movement.)

The Iranian people are becoming increasingly aware of democracy among their neighbors and politically restive at home. The mullahs, Choopan says, fear a counter-revolution and see bin Laden's fighters as a tools they can use to ensure the failure of these young democracies in Iraq and Afghanistan and the survival of mullah-dominated Iran.

Why would Iran, a predominantly Shi'ite Muslim land, work with a predominantly Sunni Muslim terror organization like bin Laden's? The short answer is personal connections, shared goals, and a common enemy. Ayman al-Zawahiri, a bona fide Sunni extremist, has received financial support from Iran since 1988.[16] Bin Laden himself is believed to have met with Iranian intelligence officials at Islamic conferences in Khartoum, Sudan, in the early 1990s.[17] Both bin Laden and the mullahs share an Islamist worldview that calls for the armed overthrow of Arab dictatorships and the restoration of a single caliph who will rule according to Shari'a law. While their visions overlap, there are, of course, significant differences about the content of Shari'a and other particulars.

Finally, they share enemies, including many Arab leaders, the United States, and the rest of the Western world.

A lot of ink has been spilled on the idea that Sunni and Shi'ite Muslims would never work together. The religious differences are dramatic and, years ago, bin Laden was quoted criticizing Shi'ites as "unbelievers." Still, the idea of a strict wall of separation between Sunni and Shi'ite terrorists seems overblown, the product of an analyst's desire to put groups in clearly categorized boxes. The reality on the ground is more complex. It is well documented that Shi'ite Iran has funded and armed Sunni warlords in Afghanistan for decades. Iran has also collaborated with Sunni terrorists in the Philippines. In Manila, I met with Parouk Hussin, the regional governor of Muslim-majority Mindanao. Significantly, he is a former leader of the Moro Islamic Liberation Front.[18] He confirmed that, over the last twenty years, he had traveled to Teheran and met with Ayatollah Khomeini and other Iranian sponsors of terror.[19] He said he had been warmly received, but did not say if the Iranians had bankrolled his terrorist outfit. Libya had been a prime supporter for years. Still Iran's "warm reception" at least indicates it does not have a blanket ban on working with Sunni terrorists.

Whether the Sunni-Shi'ite divide is as wide among radical Islamists as some analysts say, few can dispute that Iran's increasing isolation and the U.S. occupation of Afghanistan and Iraq has provided Teheran with a strong incentive to seek out new allies.

Bin Laden is not the only senior al Qaeda member who has reportedly sought sanctuary. Saad bin Laden is believed to be hiding in the western city of Kermanshah, hard on the Iraq border. Saif al-Adel, Khalid Shaikh Mohammed's successor as commander of al Qaeda's military wing, is also said to be there.

Al-Adel ordered the attacks on three housing compounds for foreign workers in eastern Riyadh on May 12, 2003, using a Thuraya satellite phone from inside Iran.[20] The three simultaneous bombings on residential compounds that were home to dozens of expatriate workers and their families killed thirty-four people, including eight Americans. Nine Saudis, including a member of the royal family, were also slain.[21] Choopan said he believed that an Iranian intelligence report including a log of the calls had been leaked to a Lebanese television network in order to send a message to Saudi Arabia.

Several senior administration officials I have spoken to have declined to talk about intelligence relating to bin Laden and Iran. Indeed, such silence on the topic seems to be Bush administration policy.

Each has said that he believes that bin Laden moves between Afghanistan and Pakistan. Administration officials expect bin Laden will most likely be captured in Pakistan. It is possible that he has not returned to Iran since 2003.

Yet policymakers would be wise to turn their attention to Iran's documented links to global terrorist networks, including bin Laden's. With vast oil revenues, a long history of supporting terrorists, and a fathomless desire to achieve its ideological aims at the expense of American lives, it certainly deserves its place on President Bush's "Axis of Evil."

CHAPTER TWO

UNHEARD THUNDER

"We have to show them we are over here. We have to show them who the mujihideen really are. We have to be like snakes. We have to strike, and then hide."

—LASED BEN HENI, PHONE INTERCEPT, MARCH 2001[1]

"We're finding out members of the al Qaeda organization, who they are, where they think they can hide. And we're slowly, but surely, bringing them to justice."

—PRESIDENT GEORGE W. BUSH, OCTOBER 1, 2001[2]

THE WHITE HOUSE—In the first nine months of 2001 and for the eight years of the Clinton administration, Osama bin Laden was at war with America. And Washington was at war with itself.

While America feuded over the 2000 presidential election, the legitimacy of the new president, the control of the Senate, and the more than three thousand officials to be appointed and approved, bin Laden patiently moved his men into position. By January 2001, al Qaeda's men would be at their posts—long before most of President George W. Bush's appointees were confirmed by the Senate.

In war, speed is as much an advantage as surprise.

Still, as this chapter will show, the Bush administration was developing a plan to strike bin Laden in Afghanistan. But bin Laden struck first, helped along by bureaucratic intransigence and partisan politics.

KANDAHAR, AFGHANISTAN—High in the hills above Kandahar, Afghanistan, lies the Khalden camp. Today it is a ruin, a few empty foundation lines and bits of trash swirling in the wind. But, in its day, it was one of many camps where al Qaeda taught its recruits to fire automatic weapons, make bombs from household chemicals, and pray under the open sky. The barracks had no heat or electric lights, the water was often contaminated, and the recruits could be as treacherous to each other as to any infidel. In a handwritten letter later found by allied Special Forces, a young recruit complained to his father that his fellow "soldiers of God" had stolen his watch and his Koran.

It was here in the Khalden camp that British intelligence believes Osama bin Laden convened a council of war sometime in the spring of 1999.[3] At that council, as an interim staff report of the 9-11 Commission confirms, bin Laden and Mohammed Atef, the al Qaeda military commander, summoned Khalid Shaikh Mohammed to present his plan for what became the September 11 attacks. In that meeting, four initial targets were chosen: the White House, the Pentagon, the U.S. Capitol, and the World Trade Center.[4]

Training would begin in the Mes Aynak camp in the fall of 1999.[5]

Throughout the Clinton impeachment trial, the 2000 presidential campaign, the Florida vote-counting scandal, and the daily battles over President Bush's appointments, the clock was ticking. The first two terrorists arrived in America on January 15, 2000.[6] By December 8, 2000, all four "pilots" of the September 11 plot were safely inside the United States.[7] George W. Bush was sworn in on January 20, 2001.

In a series of bold provocations, for eight long years, bin Laden had wanted war with America. His first attack on Americans was on U.S. Marines housed in two towering hotels in the port city of Aden, Yemen, on December 29, 1992. In February 26, 1993, his minions struck at the World Trade Center in New York. Seven Americans died.[8] He trained, armed, and encouraged the Somali militia that attacked U.S. Army Rangers in Mogadishu on October 3, 1993. In 1994, he plotted to kill Pope John Paul II and bomb twelve airliners simultaneously but failed.[9] In 1995, bin Laden's henchmen bombed an administrative office for the Saudi Arabian National Guard. Five Americans perished, along with two others. Bin Laden publicly declared war on America five times between 1996 and 1998. Yet no war with America came.

Over the next twelve months, bin Laden approved a wave of suicide attacks, increasing in scope and lethality: the August 1998 embassy bombings (which killed 224, including 12 American diplomats), the October 2000 strike on the USS *Cole* (which killed 17 sailors), and the September 11 attacks on New York and Washington. In the end, bin Laden got his wish. Over the objections of his inner circle and Taliban leader Mullah Omar, he ordered the attacks on New York and Washington. He hoped the September 11 attacks would be, in the words of the 9-11 Commission, "a recruiting and fund-raising bonanza. In his thinking, the more al Qaeda did, the more it would gain. Although he faced opposition from many of his most senior advisors—including Shura Council members Shaykh Saeed, Saif al-Adel, and Abu Hafs the Mauritanian—bin Laden effectively overruled their objections, and the attacks went forward."[10]

But why did bin Laden insist on war with America? I sought out one of French intelligence's premier counter-terrorism officials in the fourth arrondissement of Paris. He speaks Arabic, French, and English and has traveled extensively in the Muslim world. His theory about al Qaeda's quest for all-out war turns on a political and psychological analysis of bin Laden. A massive attack on America's soaring skyscrapers and public offices would compel the infidel power to invade Afghanistan, forcing a final showdown between the "house of peace" (Islam) and the "house of war" (the infidels).

Once again, bin Laden would be fighting a superpower in the cold, dry reaches of the Hindu Kush. Bin Laden likely expected that the Americans, like the Soviets, would quickly become mired in an endless, merciless ground war. Tanks and trucks would sink into the sand and snow as unseen foes picked off the occupants with rocket launchers and machine guns. Americans would be ambushed in villages they thought friendly or maimed by car bombs in cities they thought safe. In a thousand ways, bin Laden's mujihideen would use hit-and-run tactics to sap America's strength and morale. Afghanistan would become a bloody quicksand. Another Vietnam.

Indeed, many Western commentators believed the same thing.[11]

The French official told me that the jihad against the Soviets in Afghanistan had been the defining moment of bin Laden's life. Bin Laden had traded his wealth and comfort for more than two decades of jihad. It intoxicated him. It gave him purpose and direction. Now he would relive it. As he once told an interviewer: "One day of jihad is better than one thousand days praying in a mosque."[12]

THE WHITE HOUSE—Condoleezza Rice's first day in charge of America's safety was Monday morning, January 22, 2001. She faced an extraordinary set of challenges: an emerging terrorist threat, a restive China that soon held an American air crew hostage, a bitter partisan divide that would make confirming presidential appointments unusually difficult, a shorter-than-usual transition period, and a skeleton staff of Clinton holdovers who ranged from wary to hostile.

CIA Director George Tenet, whom Rice had come to trust, warned her about bin Laden in January 2001. We don't know what Tenet told her, but a month later, in February 2001, he told the Senate Select Committee on Intelligence that bin Laden and al Qaeda were America's "most immediate and serious threat."

This had been a constant theme of Tenet's public remarks for the last several years. No doubt he was equally emphatic in private.

The president's key decision-makers—the national security advisor, the director of Central Intelligence, the secretaries of State and Defense, and other important national security players—did not hold their first formal meeting on terrorism until late spring 2001. But it would be unfair to say that the administration was not concerned about terrorism from its first days. "Framing meetings" were held by administration deputy directors and deputy secretaries of Defense and State beginning in February 2001.

Rice did make some strong early moves. She made sure CIA Director Tenet was welcome at the president's daily intelligence briefing and had full access to the president, two things President Clinton did not permit his director of Central Intelligence until his second term.

She also knew that bin Laden probed for weakness, division, and indecision. He had struck twice during the transition from President George H. W. Bush to President Clinton, with the attack on American troops in Yemen in December 1992 and the bombing of the World Trade Center in February 1993. He surely wouldn't miss another opportunity.

And, Rice knew, this presidential transition was far messier than most. The 2000 presidential election was the closest since 1960 and, for the first time in living memory, there was no undisputed winner on Election Day.

AUSTIN, TEXAS—On election night, at the Four Seasons Hotel in Austin, Texas, the drinks were flowing and the mood was upbeat. Vice presidential candidate Dick Cheney and his wife, Lynne, had invited a group of two dozen longtime friends to a private room off the lobby to watch the Bush-Cheney victory on a big screen. Among them was a corporate executive named Donald Rumsfeld with his wife, Joyce, and the former arms control negotiator for President Reagan, Kenneth Adelman, and his wife, Carol.

This account is based on Adelman's recollection, an eyewitness account of an intimate gathering of Bush insiders that has not been previously reported. In 1992, the Adelmans had invited then Secretary of Defense Cheney to their Arlington, Virginia, home to watch the presidential returns. Bush had lost. Now they joined the Cheneys in Austin, hoping that this night would have a happier ending.

Then the networks announced that Bush-Cheney had lost Pennsylvania. Suddenly, Adelman told me, it no longer felt like a victory march.[13]

Adelman turned to James Baker III, a former chief of staff for President George H. W. Bush. "Okay, do the math for me. We just lost Pennsylvania."

Baker was better than the analysts on television, Adelman recalls, reeling off the combination of states Bush needed to carry to take the White House. The crowd was watchful, anxious.

An hour later, Adelman recalls, NBC announced that Gore had carried Florida. Baker was blunt: "Without Florida, we can't win."

It now felt like a wake.

Twenty minutes later, Dick Cheney's daughter Mary walked over to her parents and the Adelmans. "I'm hearing that Florida is not lost."

Soon NBC reversed itself, putting Florida in the undecided column. It would stay there for six more weeks.

Sometime after midnight, Rumsfeld turned to his old friend. "What would Shakespeare say about this?"

"A line from *Henry VI, Part III*, comes to mind," said Adelman, known for his expertise on the bard. "'How sweet a thing it is to wear a crown.'"

WASHINGTON, D.C.—While Bush did receive a majority in the Electoral College but not a majority of the popular vote—exactly the result

that President Clinton faced in both the 1992 and 1996 elections—
the press portrayed the 2000 election differently.

Whatever its merits, Vice President Al Gore's decision to challenge Florida's electoral procedures robbed the 2000 presidential election of finality and legitimacy. Unlike Vice President Richard M. Nixon, who lost the 1960 presidential poll by a whisker—amid allegations that Democratic electoral fraud had tipped the balance—Gore went to the courts. The vote-counting dispute dragged on for six agonizing weeks, with lawsuits, demonstrations, and continuous cable television coverage.

No official count put Gore in the lead, but, among partisans, hope burned—until the U.S. Supreme Court put an end to the recounts.

And, in emotional terms, it hadn't really ended. Well into 2001, America was divided over the legitimacy of the new president, with many Democrats insisting that Bush had been "selected" by the Supreme Court, not elected by the people. As a result, President Bush did not have the full moral authority usually enjoyed by a newly elected American president. There was no "honeymoon."

The bitterness of the 2000 election did not make it any easier for the new administration to consider rallying the political establishment, the press, and the people to wage war on al Qaeda, a terrorist network that few had ever heard of.

The late start of the presidential transition had weakened the Bush administration in other, more tangible ways. The outgoing Clinton administration began providing security and intelligence briefings to key officials in the incoming Bush administration only during the last two weeks of December, not in the second week of November as is customary. The Clinton administration had waited until the last possible moment to brief its successors.

In a world crowded with crises—North Korean atomic weapons plans, terror strikes in Israel, trouble in Kashmir, rising tension with China—some Bush staffers suspected that the Clinton administration briefings were shorter and seemingly less complete than usual.[14]

In some cases, departing Clinton staffers seemed hostile. One Bush advisor told me: "It was unbelievable."

But it was understandable. Many had expected to stay on in the Gore administration and then a mere five hundred votes in Florida meant that they had to brief their political opponents instead. One small sign of that hostility: The letter W was reportedly pried from dozens of computer keyboards in the White House and Old Executive Office Building, where some members of the president's national security team work.[15]

The late start also meant that the Bush administration was mostly a set of empty boxes on an organizational chart. The Bush team wasn't fully able to recruit professionals to staff the government until after the Supreme Court's ruling on December 12, 2000. (Usually, the personnel search process kicks into high gear a month earlier.) Hundreds of key positions at the Defense Department, State Department, the FBI, and the nation's thirteen intelligence agencies were staffed by Clinton holdovers or by civil servants in an "acting" capacity.

In many cases, the Bush team hadn't had time to select someone for a post. And, in the handful of cases where the incoming administration had actually identified a candidate, officials knew that they were at the beginning of a laborious vetting process with months-long FBI background checks. These nominations, in turn, would have to be formally sent to the U.S. Senate.

And the Senate, even though it was in Republican hands for the first few months of 2001, is legendary for its slow approval of presidential nominees, no matter which party is in charge.[16] The relevant committee would review the documents, meet the nominee privately, perhaps schedule a hearing, and then vote. If the committee approved the nomination, the full Senate would vote. Purely as a scheduling matter, this process usually takes weeks and months. So throughout the spring and summer of 2001, qualified nominees lingered in limbo.

By law, nominees may not start work until approved by a majority of the Senate. They cannot even sit at their appointed desks.

The few national security professionals who were at their posts were holdovers from the Clinton administration, who were just getting to know Rice. The holdovers had forged tight bonds in the many crises of the Clinton years. They drank together and ate together and fought together. They were as tightly bound as U.S. Marines emerging from Parris Island. Imagine a closed shop of union members with seniority—and then the shareholders sent in new management. Conflict was inevitable, although it was too early for either side to admit it.

The Clinton holdovers presented an almost unprecedented situation in American history. On average, national security staffers stay fewer than two years at the same job. In the Clinton administration, however, many had stayed on for four or five years. And one had been on the National Security Council for more than eight years.[17] The value of their experience—of twelve-hour days making important decisions about America's safety—is not as straightforward a calculation as it seems. In one sense, the more you do, the more you know—you learn from both mistakes and triumphs. But if you do the same task for too long, you can become too rigid and unimaginative. Unknown to the veterans of the National Security Council, the new president was inclined toward far tougher policies than his predecessor. But they had no experience of him and had no reason to believe that the president would be decisive. They wrongly assumed that President Bush would be as cautious as Clinton had been, and in need of a national security education to boot.

While the Clinton veterans certainly knew their jobs, they didn't know where they stood with Rice or the new president. They couldn't initiate aggressive action against bin Laden on their own and they didn't know how President Bush and others would respond to bold recommendations. In any White House, seeming too aggressive in a staff meeting can be a career killer. No one wanted to suggest a strong response to bin Laden until the president and his team were ready to hear it. As a result, America's antiterrorism efforts were set on cruise control.

Consider Richard Clarke, the Clinton administration's counterterrorism czar who worked under Rice on the National Security Council. He briefed her on bin Laden and Clinton's many failed attempts to kill or capture him. Clarke didn't have the same relationship with Rice as he had with Clinton's national security advisor Sandy Berger. Clarke came to like Berger, but to Clarke, Rice was a cipher, a remote personality that he cannot fathom even now:

> Now Condi Rice was in charge. She appeared to have a closer relationship with the second President Bush than any of her predecessors had with the presidents they reported to.[18]

Left unsaid is that Clarke was denied the direct access to the president that he had enjoyed under President Clinton and that he blamed Rice for his lack of access.

In different circumstances, Clarke and Rice might have gotten along well. The new national security advisor is incredibly self-disciplined, almost invariably leaving Washington parties by 10:30 and rising shortly after dawn to go back to work. Intelligent, patient, thorough, formal, and well-organized, Rice developed a reputation for puzzling out complicated and intricate problems, ranging from eighteenth-century piano compositions, which she played beautifully, to the Byzantine movements of Kremlin leaders during the Cold War, about which she wrote persuasively. As President Bush's national security advisor, she found herself in a world far from classical music and Kremlinology. Fighting terrorists was a quicksilver, deadly game. A successful player would need the political equivalent of jazz: improvising and changing while sticking to established principles.

Clarke wondered if she was up to the job. In his interviews with me, Clarke was always careful to avoid direct criticism of Rice. But, in his book *Against All Enemies*, he wrote:

> As I briefed Rice on al Qaeda, her facial expression gave me the impression that she had never heard the term before, so I added, "Most people think of it as Usama bin Laden's group, but it's much more than that. It's a network of affiliated terrorist organizations with cells in over fifty countries, including the U.S."[19]

Clarke's account misreads Rice, at best. Rice spoke knowledgably about al Qaeda during a campaign appearance on a Detroit radio station long before Clarke's briefing on the terrorist group. And Rice had doubts about Clarke's role, as he admits.

> Rice looked skeptical. She focused on the fact that my office staff was large by NSC standards (twelve people) and did operational things, including domestic security issues. She said, "The NSC looks just as it did when I worked here a few years ago, except for your operation. It's all new. It does domestic things and it is not just doing policy, it seems to be worrying about operational issues. I'm not sure we will want to keep all of this in the NSC."[20]

Rice's decision to essentially demote Clarke did not go down well:

> Rice decided that the position of National Coordinator for Counter-terrorism [Clarke's job] would also be downgraded.

No longer would the Coordinator be a member of the Principals Committee [as the Cabinet is known when the president is not present]. No longer would the CSG [Clarke's
counter-terrorism group] report to the Principals, but instead
to a committee of Deputy Secretaries. No longer would the
National Coordinator [Clarke] be supported by two NSC
Senior Directors or have the budget review mechanism with
the Associate Director of OMB. She did, however, ask me to
stay on and keep my entire staff in place. Rice and Hadley
did not seem to know anyone else whose expertise covered
what they regarded as my strange portfolio. At the same time,
Rice requested that I develop a reorganization plan to spin
out some of the security functions to someplace outside the
NSC Staff.[21]

Months before September 11, Rice informed Clarke that his
beloved Counter-terrorism Security Group would have to hand
over its operational role to another agency. Clarke would no longer
be able to bully the bureaucracy to wage war on al Qaeda. Rice's
decisions meant that Clarke would not have a ringside seat on presidential decision-making.

P. J. Crowley, spokesman for the National Security Council in
the Clinton era, told me that, during the presidential transition,
he warned Rice against dismantling Clarke's unique team.[22] He
cites two powerful arguments. The national security advisor had
to fight for influence with two powerful bureaucracies (Defense
and State). Only a strongly managed operational team can ride
herd on those bureaucracies and make sure that they get the job
done. Secondly, the NSC was designed for the Cold War, not for
new challenges. Without an operational team at the NSC, there is
no bureaucracy specifically tasked only with fighting terrorism.
Going back to the traditional NSC structure would deprive the
nation of its ability to fight bin Laden. In hindsight, Rice's deci-

sion to return to the traditional NSC she knew well may have been ill-considered.

As Clarke explained it to me in 2003, Rice's decision seemed irrational. Only he could force the bureaucracies to work together and actually fight terrorists instead of each other. He had the relationships, the experience, the staff, and the tenacity to get the job done. Working around the clock, his team had stopped the millennium plots that could have slain thousands of Americans on December 31, 1999.[23] At least six al Qaeda cells were smashed in Bosnia, Italy, and across the Middle East. Unleashed, Clarke's team could do wonders.

But Rice had a different view, colored by a different history. The last Republican administration to allow the National Security Council to carry out operations suffered the Iran-Contra scandal. It did not help matters that Clarke worked out of Colonel Oliver North's old office suite. Rice saw her job as protecting the president—and saw hard-charging Clarke as a liability. It would be safer to confine the NSC to its traditional role of analyst and coordinator and leave the field operations to the experts. That meant dismantling Clarke's beloved team and handing counter-terrorism back to the gun-shy crew at the CIA.

Clarke believed that Rice didn't understand how the national security threats to the United States had changed:

> I realized that Rice, and her deputy, Steve Hadley, were still operating with the old Cold War paradigm from when they had worked on the NSC. Condi's previous government experience had been as an NSC staffer for three years worrying about the Warsaw Pact and the Soviet Union during the Cold War. Steve Hadley had also been an NSC staffer assigned to do arms control issues with the Soviet Union. He had then been an Assistant Secretary in the Pentagon, also concerned with Soviet arms control. It struck me that

neither of them had worked on the new post–Cold War security issues.[24]

I tried to explain: "This office is new, you're right. It's post–Cold War security, not focused just on nation-state threats. The boundaries between domestic and foreign have blurred. Threats to the U.S. now are not Soviet ballistic missiles carrying bombs, they're terrorists carrying bombs. Besides, the law that established the NSC in 1947 said it should concern itself with domestic security threats too." I did not succeed entirely in making the case.[25]

Finally, in April, the full Deputies Committee met to discuss counter-terrorism policy. The first meeting, in the small wood-paneled conference room known as the Situation Room, did not go well.[26] Rice's deputy, Steve Hadley, asked Clarke to deliver a briefing. Clarke's briefing included recommendations: "We need to put pressure on both the Taliban and al Qaeda by arming the Northern Alliance and other groups in Afghanistan. Simultaneously, we need to target bin Laden and his leadership by reinitiating flights of the Predator."[27]

But the deputies did not want action; they wanted research papers. It would be months before Rice asked Clarke to develop new plans to slay his old nemesis bin Laden. But Clarke's reduced position in the bureaucracy and his demanding, bulldog personality soon undermined his valuable efforts.

Clarke held a series of brainstorming sessions around the conference table in his office on the third floor of the Old Executive Office Building. But these meetings lacked their former energy. The placard "Defenders of the Free World" that a staffer had tacked to the wall of Clarke's outer office in the heyday of the Clinton anti-terrorism effort now seemed more like a memento than a declaration.

For months, Clarke suspected that his responsibilities were about to be divided in two. In July, he learned the worst, at least from his point of view. Clarke was directed to work closely with General Wayne Downing, a tough, blunt, four-star Army general who had commanded the Special Forces during the 1991 Gulf War. General Downing had also worked with the Iraqi National Congress, a dissident Iraqi group headquartered in London, on a covert operation to topple Saddam Hussein. That plan had never received official U.S. government backing and was shelved. Downing had little time for bureaucracy or "process," things Clarke specialized in manipulating.

Once it became clear that President Bush intended to hand some of Clarke's responsibilities to General Downing, the friction between the two men became palpable.[28] Yet these two men were effectively in charge of President Bush's counter-terrorism policy in the months before September 11.

At the same time, the White House was about to announce a separate, senior post for Critical Infrastructure Protection and Cyber Security. Frustrated, Clarke asked for a transfer. He wanted to be put in charge of combating cyber-terrorism.

Rice was surprised when he asked for the job, according to Clarke. "'Perhaps,' I suggested, 'I have become too close to the terrorism issue. I have worked on it for ten years and to me it seems like a very important issue, but maybe I'm becoming like Captain Ahab with bin Laden as the white whale.'"[29]

His tone was unmistakable. Clarke had switched from fighting a covert war on bin Laden to one against Rice.

LANGLEY, VIRGINIA—The CIA's many pre–September 11 missteps stem from Clinton-era policies. The biggest mistake of the new Bush administration was not moving swiftly to reform those policies, including a glaring failure to recruit informants inside al Qaeda who might have warned America about an impending attack, and not hiring enough translators to interpret the volumes of phone intercepts and foreign broadcasts related to terrorist threats. Instead, President Bush personally assured George Tenet that his job as director of Central Intelligence was secure.

There has been a lot of speculation about why President Bush kept Tenet on as director of Central Intelligence. The first, which is bound to bring a certain amount of eye-rolling inside the Beltway, is that Bush really did want to change the tone in Washington, as he had promised on the campaign trail. When I interviewed a number of then Governor Bush's friends and associates in Austin, Texas, in the summer of 1999, I was surprised at how earnestly the Texas crowd believed they could change Washington, D.C. At lunch with Paul Burka, the managing editor of the *Texas Monthly*, the bible of Lone Star State politics, I told him that a number of Washington-based conservatives were concerned that Governor Bush went to Pete Laney's daughter's wedding. Laney was a Democrat and the Speaker of the Texas House of Representatives. Burka looked surprised. Why shouldn't Bush go? After all, he was invited, Burka said. Austin, which has a vigorous Left–Right debate, is still a clubby enough town that leaders from rival parties socialize.

"Can you imagine Bill Clinton going to Denny Hastert's daughter's wedding?" I asked. Hastert is the Republican Speaker of the U.S. House of Representatives.

"That's what's wrong with Washington," Burka said. He might be right, but that's the way Washington is.

Burka was a Democrat who had come to like and respect the Republican governor. He thought others would make the same journey. And Bush's people honestly thought they could transform Washington into something resembling Austin. Even the bitter Florida vote-counting fiasco did not seem to tarnish their idealism.

One way to make Washington more like Austin would be to keep some Democrats in top positions. One was former California congressman Norman Mineta, who became transportation secretary. Another was George Tenet, a former Senate staffer whom President Clinton had named as deputy director of Central Intelligence in 1995 and director in 1997. It was hoped that these appointments would show that the president really was a "uniter, not a divider" and mollify disappointed Democrats.

It didn't work—just as President Clinton's appointment of Republican senator Bill Cohen to defense secretary didn't dissolve GOP opposition to Clinton's policies.

Some conservative critics of Tenet maintain that he was kept on because he named a CIA building after Bush's father. This was, at best, partly true. It was the Republican-controlled Congress that actually voted to name the building after President George H. W. Bush, who had been a director of Central Intelligence in the 1970s. Tenet simply had the political sense "to make lemons into lemonade" as one CIA veteran put it, to call a press conference and invite the former president to cut the ceremonial ribbon. This certainly did Tenet no harm and, it is worth remembering, he did it during the Clinton administration.

Other Republican barons claim credit for saving Tenet's job before and after September 11. Congressman Porter Goss, a Florida Republican who Bush nominated as Tenet's replacement in August 2004, told me in December 2001 that he repeatedly advised Bush to keep Tenet. Goss has been chairman of the House of Representatives Intelligence Committee since 1997 and was known for being fiercely critical of intelligence lapses in the Clinton years.[30] But he came to respect Tenet. In addition to being Intelligence Committee chairman, Goss had served as a member of U.S. Army intelligence from 1960 to 1962 and moved on to join the CIA's clandestine service from 1962 until 1971, where he served in the hotspots of Latin America, the Caribbean, and Europe. "I've got to be harsher than the next guy because I was in the business," Goss said. "I think I'm a pretty good watchdog, because I know what to look for."[31] Goss's views certainly commanded respect inside the Bush White House. When he vouched for Tenet, it mattered.

Perhaps the most interesting reason for Tenet's survival comes from Richard Clarke. To the best of my knowledge, this account has never been published. It turns on principle and Bush family history. George H. W. Bush was CIA director when President Gerald Ford lost the closely contested 1976 presidential election. Bush went to brief President-elect Jimmy Carter. At the end of a global tour of crises, Bush added that he considered his CIA post to be nonpartisan. Just as the nonpartisan FBI directors usually stayed on from one president to the next, Bush said, he would like to continue as director of Central Intelligence.

Carter wouldn't have it. According to Clarke, Carter asked, "If it is so non-political, why is the former RNC chairman in it?"

Bush had been head of the Republican National Committee in the Nixon years. He would not be staying on in the Carter years.

Bush never forgot this rebuke, and when his son was sworn in as president in 2001, according to Clarke, he repeated the story. Another reason to keep Tenet.

Research conducted with the help of specialists at the Bush presidential library failed to uncover any letters, documents, or contemporaneous news accounts to confirm or deny Clarke's account. There are several letters to citizens in which Bush declines to comment on electoral politics, saying that he must remain nonpartisan.

Finally, there were practical political considerations. Bush's nominees for Cabinet positions immediately met stiff resistance from Democratic senators, and one, Linda Chavez, had to withdraw her name because opposition was too strong. With so many positions open, the administration had to pick its battles. The change in control of the Senate, following Senator Jim Jeffords's party switch, only underscored this point. If the Democrats filibustered Tenet's replacement, America could be left without a CIA director as global threats mounted.

So Tenet stayed on.

In addition to the director, other top posts at the CIA were held by Clinton holdovers, including the deputy director, the head of Middle Eastern Affairs, and the head of the counter-terrorism unit. No major changes in policy or personnel were announced in the nine months preceding the September 11 attacks.

In the field, problems festered. The CIA's Pakistan station, tasked with watching bin Laden in neighboring Afghanistan, was undermanned and underfunded.[32] Other CIA stations, including the ones monitoring Iran and Iraq, were also stretched thin. Morale was low.

Clinton administration rules barring the recruitment of sources from unsavory backgrounds remained. Under one of Clinton's CIA directors, John Deutch, orders were handed down to cease working with informants with criminal or otherwise embarrassing backgrounds. Thus, the agency lost many of its street-level sources in the infamous "scrub of '95" and wasn't able to recruit replacements. While most commentators fault the CIA for this radical decision, the agency really had no choice. Senator Robert Torricelli, a Democrat from New Jersey, had attached an amendment to the CIA's 1994 budget authorization bill requiring the sacking of unsavory sources. (Interestingly, Senator Torricelli's own association with unsavory sources would drive him from office in scandal.)

As for their "eyes in the sky"—those spy satellites orbiting over-head—the intelligence community was still analyzing less than 10 percent of the satellite data it received. If analysts uncovered new clues of bin Laden's pending operations, it would have been by sheer luck.

And even if intelligence from human and technological sources was forthcoming, the intelligence community often could not trans-late it. The shortage of language specialists in Arabic, Farsi, Dari, and other tongues continued—a situation essentially unchanged since Clinton's first director of Central Intelligence, James Woolsey, fought a losing battle with Senator Dennis DeConcini, an Arizona Democrat, to hire more translators in 1995.[33] "I don't bear him [Woolsey] any ill feeling," DeConcini told me. "He just wasn't in a position to get what he wanted."[34]

And neither was any other director of Central Intelligence.

RIYADH, SAUDI ARABIA—One of the biggest pre–September 11 bureaucratic failures of the Bush administration and the U.S. consulate in Jeddah, Saudi Arabia, emerged at the U.S. embassy in Riyadh in June 2001.[35] It was called "Visa Express" and essentially threw open America's gates to three of the September 11 hijackers as well as to Khalid Shaikh Mohammed, the al Qaeda planner of the attacks.

Ordinary visa programs let in the rest of the hijackers, according to a report by the Washington-based Center for Immigration Studies, as well as twenty-two other known terrorists between 1993 and 2001.[36]

The State Department consular officers are supposed to be the nation's first line of defense, an advance border guard to bar terrorists and others from the homeland. But the State Department had other priorities. Many embassies and consulates still stored terrorist watch lists on microfiche, grainy film about the size of a slice of toast.[37] Hundreds of microfiche sheets would have to be searched by hand in a special reader that displayed long columns of names. It would be easy to miss one.

Let alone that a single Arabic name can be translated into English using many combinations of letters. If these records had been computerized with state-of-the-art search programs, many fewer terrorists would have received U.S. visas.

Another problem was that consular officials had to be both guardians and diplomats, two conflicting roles. As Secretary of State Colin Powell explained to Congress in the wake of the September 11 attacks, granting visas is a key diplomatic tool. Foreign nations, including Saudi Arabia, frequently complain when influential citizens cannot secure a U.S. visa. Saudi tourists and students had also long complained about the process of getting a U.S. visa: The forms were too long, the approval process too slow, and the background checks too insulting. In order to be better diplomats, the consular officials had to streamline the visa approval process. Unfortunately, this often amounted to lowering their guard.

President Clinton appointed Mary Ryan as assistant secretary of state for consular affairs in 1993. She stayed at this vital post well past September 11, 2001. Ryan was behind a slow, incremental cultural shift at the State Department. She gradually tipped the balance away from a strict law enforcement approach to what investigative reporter Joel Mowbray has called a "courtesy culture."[38]

In the early Clinton years, Ryan's reforms were reasonable and long overdue. She instituted a "drop box" where long-term visa holders could leave their passports and have them mailed back with a new visa. This saved time and thinned the crowds at U.S. embassies. Then she spearheaded a process to effectively rewrite the rules for granting visas, even though the law had not changed. Previously, a consular official needed a positive reason to approve a visa; now, he needed a reason for *not* granting one.

Then, in the last full year of the Clinton administration, Ryan began work on "Visa Express." The plan would allow up to ten Saudi travel agencies to screen and interview applicants and even help them fill out the paperwork. All a U.S. consular officer would do is rubber stamp the application, insert a visa into the passport, and put it in the mail.

Embassy officials were ecstatic about the results. The U.S. ambassador to Saudi Arabia cabled Washington: "Using the travel agents to assure that documentation is complete and in compliance with guidelines saved the consular officers from spending valuable time pre-interviewing applicants whose paperwork was not in order."[39]

Major problems were overlooked. "It's outrageous. The travel agents had a profit motive to get everyone a visa. That's how they make their commissions," Joel Mowbray, who broke the story, told me. "And if these Saudis were too scary to have inside the embassy, why were they allowed into America?"[40]

Visa Express directly contributed to the deaths of three thousand people on September 11, but the State Department never questioned its own officials about granting visas to the hijackers. Months later, at the request of Republicans in Congress, the General Accounting Office (GAO), a federal auditing agency, investigated why the State Department had cleared terrorists for travel to the United States.[41] The "courtesy culture" inculcated by Ryan was a major cause, it found. Thanks to Mowbray's reporting and the supervision of Congressman Dan Burton, Visa Express was finally shut down in July 2002.

Burton, who was the chairman of the House Government Reform Committee, was briefed on the GAO report. He was outraged. "Moreover, it is my understanding that at least one consular officer informed the GAO that she would not have granted visas to some of the September 11 hijackers if the State Department did not have an informal policy that all Saudis were presumed to be entitled to a visa."[42]

And no wonder. Examination of the visa applications of three al Qaeda terrorists reveals that the forms should have been summarily rejected. Every application contained errors and omissions that should have triggered a refusal. Most applications left fields such as "Name and Street Address of Present Employer or School" blank. For the specific address of their U.S. destinations, the terrorists wrote: "New York," "California," "JKK Whyndham Hotel," and simply "Hotel." Consular officers are trained to reject applications like these, but the "courtesy culture" instructed them to give foreigners the benefit of the doubt. In the pre-Ryan era, the hijackers' applications would have been rejected. Under Visa Express, they were cleared for takeoff.

WASHINGTON, D.C.—Elsewhere at the State Department, officials were becoming increasingly concerned about bin Laden. The State Department issued a warning to American travelers on May 12, 2001:

> Dear American:
>
> The U.S. Government has learned that American citizens abroad may be the target of a terrorist threat from extremist groups with links to Usama Bin Ladin's Al-Qaeda organization. In the past, such individuals have not distinguished between official and civilian targets.
>
> As always, we take this information seriously. U.S. Government facilities worldwide remain at a heightened state of alert. In addition, U.S. Government facilities have and will continue to temporarily close or suspend public services as necessary to review their security posture and ensure its adequacy.
>
> In light of the above, U.S. citizens are urged to maintain a high level of vigilance and to take appropriate steps to increase their security awareness to reduce their vulnerability. Americans should maintain a low profile, vary routes and times for all required travel, and treat mail and packages from unfamiliar sources with suspicion.
>
> This Public Announcement replaces the Public Announcement—Worldwide Caution of January 5, 2001, to alert Americans that they may be the target of a terrorist threat. This Public Announcement expires on August 11, 2001.

WASHINGTON, D.C.—On the top floor of the Justice Department, the new attorney general, John Ashcroft, was learning about President Clinton's secret war on bin Laden and the mountain of work that lay ahead of him.

The Clinton administration had left some successes in the pipeline. On May 29, 2001, after years of manhunts, piles of evidence, and hours of testimony, four bin Laden operatives had been found guilty of bombing the American embassies in Kenya and Tanzania, killing 224 people, including 12 American diplomats. The terrorists would spend the summer of 2001 speculating about their sentences for the murderous bombings. Mohammed Rashid Daoud al-Owhali, a citizen of Saudi Arabia, and Khalfan Khamis Mohammed, a Tanzanian national, faced the death sentence for their role in the embassy bombings. Lebanese American Wadih el Hage and Jordanian Mohammed Saddiq Odeh faced life in prison. Ultimately, all four were sentenced to prison for life.

Grave problems festered at the Federal Bureau of Investigation, unknown to the new attorney general. FBI field offices in Phoenix, Minneapolis, and Newark had uncovered elements of bin Laden's plot to attack the United States—and had met a brick wall at FBI headquarters.

NEW YORK—The FBI's investigation into the attack on the USS *Cole*—which had cost the lives of seventeen sailors on October 12, 2000—had reached an impasse. The bull-headed John O'Neill, who ran the FBI's famed counter-terrorism unit in New York, had feuded with the U.S. ambassador to Yemen, Barbara Bodine.

In June 2001, O'Neill tried to find a plausible cover story for essentially ending the investigation. As his team flew back to New York, O'Neill leaked to the press that his investigators faced death threats: a credible excuse to leave the desert republic with its history of civil war, fanaticism, and midnight bombings. Yemen is

known for its throngs of unemployed men who listen to fundamentalist mullahs and ambush cars on major highways to take hostages.[43]

But Ambassador Bodine wasn't going to allow O'Neill to make
a dignified exit. She told reporters that she knew nothing of any
threats against the FBI. And if there had been, she insisted, she
would have been told.

Amid the bureaucratic feuding, the FBI failed to fully explore
al Qaeda's role in the attack on the USS *Cole*. While the CIA
insisted there was enough evidence to connect al Qaeda to the
attack, the FBI insisted that there was not enough evidence to persuade a grand jury. Al Qaeda had taken credit for the bombing, and
bin Laden had composed a poem in January 2001 celebrating it,
but the FBI focused on local Yemeni terrorists.

Now the Justice Department's largest ongoing terrorist investigation was stalled and Ashcroft would have to repair the damage
done with the State Department. He was not aware that the al
Qaeda connection to the bombing of the USS *Cole* was not being
pursued.

Meanwhile, many of the problems of the Clinton years continued. The Immigration and Naturalization Service, which is part of
the Justice Department, still had not implemented a terrorist tracking program that had been mandated by Congress in 1996.

And the FBI was about to lose the man who knew more about
Osama bin Laden than anyone else at the bureau—just as the
"noise level" among al Qaeda operatives increased and intelligence
analysts began to suspect a major strike against America, either at
home or abroad. On July 6, 2001, O'Neill was flying back to New
York with his longtime girlfriend. She picked up a newspaper discarded by another passenger and handed it to him without comment. O'Neill looked down at a *New York Times* article that was
intensely critical of his role in the Yemen investigation.[44] It was a
leak by an unnamed senior FBI official meant to discredit him.

Worn down by years of bureaucratic battles, O'Neill started to turn his attention away from bin Laden's next move to his own, to make plans to leave his beloved bureau before he was pushed out. On his last day, in August 2001, he waited until 6 p.m. for the paperwork to arrive; he wanted to be the one to sign the approval to send FBI investigators back into Yemen to continue the USS *Cole* investigation.[45]

O'Neill found a job as head of security at the World Trade Center. He died on September 11, 2001. His funeral procession was two miles long.

MILAN, ITALY—In July, the CIA learned that Italian police had intercepted a cell phone call in Milan. Al Qaeda had long been active in Italy: Italian police and intelligence had foiled plots to attack the U.S. embassy in Rome and had uncovered terror cells in Turin, Milan, and elsewhere. Some terrorists were arrested, but many more were the targets of roving wiretaps. What the Italians overheard surprised them. Al Qaeda seemed to be planning to assassinate President George W. Bush during his first state visit in Genoa.

Security was stepped up. The Italian military even supplied a battery of surface-to-air missiles to repel an air attack. The press treated it as simply overkill among the secret service, and never probed any deeper.

THE WHITE HOUSE—President Bush was told about the al Qaeda threat to his life in his morning intelligence briefing. He wasn't happy.

The president said that earlier attempts by President Clinton to capture or kill bin Laden were simply "swatting at flies." He wanted to "bring this guy down." He wanted a realistic action plan for killing or capturing Osama bin Laden. When he was informed that the National Security Council was already considering an interagency effort to hit bin Laden in Afghanistan, Bush reportedly told Rice that he wanted something more imaginative than a cruise missile strike, which would cost millions "to hit a camel in the butt." Bush also demanded a thorough review of all intelligence about terrorist threats from al Qaeda, including the possibility of attacks inside the United States.

CRAWFORD, TEXAS—A few weeks later, on August 6, the CIA presented its findings at Bush's small ranch house among the scrub pines near Crawford, Texas. Rice tuned in via a secure teleconferencing link from her White House office. In its entirety (except for security redactions), the briefing paper said:

> Bin Ladin Determined To Strike in US
>
> Clandestine, foreign government, and media reports indicate Bin Ladin since 1997 has wanted to conduct terrorist attacks in the US. Bin Ladin implied in US television interviews in 1997 and 1998 that his followers would follow the example of World Trade Center bomber Ramzi Yousef and "bring the fighting to America."
>
> After US missile strikes on his base in Afghanistan in 1998, Bin Ladin told followers he wanted to retaliate in Washington, according to a . . . [redacted] . . . service.
>
> An Egyptian Islamic Jihad (EIJ) operative told an . . . [redacted] . . . service at the same time that Bin Ladin was planning to exploit the operative's access to the US to mount a terrorist strike.
>
> The millennium plotting in Canada in 1999 may have been part of Bin Ladin's first serious attempt to implement a terrorist strike in the US. Convicted plotter Ahmed Ressam has told the FBI that he conceived the idea to attack Los Angeles International Airport himself, but that Bin Ladin lieutenant Abu Zubaydah encouraged him and helped facilitate the operation. Ressam also said that in 1998 Abu Zubaydah was planning his own US attack.

Ressam says Bin Ladin was aware of the Los Angeles operation.

Although Bin Ladin has not succeeded, his attacks against the US Embassies in Kenya and Tanzania in 1998 demonstrate that he prepares operations years in advance and is not deterred by setbacks. Bin Ladin associates surveilled our Embassies in Nairobi and Dar es Salaam as early as 1993, and some members of the Nairobi cell planning the bombings were arrested and deported in 1997.

Al-Qa'ida members—including some who are US citizens—have resided in or traveled to the US for years, and the group apparently maintains a support structure that could aid attacks. Two al-Qa'ida members found guilty in the conspiracy to bomb our Embassies in East Africa were US citizens, and a senior EIJ member lived in California in the mid-1990s.

A clandestine source said in 1998 that a Bin Ladin cell in New York was recruiting Muslim-American youth for attacks.

We have not been able to corroborate some of the more sensational threat reporting, such as that from a... [redacted]...service in 1998 saying that Bin Ladin wanted to hijack a US aircraft to gain the release of "Blind Shaykh" 'Umar 'Abd al-Rahman and other US-held extremists.

Nevertheless, FBI information since that time indicates patterns of suspicious activity in this country consistent with preparations for hijackings or other types of attacks, including recent surveillance of federal buildings in New York.

The FBI is conducting approximately 70 full field investigations throughout the US that it considers Bin Ladin-related. CIA and the FBI are investigating a call to our Embassy in the UAE in May saying that a group of Bin Ladin supporters was in the US planning attacks with explosives.

Neither Bush nor Rice was impressed with the briefing. Rice later described it as "vague," a rehash of existing intelligence with no new analysis. Another opportunity missed.

Later, when the briefing was made public, it was obvious why Bush was disappointed. The intelligence was mostly skimmed from news accounts and listed no targets, dates, or other specifics. What the poor August 6 briefing did not do was trigger an effort to reorganize America's flawed intelligence collection system. No more translators were hired. Rules that all but barred the recruitment of sources with shady backgrounds were not revoked or amended. Greater cooperation between the FBI and the CIA was not mandated. The August 6 briefing was not seen as evidence of systemic failure, but of a lackluster effort by a handful of individuals.

While a busy chief executive might not be expected to order large reforms on the basis of a single poor report, the failures of the intelligence community had been on display for almost a decade.

THE WHITE HOUSE—Meanwhile, Clarke and other National Security Council staffers were working flat-out on a bold, comprehensive plan to get bin Laden. As usual, Clarke's days began at 7 a.m. and lasted past 9 p.m. He kept these long hours to bring together all of the mid-level managers who would have to work in concert to defeat bin Laden: the State Department, the Defense Department, the Joint Chiefs of Staff, the National Security Agency, the CIA, and the FBI.

What no one in the federal government knew was that they were in a race against time.

By the end of August, a plan was hammered out to give the CIA some $200 million to arm the Northern Alliance, a rebel group that opposed the Taliban and bin Laden, to broaden the number of on-the-ground intelligence sources, and to increase the number of listening posts that could be used to track and target bin Laden.

The boldest part of the plan was an elaborate effort to arm the Predator, a small, unmanned, remotely controlled plane that skimmed the mountains of Afghanistan in the last days of the Clinton administration. Clarke had long hoped to persuade the Air Force to equip the plane with Hellfire missiles. The Predator had spotted bin Laden several times during the Clinton years, but the stingless drone could do nothing about it. An armed Predator could kill bin Laden.

But this was far from an easy sell. The Air Force didn't like the idea of pilotless planes, especially ones that it paid for but were essentially controlled by the CIA. The CIA feared that the Hellfire missile was too heavy and would make the plane difficult to maneuver and compromise its primary mission of gathering intelligence.

Clarke went to see Air Force General John Jumper, who had directed air operations during the Kosovo campaign and had just become a military advisor to Vice President Dick Cheney. General Jumper quickly agreed with Clarke. He remembered that during the air war over the former Yugoslavia, many targets spotted by the Predator were missed by the jet fighters sent in to destroy them. The problem was time. Sometimes it took as long as six hours from identifying a target (say, a tank hidden under the branches of a tree) to dispatching an F-16 or launching a cruise missile. If the Predator could be armed, the delay between seeing and striking the enemy could be reduced to minutes. Clarke and Jumper soon became a powerful, persuasive team.

One of the few real pre–September 11 bureaucratic triumphs of the Bush administration was the successful arming of the Predator. It would be ready by late September—and would play a critical role in the war in Afghanistan.

All of these options had been on the table in the Clinton years. Many were actively debated inside the Clinton White House. But they were ruled out. Clinton officials feared being mired in Afghanistan's decade-long civil war and allying themselves with dubious rebels suspected of human rights abuses and drug running. And, of course, there was the persistent worry that intervening in Afghanistan was "acting in Pakistan's backyard." Doing so might upset the delicate balance of power between India and Pakistan, two nuclear powers with a history of bloody wars and continual terrorism.

Now, with intelligence reports of pending attacks on Americans—one intelligence analyst, citing intercepts from Afghanistan, believed that al Qaeda could strike over the July 4 holiday—and threats to his own life, President Bush was determined to bypass the usual objections.

THE WHITE HOUSE—On September 4, 2001, the National Security Council approved the plan to strike bin Laden.[46] It had been in the works for months.

On April 1, 2004, the White House released part of this otherwise classified document, National Security Directive-9 (NSPD-9):

> The NSPD called on the Secretary of Defense to plan for military options "against Taliban targets in Afghanistan, including leadership, command-control, air and air defense, ground forces, and logistics." The NSPD also called for plans "against al Qaeda and associated terrorist facilities in Afghanistan, including leadership, command-control-communications, training, and logistics facilities."[47]

President Bush was expected to review the plan on September 10, but he was out of the White House that day. The meeting was rescheduled for the afternoon of September 11.

NEW YORK—The morning of September 11 brought confusion, mourning, anger, and growing resolve. For many Americans, that resolve took the form of a silent promise to never forget fathers, mothers, siblings, and spouses or the atrocity that cruelly took them away. By nightfall, the death toll in New York, Pennsylvania, and Virginia would be put at more than three thousand. The murdered were rich and poor; men, women, and children; Jews, Christians, Muslims, and atheists. While most of those killed were Americans, more than half the nations of the world could claim a citizen among the dead.

For weeks afterward, people would say that September 11 had changed the world, and it had. Before the politicians and the intellectuals recovered their tongues, the ordinary people of the world had their say.

In the square facing the U.S. embassy in The Hague, the Netherlands, thousands of people left notes and flowers. Some of the flowers had been bought and others were picked from backyards. I stood there awhile watching people come and lay their flowers in the rain. They were Dutch, French, German, Japanese, Russian, and on and on. No one told them to come; they just came. I found a junior American diplomat surveying the scene under an umbrella. He told me that it was his job to remove the flowers every few hours. Why? "If I didn't, they'd be waist-high by morning."

THE WHITE HOUSE—Inside the White House, in the smoldering confines of the Pentagon, and on the seventh floor of the State Department, officials faced three hard questions: What do we do now? Who attacked us? How did the system fail us? On these three questions hung the fate of the nation.

September 12, 2001, was the day America began fighting back. The CIA's elite paramilitary force was on its way into Afghanistan within twenty-four hours of the attacks. U.S. Special Forces would follow within days.

CHAPTER THREE

THE 2002 PLOT
TO KILL BUSH

"When the subject came into the embassy in August 2002, he provided the names of nine Sudanese pilots who, according to the subject, were trained in Pakistan and recruited to conduct terrorist acts against the United States, including the White House."

— CIA REPORT, MARCH 16, 2003

WASHINGTON, D.C.—As the first anniversary of the September 11 attacks approached, CIA and FBI officials were scrambling to stop a secret al Qaeda plot to assassinate President George W. Bush.

The public was never told why in August 2002 the new Department of Homeland Security raised the alert level from "yellow" to "orange"—signaling an imminent threat.[1] But the federal government had fresh, disturbing intelligence that suggested a major attack on America was slated for September 11, 2002.

Certainly, the terror network likes to strike on politically significant anniversaries.[2] The August 7, 1998, bombings of U.S. embassies in Nairobi, Kenya, and Dar Es Salaam, Tanzania—which killed a dozen American diplomats and 212 Africans—were carried out on the eighth anniversary of the arrival of American troops in Saudi Arabia.[3]

Yet, in the summer of 2002, American intelligence was *not* scrambling based on historical analysis or an inspired hunch. The CIA had received a warning that was specific and credible from a trusted source. And the plot, if it succeeded, would kill the president, destroy the White House, and shock the nation.

As it unfolded, a major CIA source would end up in an African prison, a luckless illegal immigrant would face America's new "zero tolerance" justice, and dozens of al Qaeda operatives would lose either their lives or their freedom. The "Mekki plot" would be a strange and ambivalent, yet crucial, victory in Bush's shadow war.

In August 2002, here is what the CIA thought it knew: Ali Osman Mohammed Taha, the first vice president of Sudan, was an active al Qaeda agent. Unbeknownst to Sudanese president Omar al-Bashir, Taha had recruited ten Sudanese men and sent them for flight training in Peshawar, Pakistan, in 1993. Their schooling was financed by al Qaeda and supervised by an Egyptian al Qaeda leader. Two years later, the ten returned to Sudan and were "infiltrated" into the Sudanese air force. The report, from a CIA informant who was an officer in the Sudanese military, even supplied the full names of the ten pilots. Two had subsequently died while serving in southern Sudan, where a bloody civil war had raged intermittently since 1955. Ominously, one of the ten, identified as Mekki Hamed Mekki, had vanished and was believed to be hiding in the United States. The CIA's source said that Mekki's mission was to fly a small plane into the White House and kill President Bush—on September 11, 2002.

The source, codenamed M, had a long track record. For years, he had supplied information the agency considered reliable and his position as a military officer seemed to give him access to unique intelligence. More chilling, U.S. government records confirmed elements of M's account.

American immigration records revealed that Mekki had arrived in New York on September 27, 2000—around the time that the

September 11 hijackers began to filter into the United States. A visa had been granted by the U.S. embassy in Cairo, Egypt, on July 18, 2000, for someone named "Makki Hamed Makki," perhaps an alternative spelling of Mekki's name. Translating Arabic names into the Roman alphabet frequently leads to variant spellings of the same name, although, as it later developed, Mekki was involved in a bit of subterfuge. By the time his tourist visa expired on October 16, 2000, Mekki had disappeared. There was no evidence that he had left the country. According to M, Mekki had joined an al Qaeda sleeper cell.

The report sounded strikingly similar to an al Qaeda plan found on a laptop owned by Ramzi Yousef, the mastermind of the 1993 World Trade Center bombing. The computer, captured in a 1994 raid on the Doña Josefa apartments in the Malate district of Manila, the Philippines, contained a detailed plot to pack a small plane with high explosives and kamikaze it into CIA headquarters. Yousef was captured in Islamabad, Pakistan, in 1995 and now is confined in a high-security federal prison. But his plans have a way of living on.

Years before Yousef was imprisoned, he and Khalid Shaikh Mohammed had dreamed up an early version of the September 11 attacks. The attack plan had germinated since 1992, was approved in 1998, and the first cell members were spirited into the U.S. in 2000. Was history repeating itself? Had another of Yousef's plans been put into play?

Huge measures had been taken to safeguard the president. Coast Guard boats patrolled the Potomac River. The Secret Service had initiated new, stricter procedures to protect the president and his family. Private planes had been banned from the skies over Washington, D.C. The Department of Homeland Security used helicopters to the patrol the capital's airspace, because jet fighters tended to stall out if they throttled back to the plodding speed of a Cessna or Piper Cub. Mekki was supposed to attack the White House in just such a small plane.

Even false alarms demonstrated the strong points of America's new security measures—as well as the holes just big enough for a small plane to slip through. On the night of the State of the Union address in January 2002, when President Bush was due to speak from the well of the House of Representatives, a single-engine plane flew into the "no-fly" zone radiating outward from the Capitol, the White House, and other federal landmarks. The pilot did not respond to repeated radio calls. He seemed to be making a beeline for the Capitol at the very moment President Bush was speaking.

"We read Tom Clancy just like everyone else," a Department of Homeland Security official told me. As jets scrambled and helicopters closed in, Homeland Security feared a terror strike modeled on Clancy's novel *Debt of Honor*.[4] In the book, a commercial plane smashes into the Capitol during the State of the Union address, killing the president and many members of Congress.

Homeland Security helicopters directed the plane to land at a nearby airport. Inside was an embarrassed Maryland state trooper, an amateur pilot who simply wanted to show his son an aerial view of the Capitol dome lit up at night. He had no idea that the president was delivering a speech or that air travel over Washington, D.C., was restricted to government aircraft. The incident revealed that air defenses still needed to be tightened. Fewer than nine months later, they seemed to be on the verge of being tested again—this time for real.

Meanwhile, the FBI had lost Mekki's trail. He had given one address on his immigration forms and quickly moved to another. The tenants at his first address claimed to have no idea where Mekki was—only that he didn't live there. He did not show up in a national search of phone directories or in Internet searches. If the FBI had searched state driver's license records, it would have found him in minutes. Like Mohammed Atta, Mekki had a valid driver's license in his own name.

The CIA was canvassing all of its sources and begging for help from friendly intelligence services. No luck. And the agency's source who had filed the report, M, had been sent on a military mission far from Khartoum. M could not be reached without compromising his identity as an informant and risking his life.

Seven time zones away, CIA Director George Tenet was demanding regular updates. "The station chief's balls were really getting squeezed," said a European consultant for the government of Sudan, who was briefed on the Mekki plot as the drama unfolded. "They had to do something."

KHARTOUM, SUDAN—The phone rang after midnight at the home of a senior Sudanese intelligence officer. We will call him "Sayed." The duty officer who, with his peers, covers the phone twenty-four hours a day, said the CIA chief of station urgently desired a meeting.

"Now?"

"Yes, now."

Sayed, who supplied much of this account in an exclusive interview with me in Khartoum, agreed to drive over to the rambling, run-down complex that was home to Sudan's external intelligence service, known as the Mukhabarat (Sudan's intelligence service is now housed in a new tower with Ikea-like furniture). He found the American official waiting.

The CIA was desperate and the clock was ticking. Now, in the last week of August 2002, the station chief had decided to take a calculated risk and ask the very government that was suspected of hatching a plot to kill President Bush to help locate the man thought to be the ringleader.

This was not an easy decision. Sudan had been on the U.S. State Department's list of state sponsors of terror since 1993. Osama bin Laden had lived there from April 1991, when he had been welcomed at Khartoum Airport's VIP terminal by Hassan al-Turabi, then the speaker of the parliament, to May 1996, when he was expelled at the request of the Clinton administration. Khartoum had sponsored an annual gathering of Islamic terrorists—every group from Hamas to the Moro Islamic Liberation Front—until 1996, when the conference was shut down at the request of the American government. The U.S. also believed that Sudan hid terrorist training camps and a chemical weapons program—allegations that later turned out to be false.

Relations between the United States and Sudan had long been "in the deep freeze," as one intelligence source put it. The U.S. had applied severe economic sanctions in 1997 and never eased them. A coalition of human rights and Christian groups made it politically difficult to even consider normalizing relations. Both Republicans and Democrats in Congress were pressing for tougher measures, on the grounds that Sudan's civil war had led to human rights abuses and modern-day slavery. (While these tragedies are real enough, the role of the rebels in both was overlooked.)

Sudan's many offers to help the U.S. fight terrorism were spurned by the Clinton administration. In February 1996 and again in March 1996, senior Sudanese officials in Khartoum and Washington offered to arrest bin Laden and turn him over.[5]

The Clinton administration debated the proposal and ultimately turned it down. The reasons range from the political to the procedural. If the United States took custody of bin Laden, some administration officials feared, President Clinton would be accused of negotiating with a terrorist state during the 1996 presidential campaign. Others feared that a lack of airtight evidence to guarantee a criminal conviction might lead to an embarrassing acquittal for bin Laden.

Both of these objections could have been easily finessed by asking Sudan to secretly transfer bin Laden outside of legal channels. This is known as a "rendition." Renditions of drug lords were not unknown in the Clinton years, but the Clinton team never seemed to have considered the option in bin Laden's case. Sudan might have viewed it favorably; it had rendered the infamous terrorist Carlos the Jackal to France in 1994.

But, instead, in May 1996, the Clinton administration asked Sudan, through a friendly Western intelligence service, to expel bin Laden. He left within weeks for a haven in the hills of Afghanistan.

In 1997, Sudan's president wrote a formal letter to President Clinton, offering the United States access to Sudan's voluminous intelligence files on senior al Qaeda figures. Clinton never responded. (I saw some of these files in 2002; they are a treasure trove of important details on bin Laden and his associates.)

In 1998, Sudan captured two of the planners of the East African embassy bombings. When Gutbi al-Mahdi, then the Sudanese intelligence chief, offered to turn over the two suspects to the FBI, the bureau was denied permission to travel to Khartoum to take them into custody. The White House had its reasons. Several days after spurning the offer, American cruise missiles destroyed the al-Shifa pharmaceutical plant in the Sudanese capital.

Poor intelligence—some of it based on fraudulent reports from paid informants inside Sudan—hoodwinked the U.S. into believing that the plant was owned by bin Laden and was being used to make chemical weapons. Exhibit A was a soil sample said to contain EMPTA, a precursor to VX nerve gas. But the sample could not have come from inside the plant; the ground there was covered entirely in concrete, as I noted when I toured the wreckage. And the soil sample was later shown to contain Round-Up, a common weed killer, not EMPTA. Finally, records on file with the United Nations—which had a contract with the plant to produce medicines—revealed that it had been repeatedly visited by German and other European government officials and that neither bin Laden nor any of his front companies had any ownership stake. A classic intelligence failure.

Relations between the U.S. and Sudan had begun to thaw after President Bush was sworn into office in January 20, 2001. Indeed, the shift in U.S. policy toward Sudan seems to have come directly from Bush himself. Sudanese foreign minister Mustafa Osman Ismail, sitting on the back lawn of his home overlooking the Nile River, told me an intriguing story that he said he received from a "reliable source": When Ugandan president Yoweri Museveni met with President Bush in the Oval Office in the spring of 2001, he gave the usual reasons why peace would be impossible between Christians and Muslims in Sudan. Bush was in no mood for business as usual. He interrupted Museveni, saying, "Those people need peace." There was no mistaking Bush's tone. The Ugandan president, whose government had supplied and funded the Christian rebels for years, got the message. Peace talks resumed.

While the Clinton administration had tried to unilaterally isolate and even topple the regime in Sudan, the Bush administration was trying a more realistic approach. The National Islamic Front, which ran Sudan, was not going anywhere. The Bush team, working with the European Union, initiated a strategy of limited, incremental engagement. Concerns about terrorist training camps and weapons of mass destruction were patiently investigated. Ultimately, six teams totaling 145 people would visit Sudan in the two years ending in 2002. Bush appointed a special envoy, former senator John Danforth, to broker peace talks. The peace talks would eventually succeed.

Walter H. Kansteiner III, assistant secretary of state for African affairs, met secretly with Sudan's foreign minister in Nairobi, Kenya.[6] They met again in London before September 11. These meetings are reported here for the first time. The U.S. wanted to work closely on terrorism and on promoting peace.

Intelligence cooperation was slowly resumed. On May 17, 2001, the CIA and Sudanese intelligence began a hesitant and cautious collaboration on counter-terrorism. On September 12, 2001, Sudan

provided the CIA with a list of twenty-six names of al Qaeda operatives it believed were inside Sudan. Khartoum offered to make
them available for questioning. In the following months, all twenty-
six were questioned by the CIA and FBI. Some were held and others put under surveillance. "This is probably the best set of leads
that the CIA got in the hours after September 11," said David
Hoile. "It was the beginning."

The CIA held eleven meetings with its Sudanese counterpart
from January 2001 to August 2002, according to Janet McElligott,
a onetime lobbyist for Sudan in Washington, D.C., who maintains
friendly ties with Sudan's intelligence services. Hoile puts the number of meetings between Sudanese intelligence and the CIA and
FBI at "close to one hundred" from September 2001 to June 2004.
Still, the agency remained suspicious of Sudan, which had long
been tied to terrorism.

Sudanese officials say that they wondered whether American
attitudes would ever really change. Neither side suspected that the
"Mekki plot" was about to transform their relationship. And never
before had a CIA official requested an "urgent meeting" in the
middle of the night.

The CIA chief of station gave Sayed a carefully scrubbed
account of an alleged plot to crash a plane into a major U.S. government facility, referring to his secret source only as M. He presented Sayed with a list of ten suspected pilots, including Mekki.

Sayed was guarded. "It was not the first wild allegation I'd heard
from the Americans," he told me. Previous "wild allegations"
included two post–September 11 sightings of bin Laden; one in
Darfur, in the remote reaches of western Sudan, and the other in
Juba, in its tropical, war-torn south. Both were found to be false.
"So I was not astonished."

But this was different. The account was detailed and contained
many checkable facts. If it were true, it would strangle any hopes
for better relations with the United States. If it were false and could

be proven so, it might lead the Americans to reconsider their stance. So, for Sudan, it was an opportunity wrapped in a crisis.

Then the station chief asked his urgent question: Will you help us?

Early the next morning, Sayed tracked down Mekki's commanding officer. He was told that Mekki had indeed trained as a pilot in Pakistan, but at his own expense. Until 2000, it was fairly common for Sudanese men seeking military careers to arrange their pilot training in Pakistan; Sudan's military has a relatively small training budget and preferred to recruit pilots who already knew how to fly. There was no evidence, the commander said, that Mekki had received help from al Qaeda. Oh, and Mekki had gone AWOL in July 2000. So far the CIA story was checking out.

Sayed placed a rush order for the military records of all ten pilots the CIA had named. Within hours, a stack of files had arrived via military courier. Sayed started reading.

That night, after evening prayers, Sayed met with the station chief. He got right to the point. "The backbone of the story is 100 percent true,"[7] he said. The names of the ten pilots were accurate. They were indeed sent to Pakistan for training in 1993. They had returned to Sudan in 1995. Shortly thereafter, all ten were inducted into the Sudanese air force. The two pilots who were reported to have died actually did perish in the south. And, as the CIA feared, Mekki Hamed Mekki was in fact "absent without leave" from the air force, disappearing sometime in July 2000. So far the CIA's report was dead accurate, Sayed said.

But two vital facts were wrong. The pilots had not received financial aid from al Qaeda or any bin Laden front group (they had asked their families for the money) and they had not trained in Pakistan under an Egyptian, let alone an Egyptian member of al Qaeda, but under a Pakistani who was a veteran flight trainer. Finally, there was no known relationship between these men and al Qaeda or Osama bin Laden.

The CIA official was unconvinced: "You're just trying to protect your government."

Sayed understood the situation perfectly. The CIA official believed that Sayed was either only admitting what he knew the U.S. already knew or was attempting to deceive the agency by acknowledging the less damaging parts of the story while denying the rest. Certainly, the station chief was not going to bet his career on an assurance from a Sudanese intelligence official he barely knew—especially when the president's life was on the line. The only solution was to help the CIA find Mekki. "Okay, let me start the search."

On a side street in Jimaiab, a poor neighborhood at the edge of Khartoum, Sayed found the modest home of Mekki's parents. Mekki's father, a respected high school principal, was polite but unhelpful. He said that he had no information on his son—only that he had left Sudan. Sayed got the impression that Mekki and his father had fallen out over something. But what?

Having a deep understanding of the dynamics of Sudanese Arab families, Sayed sought out Mekki's sister, saying, "You know where your brother is, don't you?"

With some reluctance, she explained the family history. Mekki wanted to chase the American dream, but his father thought it was dishonorable to desert the Sudanese military. It would make Mekki a criminal and bring shame on his family. Mekki, however, had no patience and, in his mind, no future. Father and son parted on bad terms. Mekki's sister concluded, "You can't tell [my father] that we're talking," she said, "because my father has forbidden it."

Just as Sayed had suspected, she was in furtive contact with her brother. He gently asked how he could reach Mekki.

She grudgingly provided a phone number—in North Carolina.

As soon as the time difference allowed, Sayed dialed the number. The man who answered spoke Arabic with a Sudanese accent. Sayed asked for Mekki.

The man did not want to help. Like many Sudanese, he was not in the habit of telling government officials the whereabouts of his friends. Sayed played his cards carefully. "Don't worry. The only reason we are looking for him is that there's a problem with his father. He doesn't get along with his father. His sister gave us this number. We're trying to do good with this." Sayed knew this would have the ring of truth.

"Well, why does the FBI want him?" The man told Sayed that a letter had arrived for Mekki from the FBI. Tactically, this was a stupid move on the part of America's largest domestic counter-terrorism unit and a sign of desperation. It only complicated things.

Sayed bluffed. "Oh, it's probably some immigration thing that doesn't have anything to do with us."

GREENSBORO, NORTH CAROLINA—United Yellow Cab number 50 was parked under the branches of a tree near a Harris Teeter store, along a shopping strip on West Market Street. Three other taxicabs were parked behind it. Inside number 50, four immigrants from Sudan were passing the time, waiting for the radio dispatcher to send one of them a pick-up. One of the four men, Zaher Altahair, recalls, "We were just talking, weather, sports. . . ."[8]

Suddenly two cars and a sport utility vehicle roared in, blockading the taxis. Four men in ties emerged. One was FBI special agent Michael Knapp.[9]

"Let me see your licenses," Knapp demanded.

The lanky man in the driver's seat showed Knapp a valid North Carolina driver's license. It featured his picture and his real name, in full: Mekki Hamed Mekki.

North Carolina is one of only three states that grants driver's licenses without asking for a social security card or other proof of U.S. citizenship. This policy is supposed to encourage road safety and compel illegal immigrants to get car insurance.[10] Whatever its merits, the policy made it easy for Mekki to get a license and a job.

He even enrolled as a student at North Carolina Agricultural and Technical State University, where September 11 planner Khalid Shaikh Mohammed had studied in the 1980s.[11]

Knapp wasn't satisfied. He wanted to make sure he had the right man. For all he knew, Mekki could be the Sudanese equivalent of "Smith." When he demanded further proof of identification, Knapp was setting a trap for Mekki, whether either one of them knew it or not.

Mekki offered to drive Knapp to his apartment. The address was in the heart of a Sudanese immigrant enclave. Indeed, so many of the estimated three thousand Sudanese[12] who live in Greensboro reside in this neighborhood that it is known locally as Omdurman, after a district in Khartoum.[13]

Mekki pulled up in front of the Colonial Apartments on 402 Montrose Drive. He lived there with three other Sudanese-born taxi drivers.[14]

Once inside Apartment F, Mekki opened a small closet door and withdrew a black plastic shopping bag, which is where he kept his important papers. He produced a valid Sudanese passport and U.S. immigration documents indicating that he had filed for a green card under twenty different versions of his name. Unwittingly, Mekki had just handed a FBI special agent proof of immigration fraud, a criminal offense. This evidence would become more important later, but, right now, all Knapp cared about was finding out whether this immigrant taxi driver was plotting to kill the president of the United States.

Mekki was handcuffed and led outside. His taxi would remain parked on Montrose Drive for days—a memorial to an ordinary immigrant life stopped short by extraordinary circumstances. Eventually, he arranged to lease it to a Sudanese friend and used the money to pay his legal bills.

The interrogation of Mekki began almost immediately. The more Mekki talked, the less the FBI believed.

In their initial conversation, Mekki seemed to be hiding something. Three consecutive polygraph tests confirmed these suspicions. He was lying and covering up—but what?

Mekki told the agents the kinds of things poor Africans say when they are trying to secure asylum in the United States. He said that he was forced to commit war crimes in Sudan's civil war and that when he refused he was repeatedly tortured. Fearing that the government wanted to kill him and his family, he fled. This is precisely the script someone uses to win political asylum, and the multiple, fraudulent U.S. immigration forms demonstrated that Mekki was an expert at playing the system.

When asked about bin Laden, he said he knew nothing about him. As it happened, this was the truth, but it was hidden in a welter of lies.

As a result, the FBI could not rule out that Mekki was part of a sleeper cell that was plotting a fiery, murderous atrocity. The FBI desperately needed to know the numbers and location of the other cell members and was fully aware that Mekki's arrest might have triggered a final countdown.

It was time for the CIA to take another calculated risk—an unprecedented one.

KHARTOUM, SUDAN—The lobby of the Khartoum Hilton is never quiet or empty after evening prayers. It offered the finest décor available when it opened in 1977 and has changed little since. Translucent yellow globes dangle from long chains over a rectangle of couches and uncomfortable bamboo chairs. Here men in white turbans banter with chain-smoking arms dealers, long-haired nonprofit directors, and cigar-puffing reporters.

No one noticed the tall man in the blue safari suit glide in. He found the CIA official waiting on a couch.[15]

This time the American had a surprise for his Sudanese counterpart: a copy of the cable that had launched the global manhunt for Mekki. But first the CIA officer had a question: "What made you think this information was false?"

"Well, because this is typically Sudanese."

The informant, Sayed explained, was getting paid to provide information. If he didn't have any genuine intelligence to offer, he had a powerful financial incentive to make something up. The Sudan CIA station paid anywhere from $100 to $400 per report.[16] The per capita income in Sudan is estimated at $1,400 per year.[17]

Paying for information is risky enough, but, in Sudanese terms, the agency was paying so much it was certain to corrupt its sources. A retired CIA officer who once supervised all of its Near East stations told me that it is never wise to pay for reports *at the beginning* of a relationship with an intelligence source. The truth can usually be bought by other means than money (such as appeals to pride, patriotism, or recognition), while false reports are always expensive. "You introduce money into the relationship only later," he said, "as a control factor."[18] But the Sudan station had experienced a rapid turnover since 1996 and there were few veterans to warn of the dangers of payouts to sources.

Here is how Sayed remembers the conversation:

Sayed asked, "Have you checked out the source who gave this to you?"

"Well, he's been a source for years."

"Do you think that could be why there are some problems between the CIA and the Sudanese? Why don't you check out your source?"

Perhaps the CIA still believed that Mekki was going to murder President Bush; his lie detector tests clearly showed evidence of deception.

Sayed reminded the station chief that the CIA had been repeatedly duped by false reports from Sudan. One report in 1995 warned of an assassination attempt on then National Security Advisor Anthony Lake. Lake and his family were moved to a secure location and the Secret Service stepped up security. The threat was later proven false. When I interviewed Lake in 2002, he confirmed the circumstances but claimed that he didn't give the report much credence at the time and later joked about it.[19] It was one of many small intelligence failures out of the CIA's Sudan station. A few years later, when several CIA sources failed their lie detector tests, the agency was forced to "withdraw" more than one hundred reports about Sudan.[20] Now it looked like it might have to discard one more.

"There is strong evidence that M is lying," Sayed said. "Not only should you look at this story, but, what we would do in our service is look at all of the stories he gave us. We'd suggest that you do that and go find out how many of them turn out to be true."

"Well," the station chief said, "we agree with you and we're going to do that." The CIA officer then gave up the name and rank of his source.

"This was the turning point in the relationship with the Americans. It is not normal that an agency gives up a source," Sayed told me. "I praise him [the station chief] for doing this."

It turned out that M was a Sudanese army captain named Bilal Awad Sulayman. Together, the two intelligence officers conspired to snare him.

The next day, still carrying a travel bag from his assignment in the southern war zone, Bilal was met by plainclothes intelligence officers and escorted from the Khartoum military airport to the Mukhabarat headquarters. If he was nervous or had questions, he was too clever to ask his escorts.

Eventually he was ushered in to see Sayed. Bilal demanded to know why he had been brought in.

Sayed expertly seized control. "You have been chosen for a special intelligence assignment. Ask no questions. I need you to go into the next room and answer truthfully all the questions asked of you by the people who are in there."

Bilal said nothing. He had only one option—to brazen it out and hope, like Benedict Arnold, he would survive.

Sayed told Bilal to change out of his military uniform and into civilian clothes. As the captain snapped back the locks on his suitcase, Sayed stepped outside.

A few minutes later, Bilal emerged in "civvies." Sayed pointed to the closed door of a conference room. Bilal twisted the knob, not knowing what to expect.

He was surprised to find two middle-aged Americans inside. One was setting up a polygraph, laying out the lie detector's telltale wires and cords. The other addressed him in clear, non-Sudanese Arabic. They identified themselves as CIA officers.

CIA? Working *inside* Sudanese intelligence headquarters? Bilal couldn't believe it. "It was a great shock to him," Sayed said dryly.

For more than an hour, Bilal sat in stony silence as an old CIA hand tried to coax and coach him. Bilal's thoughts must have raced. Perhaps it really was some kind of Sudanese intelligence operation. Or was it a trap?

The polygraph operator was a very skillful interlocutor. He had interrogated people for the CIA for some twenty-six years. We don't know what he said, but we know the result. Bilal broke.

Wires were attached to his fingers, forehead, and chest. The polygraph needles jumped and the readings scrolled out. The interrogation lasted three and a half hours.

While Bilal debated his nonexistent options, Sayed met with the station chief in another office in Mukhabarat headquarters. "You might assume that this man is not the right one, so I wanted to put all of those suspicions aside," Sayed said.

He picked up a military ID card, which he had plucked from Bilal's uniform pocket. The station chief had a photocopy of Bilal's ID card that had been made about two years earlier. They put the two side by side. A perfect match.

If the station chief suspected that the Sudanese had supplied a ringer, he did not let on. But he had no doubt now that the man in the next room was M, his source. It would be dawn before he knew whether his source was reliable—and whether the president's life was actually in danger.

Early the next morning, CIA officials pored over the polygraph results. There was no doubt: Bilal had been lying to the CIA for years. There was no plot to kill the president. It was an ingenious scam, a great lie propped up by many small truths. Or, as a CIA polygraph report concluded: "information that subject had concerning an attack on the White House was a fabrication."[21]

Bilal had a mix of personal, financial, and political motives. He disliked Mekki and some of the other ten pilots he had named; he was paid hundreds of dollars for each false report and he liked the folding money. He was in the midst of building a large house in Khartoum which was "very expensive and would have been beyond the reach of an army officer," Sayed told me. The house could not have been built with family money: Bilal never married, and his parents, who were divorced, had little themselves. "Lies and CIA cash built that house," David Hoile told me.

Bilal also had ideological and personal reasons to detest the regime. His family was known for its history of anti-government sentiments. And he smoked hashish, a serious crime in the Sudan—and the threat of punishment no doubt concentrated his mind. Finally, the CIA had promised him that if things got too dangerous for him in Sudan, the agency would give him a U.S. visa and help him get a job in the United States. If Bilal had had the wit to lie about assassination attempts on his own life instead of George Bush's, he might have moved to the green, prosperous suburbs of Washington, D.C.

Instead, he never made it out of Sudan. In the coming weeks, he would be tried and convicted of espionage. Today he is incarcerated in the al-Khobar prison, an old British-built penitentiary with whitewashed walls and narrow guard towers in Khartoum.[22] "When we recruit a source," a former CIA station chief explained to me, "we are seducing people into betraying their country."[23] Bilal was a traitor who lied to the CIA and got caught. There was no mercy for him now.

Some might feel sympathy for Bilal, thinking he was simply a poor man on the make. Citing such impersonal forces—such as poverty—is always a dodge for individual responsibility. Bilal swore an oath to defend his country and he betrayed it. He also betrayed the trust of his American friends for profit and self-aggrandizement. His lies led hundreds of FBI, CIA, and Homeland Security staffers to waste their time on a plot conjured out of his imagination. As any firefighter knows, a false alarm across town can keep the fire department from responding if a fire starts next door. His fabrications temporarily poisoned relations between the U.S. and Sudan, at the very moment when President Bush badly needed allies in East Africa to wage war on al Qaeda.

Meanwhile, on September 13, Mekki was being held in Forsyth County Jail in Greensboro, North Carolina, awaiting arraignment. He had no idea how his freedom had been taken, through incredible circumstances, by his old acquaintance Bilal.

GREENSBORO, NORTH CAROLINA—U.S. attorney Anna Mills Waggoner heard the news from the FBI. There was no easy way to explain that the bureau—indeed, the entire federal government—had been duped by false intelligence. Mekki was not at the center of an al Qaeda plot to kill President Bush; he was a pawn in a scam to defraud the CIA.

In principle, Waggoner could have decided not to pursue the case against Mekki at that point. But leniency was actually against U.S. policy.

The head of the FBI's international counter-terrorism division, Michael E. Rolince, had written a secret seven-page document distributed to all federal prosecutors. It was used to secure the strongest sentences possible, even for minor offenses, if a link to terrorism were suspected.[24]

Attorney General John Ashcroft publicly endorsed this policy in a speech before the U.S. Conference of Mayors in October 2001: "Robert Kennedy's Justice Department, it is said, would arrest mobsters spitting on the sidewalk if it would help in the battle against organized crime.... It has been and will be the policy of the Department of Justice to use the same aggressive arrest and detention tactics in the War on Terror. Let the terrorists among us be warned: If you overstay your visa—even one day—we will arrest you."[25]

Mekki had overstayed his visa by almost two years. The fraud charges would be harder to prove.

"Does the government intend to pursue this case?" asked U.S. Magistrate Russell Eliason.[26]

Assistant U.S. attorney Patrick Auld had his marching orders. "Yes, your honor, and there's the possibility that other charges will be brought."[27]

Actually, as the judge hinted, the government's case was weak. Even FBI special agent Knapp admitted under oath that the immigration processing center in Lexington, Kentucky, had no record of Mekki's fraudulent applications. The facility regularly trashed all applications it denied. So there was no hard evidence, aside from the documents handed over by Mekki, that the defendant had defrauded anyone.

Gregory Davis, one of the public defenders fighting for Mekki, was outraged. "It's almost like saying somebody's dead and there's no body," he said. "I think they've jumped the gun and held him... when there was really some other motive for holding him."[28] But, as far as I have been able to determine, no one ever told Davis or Mekki the true story.

Some forty of Mekki's friends, mostly Sudanese-born cab drivers, sat in the courtroom. They had helped raise almost $2,500 for

Mekki's legal defense, a princely sum in the minimum-wage world. Outside the courtroom, they told reporters that the prosecution of Mekki was more evidence of anti-Muslim bias in post–September 11 America. The familiar script of grievance and selective prosecution would take over. One of their own was being sent away and to them it was easy to suspect persecution. A bitter little taste of what they had left behind. After all, the government wasn't deporting Mexicans and other Roman Catholics who entered the country illegally. Only hardworking Muslims like Mekki.

A moment's reflection would dissolve these claims. More Latin Americans are deported from the United States than people from any other region in the world. Besides, no one argues that immigration cases should be litigated using some form of affirmative-action quota system.

Few knew or admitted that Mekki had supplied physical evidence of and admitted to committing a number of immigration crimes. These facts might not count for much in Greensboro's Omdurman. Illegal aliens from all over the world had done the same thing, including perhaps Mekki's neighbors. To them, it was a paperwork violation. And it was. But as federal prosecutors could point out, similar violations had helped cost three thousand people their lives on September 11, 2001.

And, in the unlikely event Mekki did turn out to be a terrorist, releasing him would shame the Justice Department and cripple some careers. The easy decision would be to let the wheels of justice grind on. That is what happened.

In an ideal world, Mekki might have been allowed to stay in the United States. After his unlawful entry, he had done all of the right things; he worked hard, paid his bills, helped others, and pursued an education to further better himself. He was unknown in both the police department and the welfare office. Government certainly has the power of selective prosecution; it does not have to charge every lawbreaker it runs across. It can set priorities. It cannot possibly prosecute every malefactor—there isn't money enough or time. But that is not to say that Mekki was not guilty, only that he was unlucky.

Welcome to the post–September 11 world. It isn't ideal. It is full of hard choices. A nation at war is not disposed to take chances on mercy. Remember the visible and invisible aspects of such tough law enforcement. We see Mekki and his destroyed life. We don't see the terrorists who might have been deterred when his sad story circulates in the immigrant community—or the lives saved by tougher immigration measures. Not everyone who cheats the system, like Mekki, is harmless.

Due to poor intelligence, the CIA and FBI had spent thousands of man-hours and hundreds of thousands of dollars to arrest a taxi driver with a stack of falsified immigration documents. The CIA's fabricating source was imprisoned and Mekki was on his way to being deported.

Yet, strangely, the sad Mekki case was a net victory in the War on Terror—at least from the viewpoints of the CIA and the Sudanese.

The so-called Mekki plot pushed the CIA to purge its poor intelligence sources in Sudan and led to a newer, stronger relationship with Sudanese intelligence officers. As a result of this new cooperation, since September 2002, the Sudanese have arrested or detained for questioning nearly seventy al Qaeda operatives or associates, according to documents shown to me by a Washington-based Sudanese official who works with the CIA. Another four hundred were expelled or handed over to other Arab security services, including those in Egypt and Jordan.[29]

Mekki's sad case might even have prevented a covert war. In 2002, the Defense Department established the Combined Joint Task Force–Horn of Africa, known in Pentagonese as "CJTF-HOA." Under the umbrella of U.S. Central Command, CJTF-HOA is headquartered in Djibouti, a former French colony on the Red Sea. With more than 1,800 soldiers, a multinational naval force, and several wings of attack helicopters, it is the largest American force deployed in the region since the ill-fated 1993 humanitarian effort in Somalia. Enhanced cooperation with Sudan was pivotal in persuading the Bush administration against deploying Special Forces in Somalia in 2003.

Like Afghanistan, Somalia is remote, lawless, and has a long history of Islamic radicalism. Al-Ittihad al-Islamiya, a Somali terror group modeled on the Taliban and associated with Osama bin Laden since 1993, had sheltered a number of al Qaeda terrorists. The Pentagon had planned for an assault on Somalia with supplies and men on the island of Diego Garcia. This buildup fooled several Arab intelligence services into believing that the Americans were simply over-preparing for the Iraq War.

But a stronger relationship with Sudan made other options more plausible. Sudanese intelligence understood the people and politics of Somalia very well. Many of the leaders of al-Ittihad al-Islamiya had studied in Khartoum and had been routinely watched by the Mukhabarat. While most of the money for the Somali terror group came from Saudi Arabia, Kuwait, and other Persian Gulf states, many of its low-level staff had passed through Sudan.

In June 2003, the U.S. unveiled a $100 million package for fighting terrorism on the Horn of Africa, including coastal patrols and tighter border security.[30]

With the help of several governments, dozens of al Qaeda operatives were captured and joint covert operations were carried out. Bin Laden's network was denied a critical base on the Horn of Africa. A shadow war against al Qaeda in East Africa was just beginning.

CHAPTER FOUR

THE NEW AFGHANISTAN AND THE NEXT BATTLEFIELD?

"An agreement between the two [African rebels and al Qaeda] which aims at providing assistance in their sacred war [in the] west of Sudan in return for certain support and security arrangements for them and those [al Qaeda] members on the run."

—SECRET SUDANESE INTELLIGENCE MEMO, JULY 2004

"We want to be preventative, so that we don't have to put boots on the ground here in North Africa as we did in Afghanistan."

—LT. COLONEL POWELL SMITH, CHIEF OF COUNTER-
TERRORISM, U.S. ARMY EUROPEAN COMMAND

GARDEZ, AFGANISTAN—By November 2001, al Qaeda's strategic situation was desperate.

It had barely noticed the careful preparations of CIA paramilitary and U.S. Special Forces in September. Fewer than thirty days after September 11, on October 7, American and allied air forces appeared overhead, supporting Northern Alliance attacks coordinated by Special Forces. Neither al Qaeda nor the Taliban (nor indeed anyone else in Afghanistan) had ever experienced "close air support" before. The accurate and continual delivery of bombs to clear opposition for a fast-moving land assault was a shock and a surprise. The Soviets had used massive aerial bombardments and artillery barrages, which ended on a fixed schedule followed by a lull to allow the infantry to move in. This is how the Soviets, and everyone else, had fought World War II. In 1979, the Soviets brought the same tactics to Afghanistan. No doubt al Qaeda expected more of the same.

Yet the Americans were trained and equipped to fight a new war in a new way. Air and ground efforts were synchronized and simultaneous. The bombs, even the dumb ones, were more precisely delivered than any other munitions in the history of warfare.

Al Qaeda was accustomed to the slow pace and low intensity of the Afghan warlord battles during the 1990s. The Islamist fighters were willing to die, and many did, but their commanders were expecting a contest of wills like the duels fought between mountain warlords—not the new face of war.

Operating out of a war room that looked a lot like NASA's mission control, American military commanders were able to use advance communications, aerial surveillance, and computer imaging to make decisions faster than their enemies could. As a result, the pace of the terrorists' retreat was mainly determined by the speed of Northern Alliance trucks.

Al Qaeda had to make a strategic decision—quickly.

Concentrating its forces now seemed unwise. There was no sanctuary from the American bombers. Even the forbidding terrain of Tora Bora offered little refuge. It guaranteed only that they would all die together.

New bases and rally points would have to be found. These new havens would have to be small, secret, and spread across the Muslim world from Morocco to Malaysia. Like a cancer, al Qaeda would have to metastasize.

What follows is my own surmise of the strategic picture, drawing on observations gleaned from sources in Southeast Asia and the Middle East as well as senior Bush administration officials. This analysis is not based on the account of any single source, but is a compilation. Even Bush administration officials who were willing to confirm many details refused to confirm or deny my view of the big picture. So consider it an informed surmise.

In November 2001, bin Laden's inner circle was composed almost exclusively of Egyptians, Saudis, and Chechens. No doubt Chechnya or elsewhere in Central Asia was considered as a new headquarters and staging area. While al Qaeda activity did seem to pick up in the region in December 2001, the Russians and the dictators who run the former Soviet republics of Central Asia have proved far too brutal to make the region an attractive refuge for al Qaeda.

Southeast Asia offered a number of advantages. Al Qaeda and its affiliates (including Jemaah Islamiya) already had an extensive network of camps and safe houses in the Philippines, Malaysia, and elsewhere. Southeast Asia is also conveniently littered with American and allied targets.

Over the next year, the bin Laden terror network killed hundreds in two night clubs in Bali and dozens in two hotels frequented by Westerners in Kuala Lumpur. Others died in al Qaeda attacks in Thailand, Indonesia, and Malaysia.

Al Qaeda also attempted many more attacks. It tried to bomb the U.S. embassy in Kuala Lumpur, the U.S. embassy in Singapore (including a plot to assassinate U.S. ambassador Frank Lavin), and a U.S. naval base in Singapore, among others. The unraveling of the Singapore plots is a dramatic tale of the quiet surveillance of several cells followed by lightning-fast arrests of nearly forty terrorists. All the while, Ambassador Lavin went about his daily routine, trying not to reveal to his staff, his children, or the outside world that he knew his life was in danger. Lavin and Singapore intelligence officials shared the story with me on a "background" basis. Suffice it to say that by the end of 2002 al Qaeda was in full retreat in Southeast Asia: Its major operatives were arrested (including Hambali, Southeast Asia's bin Laden, who was captured in Thailand), or killed, its camps destroyed, its network in disarray. Renewed attempts to restart activities in the three southernmost Muslim-majority provinces of Thailand have been crushed.

Denied sanctuary in both Central and Southeast Asia, bin Laden's forces began to rebuild in the vast collection of failed states known as North Africa.

NORTH AFRICA—The Sahara is the world's largest desert and its most lawless region. Its slowly shifting dunes and green flecks of oases stretch from the Atlas Mountains of Morocco to the Red Sea of Egypt, covering roughly 1.5 million square miles.[1] Below the Sahara lies a dry belt of scrub bush, butte, and sunburned rock known as the Sahel, Arabic for "margin."

These two inhospitable regions stretch over nine North African nations, which are too poor and too poorly equipped to patrol these furnace-hot wastelands. They are the home and hideout for legions of nomads, smugglers, gun runners, marauders, bandits, rebels— and now, al Qaeda terrorists.

In this desolate landscape, al Qaeda and its affiliated terrorist groups have established more than a dozen training camps and safe havens, according to interviews with North African intelligence officials, intelligence documents, and U.S. Defense Department reports. The consensus of opinion among the sources I have consulted is that al Qaeda is in the Sahara and the Sahel to create a "new Afghanistan."

Al Qaeda and its affiliates need safe places to plan attacks and train fighters. Since 2002, it has established bases of varying sizes across the region, including a secret stronghold near where the borders of Algeria, Niger, and Mali meet.[2] Other reports indicate bases in northern Chad, Sudan, and Mali.[3]

Finding these bases is more difficult than a layman might believe. While there is little vegetation, the land is far from flat or featureless: It rises to more than eleven thousand feet and drops to more than one hundred feet below sea level, with many ravines, ridges, and revetments. The National Security Agency, which studies the output of spy satellites, is trained to look for telltale collections of buildings or sources of electric light at night. Yet the Sahara and the Sahel contain thousands of uncharted settlements; a terror encampment, viewed from an orbiting satellite, can easily be confused with a herding community or a base for smugglers, rebels, or other outlaws.

Even ground-level searches are difficult. The terrain is vast and unforgiving. The old African trick of "staking out the waterholes," as one former African special forces operative told me, is also difficult. There are many small springs known only to locals, and many different groups frequent the bigger ones.[4] Several thousand men, especially if they divide into groups of a dozen or so, can easily blend in.

Despite the difficulties, America is fighting back with special forces, new CIA posts, and a wide-ranging diplomatic initiative. America and its allies are using joint covert operations, P-3 Orion surveillance aircraft, and African ground troops to wage search-and-destroy missions against al Qaeda. The U.S. has established a clandestine listening post deep in the Algerian Sahara to monitor al Qaeda's movements there.[5]

Bush administration officials convened a conference in October 2003 with senior intelligence officials from across North Africa. The so-called Bamako Conference led to the creation of a regional intelligence-sharing scheme and a counter-terrorism task force. U.S. officials later unveiled an unprecedented aid package, known as the "Pan-Sahel Initiative," to Mali and other North African nations. The initiative includes both economic aid and military assistance.

Fought largely by forces from the U.S. Army's European Command (which is responsible for North Africa), the CIA, French intelligence (many of the Saharan countries are former French colonies), and a panoply of African allies, the war on al Qaeda in North Africa has gone largely unnoticed in the American media. At the very least, this war shows that the Iraq War was not a distraction from President Bush's War on Terror, only a distraction for the press.

Why did al Qaeda select North Africa as its staging ground? In short, opportunity and necessity.

The region is much like Afghanistan. It is mostly Muslim and largely undeveloped, with only a few hundred miles of paved roads in more than one million square miles of territory. In vast tracks of the Sahara and the Sahel, the only local authority is a warlord and his private army. Here guns outnumber people. The rugged and remote region is crisscrossed by roving bands of armed men. Irregular army units and some eighty Arab tribal militias patrol the landscape on camel and horseback. Add to them the wandering nomads with dirty white turbans, flowing robes, and camel trains who could easily be figures from millennia ago—but for the AK-47s slung over their shoulders. Then there are the gun-toting bandits who range over the desert, seeking women and loot.

Next there is the constellation of groups loosely known as "rebels," including the professionally trained insurgents of the Justice and Equality Movement (backed by the now jailed former speaker of Sudan's parliament, Hassan al-Turabi); the Sudan Liberation Army (a new name for the Darfur Liberation Front, believed to be trained by Eritrea and not to be confused with the Sudanese People's Liberation Army, which has waged war on behalf of the predominantly Christian and animist south of Sudan for some three decades); the Eritrean Federal Democratic Movement (whose armed cadres specialized in shooting policemen); the Polisario Front, a rebel group seeking independence for "Western Sahara" inside the present borders of Morocco; the rebels who seek to overthrow the central government of Chad; and half a dozen other rebel movements. Then there are the Janjaweed, Arabic-speaking raiders now infamous for their attacks on the "blacks" of Darfur. Next are the African tribal militias, one of which calls itself "Tora Bora" in homage to bin Laden's fighters. "Outside the major market towns," David Hoile told me, "men carry guns as casually as women in Chelmsford would carry handbags."[6]

Nor does the region lack for Islamic militants. An exhaustive list would fill pages, so let's stick to the major ones. In Egypt—as well as in Sudan, Libya, Tunisia, Algeria, and Morocco—is the Muslim Brotherhood, the oldest of modern Islamic terror groups and the source of much of radical Islam's ideology. In Algeria there are two Muslim terror groups known as the GIA (Armed Islamic Group) and the GSPC (Group Salafi for Preaching and Combat) who have perhaps killed more people since 1992 than any other non-governmental organization.

Across North Africa, the rough terrain impedes allied forces and the collection of human intelligence. The reach of central governments is minimal and incapable of punishing terrorists. Rebels and warlords can make for useful al Qaeda allies, and local Muslim militants provide a recruiting base. Finally, the severe brand of Islam often practiced in this harsh climate provides al Qaeda with at least the sympathy and often the cooperation of the locals.

Al Qaeda thrives in cruel environments like these.

ALGIERS, ALGERIA—His real name was Amara Saifi but he was perhaps best known by his terrorist alias: Abderrezak al-Para.

He was born in the Algerian village of Kef el-Rih, which means "ravine of the wind." Like many ambitious but unemployed young men in Algeria, he joined the army. He was accepted into Algeria's elite paratrooper training school in 1988. But before he could complete his training in 1989 he was dismissed as "physically unqualified."[7] He gravitated toward radical Islamic groups. Eventually, he ended up as a member of the Islamic Salvation Front, a radical religious party that had won the January 1991 elections but was denied power by Algerian military leaders. Ironically, the Algerian military coup might have saved hopes for a democratic Algeria. The Islamic Salvation Front had promised that if it came to power it would abolish the parliament and all elections because "after that God will be in charge." Denied power, the Front mutated into a terrorist organization. Saifi was put in charge of his home region of Aures. By the mid-1990s Saifi was linked to a series of massacres in Aures and was believed to be in touch with Abu Qatada, the head of al Qaeda in Europe. When al Qaeda issued a declaration condemning the GIA for slaughtering villagers instead of soldiers, the splinter group GSPC formed. In time, the GSPC would be largely funded by al Qaeda and Saifi would deal directly with Mohammed Atef, then the head of al Qaeda's military wing. In May 2001, Saifi met with Imad Alwan, an emissary from bin Laden sent to unite the North African Islamic group.

In February 2003, Saifi masterminded the kidnapping of thirty-two tourists in southern Algeria. The Algerian army immediately began tracking the terrorist kidnappers. Saifi divided the hostages into two groups. The first group was discovered by Algerian troops on May 13, 2003. Following a shootout, all seventeen hostages were safely rescued. The second group was force-marched into the deserts of northern Mali. On the march, a forty-six-year-old German mother of two died of sunstroke and dehydration. Saifi negotiated for ransom through the tribal chieftains of northern Mali. By some accounts, the German government paid some six million euros. (Sixteen of the hostages were German.) Other accounts suggest that the Libyans paid the ransom at the German government's behest.

When the hostages were released and Saifi had his money on August 18, 2003, he went on a buying spree—purchasing new trucks, automatic weapons, and satellite phones.

BAMAKO, MALI—Ever since 2000, Mali's intelligence service had been receiving reports that the Algerian-based GSPC had been filtering into remote villages in northern Mali. The terrorists had systematically married into local Muslim tribes, developing a network of allies who would not cooperate with the central government in arresting their new in-laws. Al Qaeda had used a similar strategy in Afghanistan.

In May 2004, Mali received detailed and timely intelligence that several high-ranking GSPC terrorists were in a particular village in northern Mali. Mali planned a joint special forces operation with neighboring Algeria, an increasingly important American ally in the War on Terror.

They arrived by truck and encircled the village. But the terrorists had been tipped off and had fled. In their hurry, the GSPC fighters left behind a cache of documents.

The elite Malian and Algerian troops seized several fake French passports, $5,000 in cash, and line drawings of a truck bomb plot strikingly similar to the simultaneous East African embassy bombings that had killed 224 people on August 7, 1998. Yet the drawing was not about the past, but the future. Careful study by Malian intelligence of the drawing and other captured documents revealed a developing plot: to use trucks to bomb the U.S. embassy in Bamako, Mali's sandblasted capital.[8]

BAMAKO, MALI—The Paris–Dakar Rally is one of the world's most popular automobile races. Souped-up cars and motorcycles compete over tough terrain in a race broadcast around the globe.

French intelligence learned that Saifi had moved one hundred of his fighters into the Sokolo region of central Mali to kidnap leading French driver Stéphane Peterhansel and Spanish motorcyclist Nani Roma.[9] French intelligence immediately warned Mali's intelligence service. U.S. intelligence confirmed that a large convoy of trucks and some one hundred men were seen heading toward Sokolo.

Hostage-taking had proved to be a lucrative business for Saifi, but this adventure would become a turning point in the War on Terror.

Two sections of the rally that passed through Sokolo were immediately cancelled, depriving Saifi of any hope of hostages. A U.S. Navy P-3 Orion surveillance aircraft, operating out of Algeria, was deployed to track the terrorist band. Malian troops, newly trained by American specialists, moved in to attack. They pursued Saifi's forces into Niger, a landlocked Muslim nation that had recently joined President Bush's anti-terror alliance. Outnumbered, the GSPC continued to flee. It did not turn north to Algeria, as expected. Saifi probably assumed (correctly) that Algerian soldiers were waiting to intercept him.

Instead, Saifi and his men crossed into northern Chad in search of the Movement for Democracy and Justice, a rebel group known to infest the Tibesti Mountains.

Before he could reach the mountains, Chad's army found him. Guided by U.S. aircraft, Chadian soldiers zeroed in and attacked the terrorist convoy. Saifi's men made a desperate last stand. Forty-three out of the one hundred terrorists who had set out to kidnap the rally drivers were killed. All but a dozen of the remainder were rounded up.

Saifi was one of the few who got away.

NORTHERN CHAD—The reception was not what he expected.

The Chadian rebels first reported him dead—claiming that he had slipped off a cliff—and later decided to sell Saifi to the highest bidder.

For a time, the Bush administration, as well as its allies in Africa and Europe, was uninterested. Officials offered different rationales, from disputing that the rebels actually had Saifi to citing the complex calculus of African diplomacy. No one wanted to give the Chadian rebels the patina of respectability by negotiating with them, a group opposed to the government of an African ally.

Saifi had clearly miscalculated. Like his own terror group, the Movement for Democracy and Justice needed money and there is no honor among terrorists. He also did not realize that a seismic shift had rocked the Chadian organization, shaking loose the grip of the "Saudis"—a faction of Chadian rebels educated at Wahhabi schools in the Arabian peninsula. The new ruling faction saw bin Laden as a rival who would shower support on the defeated "Saudis." Why help one of his men?

Eventually, the Algerians paid the ransom for Saifi and took him into custody. We don't know the price that was paid, but we do know that al Qaeda's most effective operator in North Africa is now out of action. He will not be easy to replace.

NORTH DARFUR, SUDAN—For centuries, the dirty collection of mud-brick buildings and grass-roofed huts known as al-Fasher has been a way station for camel trains bound for Libya. Now it is a rest stop for al Qaeda.

Darfur, a collection of three Sudanese states on the edge of the Sahara, covering an area the size of California, is a center of African misery. Famine, drought, and disease are familiar visitors. But most of the hardship is man-made: abduction, rape, and war.

Al Qaeda appeared before the headline-making misery like the lightning bolt before the thunder.

This remote region of western Sudan is well known for its Spartan interpretation of Islam. It supplied the foot soldiers of the Mahdi, an Islamic "holy man" who killed British general Charles "Chinese" Gordon in Khartoum in 1885, and provided the legions who fought under the Mahdist banner against Lord Kitchener (and the young Winston Churchill) at Omdurman in 1898. Suicidal waves of camel cavalry charged British Maxim guns. They fell by the thousands, with the promise of a martyr's paradise in their hearts.

Darfur made headlines in the spring of 2004 when two hundred thousand refugees poured over the border into Chad, desperate, hungry, sick, and fearful. An estimated thirty thousand were killed by machine gun, sword, or starvation. Another one million—almost one-quarter of the population of Darfur—fled to one of 132 makeshift camps scattered across Sudan. Charges of mass murder and mass rape, genocide and ethnic cleansing, as well as tales of marauders looting and torching villages, abounded. The United Nations pronounced it the worst humanitarian crisis in the world.

The crisis began when a surprisingly well-armed rebel movement launched a series of well-coordinated attacks and seized control of state capitals and market capitals across the three Darfur states. The revolt triggered a ferocious response from mainly Arab militias, backed by the government in Khartoum. Humanitarian groups and major newspapers, relying on the accounts of desperate refugees, quickly blamed the Janjaweed, which is an Arabic word meaning "demon on horseback." There is no doubt that these demons have burned countless villages and hacked and shot thousands of men and boys while raping women or driving them into the desert to die. Nonprofit groups active in the region were quick to claim that these horsemen were backed by the government of Sudan and accusations of mass murder, mass rape, and even genocide on the scale of Rwanda soon followed.

While true in part, this account is too simple and utterly misses the role of other outside groups, including bin Laden's network. Human rights activists, especially Human Rights Watch, seem to lump together all armed marauders—everything from bandits to tribal militias—as Janjaweed. Sudan, which has admitted arming the tribal militias, does not consider them to be Janjaweed. The Sudanese government sees the Janjaweed as a purely criminal force, including rebels and bandits, while it embraces the tribal militias as a semi-official law enforcement arm. There is some precedent for this view. Beginning in 1916, under British rule, the tribes did indeed carry out some law enforcement duties and this role has continued under all of Sudan's independent governments. Nonetheless, there is little doubt that these Arab posses have committed many human rights abuses, including wholesale slaughter of African tribes.

The victims of Janjaweed and other forces are not hard to find in the internally displaced persons camp near the Chad border. At the Sayalabe camp, an hour outside of Nyala in South Darfur, beside a village of mud huts, refugees tell a story that sounds a lot like ethnic cleansing. On May 22, 2004, Janjaweed attacked their village on foot. As a helicopter hovered nearby, one refugee woman told me, more than a dozen gunmen sought out the Africans for murder while sparing the Arabs.

How could the marauders tell the "Arabs" from the "Africans?" Both Arabs and Africans in the Darfur region are dark black and practice the same form of Islam. What makes one either "Arab" or "African" is simply tribal. "Arab is culture, not roots," one explained. They were massacred on the basis of their tribal heritage, not their appearance. The killers needed the help of treacherous neighbors to point out the "Africans" among the "Arabs."

To many, Darfur was on the verge of becoming another Rwanda, a hideous scene of death and destruction on a desolate African landscape. In reality, it is another Somalia, where tribal warfare and ideological hatred foster anarchy, murder, and starvation. And, as in Somalia in the early 1990s, al Qaeda plays a role.

While Sudan is listed as a state sponsor of terrorism by the U.S. State Department, and its government bears some responsibility for the massacre, Khartoum's ability to enforce its will in Darfur is doubtful. Over the 196,404 square miles of Darfur, there are only 15 paved roads, many in poor repair. The rainy season turns them into mires. The Sudanese army arrived long after the misery began and, even by August 2004, it was only able to garrison the major cities.

Let's go back to the beginning and examine the untold origins of the Darfur crisis. Meeting at an undisclosed location in Algeria, representatives of al Qaeda and the GSPC received a liaison officer from Sudan's Popular Congress Party, an opposition group.

A secret Sudanese intelligence memo, which I obtained in Khartoum, details what happened next (see Appendix A). Citing Algerian intelligence reports, the memo describes a February 2003 meeting in Algeria between Hassan al-Turabi's aides and bin

Laden's deputies. That meeting "resulted in an agreement between the two [African rebels and al Qaeda] which aims at providing assistance in their sacred war [in the] west of Sudan in return for certain support and security arrangements for them and those [al Qaeda] members on the run," the secret memo said.

The secret Sudanese memo details an alliance between al Qaeda, the GSPC, and the Popular Congress Party, which is headed by al-Turabi, the now jailed former speaker of Sudan's parliament.

This is the same al-Turabi who welcomed bin Laden into Africa's largest country in April 1991 and, reluctantly bowing to U.S. pressure, agreed to his departure in May 1996.[10] A senior Sudanese intelligence official in Khartoum told me that the link between the fiery Islamist and bin Laden's network has strengthened in recent years.[11]

Since 1999, al-Turabi has been a determined foe of the Khartoum government. He opposes the government's efforts to negotiate peace with the predominately Christian and animist South, prolonging a bloody civil war that has claimed an estimated two million lives since 1983.

Now, according to Sudanese intelligence, Darfur is providing the shock troops of al-Turabi's Justice and Equality Movement—a fierce rebel movement that touched off the conflagration in Darfur. These forces murdered some 550 policemen—one-third of the total constabulary body—and routed the rest, spreading anarchy across Darfur. They killed anyone who dared oppose them and conscripted men and boys to be their foot soldiers. This is the same strategy used by the Taliban to conquer Afghanistan.

Khartoum responded by arming the Arab tribal militias whose wanton slaughter made headlines.

Relying on intelligence reports from Algeria, Chad, Niger, Mali, and Pakistan as well as its own informants, the Sudanese intelligence document concludes that al Qaeda is operating in new training camps inside Chad, near its border with Sudan.

Following the pact made between al Qaeda and al-Turabi, the secret memo alleges, five al Qaeda trainers were dispatched to three training camps in northern Chad, where al-Turabi's militants trained for war against Sudan. Three of the al Qaeda operatives were specialists in guerrilla and urban warfare and two were "specialists in organizing logistical support in desert and mountainous areas similar to the territory of western Sudan." The report does not name the al Qaeda instructors.

The secret memo provides five additional sightings from other intelligence services, a pattern that suggests a continuing influx of al Qaeda terrorists into the troubled region. According to the memo, six terrorist instructors were seen travelling through Abache in April. In N'Djamena, the capital of Chad, three other terror instructors were identified, posing as businessmen who claimed to be "friends" of the older brother of Chad's president. The president and his brother hail from the Zhargawa tribe, a key combatant in the tribal warfare in Darfur.

A Sudanese intelligence official insisted that Chad's president is not in league with al Qaeda or the Sudanese rebels in the Darfur conflict and indeed has been a key anti-terror leader in the region.

Finally, Pakistan's Inter-Services Intelligence, Islamabad's feared intelligence service, told Sudan that the physical descriptions of some of the al Qaeda operatives match those of jihadis who went missing from Pakistan in 2003.

The central government has been reluctant to publicly make the case that outside groups have participated in the Darfur tragedy, the official said, because the news might encourage al-Turabi's rebellion, entice the southern rebels to hold out for better terms in the peace process, and set the stage for United Nations or Western military intervention in Darfur—which Khartoum resolutely opposes.

While the details of the secret memo are impossible to verify independently, the Sudanese document dovetails with other reports from North Africa. The desert wastes have become al Qaeda's latest battleground.

AL-FASHER, SUDAN—Through rough terrain reminiscent of Afghanistan, I went looking for a bandit king. I was hoping to verify Sudanese intelligence reports that the Janjaweed were not backed by the government and that some had received help from al Qaeda.

After passing through the Sudanese army cordon around al-Fasher in a rented Land Rover, I crossed over miles of sandy wasteland. After the Land Rover fishtailed across the trackless plain, it stopped before a steep wall of rock-strewn hills. I was obliged to continue on foot. After hiking over hills more than 150 feet high under a baking sun, a gun-wielding man in a white turban appeared on a ridge overhead. He was a Janjaweed lookout.

My translator and I were told to wait: A signal was obviously being passed.

From the steep lifeless hills I could see for miles. Eventually a truck emerged in the distance. As the white dot grew, I could see it was a pickup truck with a number of armed men in the back. It stopped somewhere out of sight and about twenty minutes later, I was given the signal to continue into the stony ravines.

There, in bug-infested scrubland, I found a tall black man who had rearranged his turban to cover all but his eyes and the crown of his head. He was very dark black and his hair was tightly curled. He said he was "an Arab." His name was Musa Khaber.

He was a bandit king, the head of a fearsome band of marauders, one of the Janjaweed.

Khaber's bodyguards, a contingent of hard men carrying AK-47s, FN-FAL rifles, and G3 assault weapons, took up fighting positions in the rocks above.

Musa's eyes glared menacingly, oblivious to the two flies crawling on his eyelids. He issued a warning to those who proposed to send an international peacekeeping force into Darfur. "We will fight them, we hate them, and we will attack the foreigners just like we attacked the government. We refuse to be like Iraq, surrendered, confused, and occupied."

He made his hand into the shape of a pistol. "We will fight them, more than the mujihideen in Afghanistan."

In this rough terrain there are many similarities with Afghanistan: dry, boulder-strewn hills, a welter of independent, tough tribesmen, a tradition of Islamic extremism, and a multitude of weapons.

This Janjaweed leader is allied with no one—he is a pure force of anarchy. "We are not with the rebels, we are not with the government, we are in hell. But we look for our due."

What does he consider his due? Development. When I point out that the number of schools has tripled in Darfur in the last ten years and there are three hospitals and one university when before there were none, he simply got angry. "I am from Krniui village. They have built nothing in my village."

He is from the Berti tribe, but his band is a mixture of many African and Arab tribes, including the Mussalit, the Zhargawa, and the Rezeigat. All they have in common is the taste for war and loot.

Some, including Human Rights Watch, allege that the Janjaweed are funded and controlled by the national government. Khartoum has long denied the charges. Musa Khaber denies any government support. "We fight all governments in Sudan, we fight Nimeri's, Sadik's, Mahdi's, and now we fight Omar Bashir [the president of Sudan]. We get nothing from the government," he said, adding that he has some relatives in the local government who provide assistance from time to time.

The interview ended abruptly when the lookout sounded that the Sudanese army was approaching. Men with rocket-propelled grenade launchers and heavy machine guns climbed into the crags above, clearly preparing for a shootout. Musa stood up suddenly and ran to Dafalla Hajar, his number two man. They argued urgently in Arabic. They were clearly outnumbered by the army. As the Janjaweed fled north into the high ground, I retraced my steps, hoping to avoid the army and arrest.

North Africa is only one important battlefield in the War on Terror, and it is far from the only one. The war extends far beyond the desert, to the sea lanes of the world.

CHAPTER FIVE

TERROR AT SEA

"If the terrorists are not able to attack targets on land, because we have hardened these, or in the air, because we now have air marshals and our airlines are taking precautions, the next alternative is to attack by sea."

   —TONY TAN, DEPUTY PRIME MINISTER OF SINGAPORE AND
   COORDINATING MINISTER FOR SECURITY AND DEFENSE[1]

"If a boat that didn't cost $1,000 managed to devastate an oil tanker of that magnitude, imagine the extent of the danger that threatens the West's commercial lifeline, which is petroleum."

   —A COMMUNIQUÉ ISSUED BY AL QAEDA'S POLITICAL BUREAU
   ON OCTOBER 13, 2003

GIOIA TAURO, ITALY—On October 18, 2001, port inspectors in this small southern Italian seaside town were making a routine inspection of a cargo ship. They were looking for illegal migrants, as people-smuggling is common on that coast. But they had never seen anything like this.

Inside a shipping container, they found an Egyptian man with a virtual hotel room—including a bed, toilet, heater, and fresh water. They also found two laptops, a cell phone, a satellite phone, and airport security passes for Kennedy International Airport in New York, Newark International Airport in New Jersey, Los Angeles International Airport, and Chicago O'Hare Airport.[2] Also found were papers identifying the man as an airplane mechanic.[3]

Italian intelligence officials declined to provide me with any information on the case except to say that the suspected al Qaeda terrorist was in the custody of a "non-European country."[4]

American military and intelligence officials were about to learn that fewer than four months after the September 11 attacks, al Qaeda was opening a new front in the War on Terror: the sea lanes.

This is the story of that war, one that America and its allies have unequivocally won so far. It is the largely untold tale of ingenious terrorist plots, modern-day pirates, an attack on a French-flagged oil tanker, the high-speed pursuit of bin Laden's fifteen-ship fleet, the capture of the "al Qaeda admiral," the killings of two key al Qaeda operatives, and the ominous designs of deep-sea terrorists who wanted to learn how to dive but not to resurface.

CAMP DELTA, CUBA—In December 2001, in an American detention center on the western tip of Cuba, the U.S. got its first big break about an impending al Qaeda seaborne attack.

Three Moroccan prisoners captured in Afghanistan told interrogators about an al Qaeda cell forming in Morocco.

In time, American intelligence would learn that the Morocco cell was targeting American and British warships moving through the Straits of Gibraltar, a channel that narrows to barely fifteen miles wide between Spain and Morocco.

Bin Laden could hardly have chosen a more strategic spot. Hotly contested in both world wars, Gibraltar is the only outlet of the Mediterranean Sea to the Atlantic Ocean. Much of Europe's food, oil, and trade moves through this vital channel. A strike in the straits, which the Arabs know as Bab al Zakak, could kill hundreds and choke Europe's economy—the world's second largest.

Months of interrogation had provided some clues of an attack.

But vital pieces of the puzzle were missing. When would they attack? How? Planes, boats, submersible bombs? Where was the cell? Who controlled it?

The interrogations were hobbled by the crawling pace of translations and by the fact that one of the best interrogators was a woman, which irritated the Arab men held in camps in Guantanamo Bay. She would turn their vexation to her advantage and skillfully gather many of the important early clues.

Slowly, a picture came into focus. In seemingly stray comments gathered from repeated interviews, detainees described the cell leader—a mysterious Saudi man that they knew only as "Zuher."

Was it a real name? Al Qaeda operatives are known to use aliases even inside their own training camps. Even if it was a real name, it was only part of one.

The intelligence gaps were agonizing and the Guantanamo Bay interrogators did not know how much time they had before Zuher's cell attacked.

RABAT, MOROCCO—In hopes of a breakthrough, CIA Director George Tenet flew to Rabat. Morocco's busy capital city is a metropolis of whitewashed buildings, broad boulevards, palm trees, and aging Art Deco hotels near the Atlantic Ocean. In February 2002, Tenet was there to meet Morocco's king, Mohammed VI, and his portly intelligence chief, General Hamidou Laanigri.

Tenet was received in the grand style preferred by the Moroccans. He got down to business. The CIA director told the king and the spy chief that Moroccan prisoners in America's Cuban holding pen were talking about a mysterious al Qaeda cell leader who might be hiding in their country and plotting to attack ships in the Straits of Gibraltar. King Mohammed agreed to help Tenet find the terrorist leader.

CAMP DELTA, CUBA—Two Moroccan intelligence agents were sent to America's Cuban base and went right to work sizing up the Moroccan prisoners.

The agents had considerable advantages over their American counterparts. In addition to Arabic, they were familiar with Moroccan idioms and regional accents. They knew the family history of the kingdom's radical Islamist leaders, who are far fewer in number than in neighboring Algeria. That knowledge allowed them to make connections that Americans might miss. Most important, they accidentally created a climate of panic and fear without ever issuing a single harsh word. The prisoners knew the Moroccan intelligence service could take them home; they feared that their countrymen could use *other* methods of persuasion once they were far from the reach of American law.

Though they didn't need interpreters, it was still slow going. The Moroccans patiently gathered clues. "Zuher" appeared to be a real name. They did not know, however, if he was Moroccan, Saudi, or some other Arab nationality, or how long he might remain in Morocco. But, they learned, he was married to a Moroccan woman, and, with any luck, Zuher or his wife would show up in Moroccan government records.

Then they hit pay dirt. One prisoner remembered the name of a relative of Zuher's wife who lived in Casablanca. At last, a solid lead.

CASABLANCA, MOROCCO—Moroccan police tracked down Zuher's in-laws in Casablanca, a sprawling, charmless industrial city on the Atlantic coast.[5] Where was Zuher? The in-laws insisted they did not know.

In the course of the interview, a police sketch artist was brought in. As police questioned the family about Zuher's appearance, the artist used a charcoal pencil to scratch out an image of the mysterious mastermind's face. He showed the family members the likeness. They agreed that it was Zuher. In the drawing, Zuher had a broad face, a thick beard, and deep-set dark eyes.

Meanwhile, intelligence officials searched government records, looking for any sign of "Zuher." They looked at national identity cards and hotel records as well as customs and immigration documents. It wasn't easy. Few of these records were computerized. Card files had to be searched by hand and there were millions of pages to sort through. Nothing substantial turned up, except the identity card of Zuher's wife. Now they had a home address.

By mid-March 2002, surveillance teams had staked out Zuher's home, and shadowed him on the few occasions that he ventured outside.

They noticed a pattern of secretive behavior. He had never applied for a Moroccan identity card or registered with the police, both of which are required by law in Morocco. He stayed indoors for long periods of time—which is unusual in a hot climate, especially in an apartment that lacked even a single air conditioner. (Many similarly situated Moroccans prefer to sit outside in the cool night air.) He didn't rent an apartment in his own name, but insisted that he and his young Moroccan wife live with her relatives. He paid cash for every purchase and never opened a bank account in his own name. He seemed incredibly disciplined, as if trained by an intelligence service.

As it turned out, he made one crucial mistake: He relied on funds wired from Pakistan to the bank accounts of his wife's relatives. This suggested to Moroccan intelligence that they were watching either the right man or someone they should be watching anyway.

Then Zuher's travels suddenly increased. An informant spotted him at the border post of Melilla, a Spanish territory inside northern Morocco. He was seen again entering Ceuta, a Spanish enclave directly across the water from Gibraltar. He was also observed negotiating in maritime shops, trying to buy several Zodiac speedboats.

The Moroccan intelligence service read his e-mails, listened in on his phone calls, and watched him around the clock. While Morocco is an emerging democratic society, roving wiretaps are far easier to get in the kingdom than in the United States, even under the Patriot Act. As Moroccan intelligence officials gathered information, they quickly concluded that Zuher was a major al Qaeda figure.

From his e-mails and other communications, they knew that he had survived the U.S. bombing of the Tora Bora region, one of bin Laden's Afghanistan strongholds, in November 2001. And he was clearly following orders from an al Qaeda commander, who seemed to be holed up somewhere near the Afghanistan–Pakistan border. That commander, known from his e-mails to Zuher, called himself simply "Abu Bilal."

Bilal is believed to be the nom de guerre of Abdul Rahim al-Nashiri, one of the senior planners of the attack on the USS *Cole*.[6] Later, Arab intelligence officers would jokingly call al-Nashiri the "al Qaeda admiral," as he was directing bin Laden's attacks at sea.

In April 2002, Zuher's e-mails revealed that al-Nashiri wanted him and an associate to fly to Saudi Arabia for further instructions. It is a well-established protocol within the bin Laden network, as outlined in the writings of Ayman al-Zawahiri, al Qaeda's number two man, to conduct all operational conversations in person. Something big was in the works.

The Casablanca airport is a dingy temple to 1960s modernism. Zuher and another Saudi man, Hilal Jaber al-Assiri, and their two Moroccan wives were discovered in the passenger lounge. The police closed in.

Once in custody, their discipline broke. They gave investigators the name and whereabouts of a third cell member, who was soon arrested. They admitted to training in bin Laden's camps in Afghanistan. One said he had dined with bin Laden "many times" and that he last saw bin Laden alive near the town of Gardez, Afghanistan.[7]

Their plot may have been only weeks away from completion. They were waiting for an al Qaeda logistics team to make and load the explosives. The plan was simple and lethal: Zodiac boats would be packed with high explosives and rammed into the hulls of American and British warships. Clearly, al-Nashiri hoped to reenact his successful attack on the USS *Cole*.

Moroccan intelligence officials seemed impressed with their quarry. "They are not foot soldiers. They are educated, ideologically formed, and they are technically proficient."[8]

It was a clear-cut victory. A major cell was smashed, vital intelligence collected, and potentially hundreds of lives saved. But it was only the beginning.

RIYADH, SAUDI ARABIA—He was known sometimes as "the prince of the sea" or the "al Qaeda admiral." His full legal name, intelligence officers would learn, was Abdul Rahim Mohammed Hussein Abda al-Nashiri.

Al-Nashiri was born in Mecca and, like bin Laden, he was a Saudi from Yemeni stock. He had trained and fought alongside bin Laden since the 1980s, and was involved in most of al Qaeda's strikes against Americans. He arranged for the shipment of explosives for the 1998 embassy bombings in Kenya and Tanzania and telephoned the suicide bombers to approve the murderous attack on the USS *Cole* in October 2000.[9] With a $25 million price on his head, al-Nashiri was listed in 2001 as "one of the most dangerous" of twenty top al Qaeda operatives still at large.[10]

Al-Nashiri had been steadily promoted inside al Qaeda. As top al Qaeda members were killed or captured—including military commander Mohammed Atef; September 11 operational planner Khalid Shaikh Mohammed; his replacement, Abu Zubaydah; September 11 manager Ramzi Binalshibh; and Southeast Asia commander Hambali, who masterminded the Bali bombing—bin Laden increasingly relied on al-Nashiri. He was one of the few experienced managers left and he was lethally efficient.

At the height of his powers, al-Nashiri commanded a fleet of some fifteen cargo ships, which he dispatched to smuggle terrorists, tons of explosives, and cartons of cash or drugs. He even had the power to order the conversion of freighters into floating bombs.

The al Qaeda fleet is not a new development. Bin Laden has leased and owned cargo vessels since the early 1990s, using the vessels to transport sesame seeds as well as explosives. Sometimes the flotilla was used to smuggle terrorists into Europe or move drugs to Asia.[11]

The terror network had a history of maritime attacks. Bin Laden's crew tried to sink the USS *The Sullivans* in January 2000, but the heavy explosives sank the terrorists' dinghy. Later that year, off the coast of Aden, Yemen, a bomb-laden boat detonated beside the USS *Cole*, killing or wounding sixty-one sailors. For two days, naval commanders feared the *Cole* would sink; only the heroic efforts of the crew saved it.

What was new was al Qaeda's bold, strategic vision. The terror network relentlessly probed for weakness. Bin Laden had clearly found the soft spots in air travel. Even after September 11, al Qaeda continued to test airport security with Richard Reid, the so-called shoe bomber.[12]

Shipping is another big target. Eighty percent of the some six billion tons of goods sold each year is carried by ship.[13] It is impossible to track every cargo vessel; more than 46,000 ships ply their trade at the world's 2,800 ports.[14] Many are registered in shady Third World nations, which do not even try to police their carriers. Seventy-five percent of ocean-going trade moves through five chokepoints: the Panama Canal, the Suez Canal, the Straits of Gibraltar, the Straits of Malacca, and the Straits of Hormuz—a fact that has not escaped the attention of terrorists.[15]

Perhaps the most vulnerable is the Straits of Malacca, between Indonesia and the Malay Peninsula. It is the lifeline of Singapore, the world's busiest port. Half of all oil shipments thread through these straits, which shrink to less than two miles wide at their narrowest point. Sinking even a single ship in the straits would immediately raise oil prices around the world and wreck the economies of the city-state of Singapore and its Southeast Asian neighbors. This is not just a threat to America's allies, but to America itself. The 1997 Asian financial crisis demonstrates how faraway events can rock Wall Street and erase investments in the 401(k)s of seventy million Americans.

The ultimate al Qaeda target is our economy, according to Admiral James M. Loy, deputy secretary of the Department of Homeland Security. "Our link to the global economy is by water— 95 percent of what comes and goes to this country comes and goes by ships."[16]

After September 11, the U.S. Navy and Coast Guard realized that they could not risk being reactive, waiting for intelligence about looming terror attacks. So they adapted the classic Bush strategy of preemption. "If all you do is wait for ships to come to you, you're not doing your job," chief of U.S. Coast Guard intelligence Frances Fragos-Townsend said. "The idea is to push the borders out."[17]

Throughout 2002 and 2003, American and allied navies and intelligence services scrambled to track and seize terrorist ships in the Mediterranean, the Black Sea, the Red Sea, and the Indian Ocean.

In what was probably the largest joint naval operation since the end of World War II, America and its allies used every weapon in their arsenals: spy satellites, surveillance planes, naval patrols, even paid informants in remote ports.[18] The U.S. Navy and its allies in Europe and Asia tracked and boarded many vessels that military officials call "ships of concern" with evocative names like the *Baltic Sky* and the *Cristi*. Sometimes the al Qaeda ships would slip through the net and vanish to emerge renamed, repainted, and reflagged. Then the hunt would begin again.

TRIESTE, ITALY—Italian police boarded the *Twillinger*, a cargo vessel docked in Trieste, on February 19, 2002.

Eight crewmen—all Pakistani nationals—were arrested on suspicion that they were linked to al Qaeda, which is believed to operate training camps in the semi-autonomous tribal lands in eastern Pakistan.

Investigators found false identity documents and "other material judged incompatible with their position as ordinary seamen" on their persons and in their sea lockers.[19] The crewmen were deported to Pakistan and are believed to have been questioned by Pakistani intelligence.

SICILY, ITALY—Italian anti-terror police again swung into action after the *Sara*, a cargo vessel, sent out a distress call on August 5, 2002. Italian and other intelligence services had been monitoring the ship for some time. It was towed into port and fifteen men aboard were arrested. In the crew's possession, investigators found fake identity cards, $30,000 in cash, and maps of several Italian cities and the Vatican. The fifteen arrested men were held for questioning at an Italian facility in Caltanissetta.

Naval intelligence had suspicions about the ship's owners. The *Sara*, originally known as the *Ryno*, was owned by a Pakistani American, Rifat Muhammed, and Dimitris Kokkos, a Romanian who is wanted by the Greek government for smuggling and other activities. He was also part owner of the *Karine-A*, which the Israeli navy intercepted hauling short-range missiles bound for the Palestinian authority in the Gaza Strip.[20] He has since disappeared.

Sara captain Adrian Pop Sorian claimed he was boarded off the North African coast and made to transport the suspected terrorists. He said he issued the distress call when his Pakistani "passengers" threatened to kill his crew. Captain Sorian also said that he overheard one of the fifteen Pakistanis, suspected of being an al Qaeda operative, talking to radical Islamists in Afghanistan. He thought the man on the other end of the phone was "Taliban."[21]

EASTERN MEDITERRANEAN—The *Cristi* had disappeared. NATO intelligence believed that the 1,600-ton cargo vessel was ferrying wanted men linked to al Qaeda.

The *Cristi* was believed to be registered in Tonga, a Pacific island run by a corrupt monarchy that serves as a "flag of convenience" for shippers who don't want to answer too many questions.

If the records are correct—and it later turned out that Tongan paperwork was incomplete—the *Cristi,* like the *Twillinger* and the *Sara,* was partly owned by Dimitris Kokkos.

The hunt was on. The U.S. Navy deployed ships and aircraft. The Greek and Israeli navies fanned across the eastern Mediterranean and the Aegean seas.

OFF THE COAST OF AL-MUKALLA, YEMEN—A French-flagged oil tanker, the *Limburg*, was approaching Ash Shihr oil terminal on October 6, 2002. On board were three hundred thousand barrels of Iranian crude oil and nineteen crewmen.

Members of al Qaeda were waiting in a small, explosives-packed fishing boat that was hoping to spill not just oil, but blood. But the terrorists couldn't find their primary target, a U.S. warship, so they steered for the *Limburg*. "We would have preferred to hit a U.S. frigate," a terrorist from the Islamic Army of Aden said, "but no problem, because they are all infidels."[22]

As the tanker was idling three miles off shore, a junior officer saw the fishing boat coming. There was nothing anyone could do. The approaching craft was too small and too fast, and oil tankers weighing hundreds of tons cannot be easily turned. They were helpless.

The blast ripped through the *Limburg*'s double-steel hull. The oil poured into the sea and caught fire, sending black smoke almost a mile into the sky. Ninety thousand barrels of oil poured into the waves, polluting forty-five miles of Yemen's rocky coast.[23]

The crew jumped from the pitching deck of the burning *Limburg* into the wine-dark sea some two stories below. One crewman, a Bulgarian, drowned. His body washed up on shore several days later.[24] The other eighteen sailors and the skipper were soon pulled aboard boats manned by workers from an oil terminal operated by a Canadian firm, Nexen Inc. "We owe them our lives," Captain Peter Raes said.

U.S. intelligence had e-mailed a warning days before to counterterrorism agents worldwide detailing a possible attack on ships in the Persian Gulf or Yemen.[25] The report was maddeningly vague; the Americans knew an attack might be coming, but did not know enough to stop it.

The attack was astonishingly easy. Yemen has no coast guard, though the U.S. is now helping it launch one.[26] Tankers are defenseless.

Somehow, the wounded tanker stayed afloat. American, French, and Yemeni intelligence officials cautiously approached in small boats. They studied the massive hole in the tanker's side. Forensic investigators found shards of a fiberglass boat and trace amounts of TNT. No human remains of the terrorists were found. In the aftermath of the USS *Cole* attack, experts had found human teeth embedded in the ship's hull—a clue that helped intelligence learn the perpetrators' identities. This time, the investigation would be harder.

Still, al Qaeda swiftly took credit. Al Qaeda's political bureau issued a short communiqué on October 13, 2002: "If a boat that didn't cost $1,000 managed to devastate an oil tanker of that magnitude, imagine the extent of the danger that threatens the West's commercial lifeline, which is petroleum."

This was not an empty threat. According to American and Saudi sources, months before the *Limburg* attack, allied counter-terrorist operatives had thwarted a plot to blow up the Ras Tanura oil terminal, where some 6 percent of the world's oil is processed each day. Saudi police and intelligence officers arrested more than twenty people.[27]

Yemeni intelligence, with leads from the CIA and French intelligence, slowly began to unravel the *Limburg* plot. Over the next two months, some twenty suspects were rounded up. Two men confessed to loading the suicide boat with high explosives. Others revealed the identity of the operational commander, Abdul Hakim Bazib, who was linked to al Qaeda. The manhunt seemed about to end on December 19, 2002, when a group of terrorists was cornered in a three-story house in Hadramaut province, the land where bin Laden's father was born. Roadblocks were set up and police settled in for a long siege. It didn't last long. The terrorists opened fire with automatic weapons and lobbed grenades.[28]

The terrorists shot their way to freedom. Two policemen died and two others were wounded. Only two injured gunmen were captured. The rest disappeared into the night. Bazib is still at large, but the bulk of his cell is either dead or in custody. Mohsen al-Fadhli, one of the al Qaeda planners of the *Limburg* attack, was not one of the lucky ones. As he was planning an attack on an American housing complex in Yemen's capital, Yemeni intelligence nabbed him. The twenty-one-year-old Fadhli is a Kuwaiti citizen. One Kuwaiti government source described the arrest as "a significant blow to al Qaeda. This is one of their main organizers and fund-raisers."[29] Another victory against al Qaeda's war to bring terror to the seas.

As the crippled supertanker was towed to Abu Dhabi in the United Arab Emirates for repairs, Yemen was just beginning to calculate its economic losses. Shipping insurers immediately raised the "war risk surcharges" by $150,000 for any ship bound for a Yemeni port—a 300 percent increase.[30] Business at Yemen's two main ports, Aden and Hodeidah, plunged by 50 percent. As oil tankers were rerouted to Djibouti and Oman, Yemen would lose some $4 million per month in fees.

Still, Americans feel the price of al Qaeda's attempted seaborne terrorism at the pump. One of the reasons that gasoline prices have climbed so sharply since 2001 is the attack on the *Limburg* and the ever-present threat of attacks like it.

OFF ANTALYA, TURKEY—The USS *Monterey* found the *Cristi* at 4 a.m. on October 23, 2002, some seventy nautical miles south of Antalya, Turkey, in the eastern Mediterranean. As the U.S. Navy's board-and-search team approached, they noticed the cargo vessel had been crudely repainted and renamed the *Tara*.

After several hours' search, the Navy allowed the ship to continue. If there had been contraband on the ship, it had been offloaded sometime after the vessel disappeared.

But the pursuit and boarding of the *Cristi* was still a valuable exercise. "We believe that if a global terrorist network wants to move people or material, they will likely try to do that through shipping," said Commander Bob Ross, spokesman for the U.S. 6th Fleet in Gaeta, Italy. "The first objective is to protect shipping and the second is to disrupt, deter, or degrade potential terrorist activity."[31]

UMM AL QAIWAN, UNITED ARAB EMIRATES (UAE)—Umm al Qaiwan is one of the poorest of the UAE's emirates and one of its least inhabited. It was a perfect hideout for one of the world's most wanted terrorists.

But it was more than a safe haven. From Umm al Qaiwan, al-Nashiri could watch the sea lanes of the Persian Gulf. Unknown to American and allied intelligence at the time, al-Nashiri was plotting to attack the headquarters of the U.S. Navy's 5th Fleet, based in nearby Bahrain.

An informant reported that al-Nashiri was taking flight lessons there. Why did the "prince of the sea" want to fly? Most likely, he wanted an international pilot's license because it would legally admit him to most of the world's major seaports. This bureaucratic courtesy had its uses—al-Nashiri could legally wander into secure areas to do reconnaissance for future attacks on seaports.

It was his satellite phone that betrayed him. Like most phones, when it receives a call, it automatically broadcasts its location. Unfortunately for al-Nashiri, the National Security Agency's satellites were listening in. The CIA station chief in Abu Dhabi relayed the information to UAE intelligence.[32] Agents nabbed al-Nashiri within hours.

In his possession were two fake Saudi passports, a laptop, and a satellite phone—both of which were mined for clues.

Capturing al-Nashiri may prove to be the equivalent of shooting down Japanese admiral Yamato's plane during World War II—a turning point in the war at sea. Al-Nashiri's arrest was kept secret for several months in the hopes of rolling up other terrorists in Yemen and Saudi Arabia. One Bush administration official said: "This is definitely a big fish."[33]

Al-Nashiri was turned over to the CIA, the state-run Emirates News Agency reported, "as part of the ongoing cooperation between the two sides in the fight against international terrorism." The UAE intelligence alliance with the U.S. is just one of many that the Bush administration has negotiated—and others are said to be just as productive. With its dizzying number of alliances, the Bush administration's War on Terror is anything but unilateral.

Al-Nashiri was reportedly shipped to a special interrogation center in Jordan.[34] This is an increasingly busy facility, according to an Arab intelligence source I interviewed in 2003, and it uses "methods denied to Americans."[35] He would not elaborate, but it seems safe to conclude that it is far tougher than Abu Ghraib. Whatever the reason, al-Nashiri is said to be "cooperating."[36] For bin Laden, this couldn't have been worse news.

NORTHWEST YEMEN—Qaed Salem Sinan al-Harethi[37] thought he was safe. The al Qaeda terrorist had evaded capture by Yemeni security forces and was now deep into the lawless region of northern Yemen, a redoubt of Islamic radicals that the central government has not been able to subdue after years of civil war.

He was one of al-Nashiri's lieutenants and did not know his superior had been captured and compromised. On November 3, 2002, his ignorance would kill him.

Terrorism is often a trade of close calls. Al-Nashiri himself, while posing as the owner of the Yemen-based Al Mur Honey Company, had been arrested by Saudi Arabia in 1998 and released in 1999. "He was like a trout out of season," a UAE intelligence official jokingly told me.[38] (But in 2002, the CIA was not playing catch-and-release with terrorists.) Al-Harethi too had his scrapes with the law, but money, connections, and luck had always saved him. In December 2001, he had evaded Yemeni troops in the Marib province, an operation that cost eighteen Yemeni soldiers their lives. Now his luck was running out.

As al-Harethi and five other known terrorists barreled down a two-lane highway in the dry expanse of northern Yemen, a slow-moving bat-like plane found them. Its high-resolution black-and-white video images were beamed back to a control room in Djibouti, some 160 miles away. The CIA team there had no difficulty recognizing al-Harethi; they had been hunting him for months.

The Predator launched its sole Hellfire missile. Direct hit. Al-Harethi, his companions, and their vehicle disappeared in a ball of fire. In the charred chassis, Yemeni intelligence found weapons and explosives.

If al-Nashiri had given al-Harethi any final orders to attack U.S. ships, he did not live to carry them out.

LONDON—Barbar Ahmad is a thirty-year-old British subject who ran websites and other businesses that American and British investigators believe were used to fund and recruit for Taliban and Chechen terrorists. On August 6, 2004, he appeared in a London court to hear charges read against him.[39] Of course, he denied them.

However, a look at his computer's hard drive told a different story. E-mail records revealed that he had received communications from a sailor aboard the USS *Benfold*, an American guided-missile destroyer. The writer said he was a "U.S. naval enlistee" who was "sympathetic to the jihad movement."[40] The sailor (who authorities do not want to name) praised the Islamic terrorists in Afghanistan, Bosnia, and Chechnya. This might not have been the sailor's first e-mail.

Ahmad's computer revealed that he had received sensitive U.S. naval documents on April 29, 2001, showing the precise *future* movements of the Constellation battle group—of which the *Benfold* was a member. The mysterious e-mailer noted: "They have nothing to stop a small craft with rocket-propelled grenades etc., except their Seal's Stinger missiles."[41] U.S. Navy SEAL teams, usually composed of four men, operate in small boats near naval vessels and are equipped with shoulder-launched Stinger missiles.

Documents found on Ahmad's computer detailed the specific assignment of each ship, the battle group's planned movements, and a drawing of the battle group's formation.[42]

Investigators won't say if Ahmad passed these documents to the Taliban or al Qaeda. If he is extradited to the United States, Ahmad faces a thirty-one-page indictment in a federal court in Connecticut. Only then will we know why the terrorists failed to strike and who the traitorous mole aboard the USS *Benfold* was.

OFF SABAH, THE STRAITS OF MALACCA—It was 3 a.m. on a Wednesday in one of the busiest waterways in the world. From the deck of the chemical tanker *Dewi Madrim* on March 26, 2003, one could see the lights of oil tankers bound for Korea and Japan and U.S. military vessels hauling food and ammunition to Iraq. In the humid haze above the darkened coastline of the island of Sumatra, no one saw the speedboat.

It was alongside the lumbering tanker before anyone could sound the alarm. Ten armed men climbed aboard. The modern-day pirates seized control of the ship while most of the crew was still asleep. While piracy is an all-too-common occurrence in these seas, it is what happened next that got the attention of intelligence officials around the world.

The men, carrying assault rifles, did not attempt to offload the cargo or the crew, who could be held for ransom. (Chinese and Malaysian ship owners, among others, have been known to pay as much as $1 million to free a captive crewman).

Instead, these "pirates" expertly disabled the ship-to-shore radio and switched on their own portable VHF communication system. Once they had control of the bridge, they reduced the tanker's speed and practiced steering the vessel.

By 4:05 a.m., they were gone. They took a few valuables from the crew and two of the ship's senior officers. No request for ransom was ever made and, more than a year after their disappearance, the officers are feared dead.

Noel Choong, who runs the International Maritime Bureau's Piracy Reporting Center in Kuala Lumpur, Malaysia, was concerned about "three things—the automatic weapons, the fact that chemical tankers were targeted, and finally, the fact that they know how to operate the tankers. . . . They are obviously very well organized."[43]

Pirates in the South Pacific rarely use automatic weapons. They usually target oil and diesel tankers—which have cargos that are easily sold in black markets—not chemical tankers. And, of course, pirates are primarily interested in money; the ones who took over the *Dewi Madrim* had only a passing interest in loot.

It looked like an al Qaeda training mission, according to Aegis, a London-based defense consulting outfit. The seizure of the *Dewi Madrim* was, in the words of *The Economist*, "the equivalent of al

Qaeda hijackers who perpetuated the September 11 attacks going to flight school in Florida."

What could these pirates-cum-terrorists be training for? Choong offers a plausible nightmare scenario. "Our concern is that terrorist groups could use a chemical tanker as a weapon. Simply set the vessel on autopilot and aim it at another ship or a Singapore oil refinery and get off the ship" before it exploded.[44] It doesn't have to be a suicide mission to be deadly and dramatic.

Singaporean officials were alarmed. "This may signal the start of serious preparations for a maritime terrorist attack as terrorists learn to navigate tankers to use them as floating bombs against other vessels, key installations, naval bases or port facilities," said Singapore's deputy prime minister, Tony Tan.[45]

Other developments also suggest that al Qaeda's seaborne terrorism will continue. In 2000, an engineer who was fond of deep-sea diving was kidnapped by Abu Sayyaf, an Islamic terror group based in the Philippines that has long been linked to al Qaeda. Abu Sayyaf has terrorized Filipinos for years in the hopes of carving out an independent state for Muslims in the southern Philippines, but it has never made a waterborne attack. The engineer, when he was released in June 2003, was interviewed by Filipino intelligence officials. What he told them was disturbing: The terrorists wanted to be taught to dive—but not to resurface.[46]

At the same time, the owner of a diving school in Kuala Lumpur said a number of ethnic Malays had enrolled. "Strangely, they are seemingly uninterested in decompression techniques."[47] Divers must decompress as they resurface or they may be fatally injured.

Three former students at the Safe Dive Club in Eindhoven, the Netherlands, were detained and questioned by Dutch police. One of the diving students questioned was linked to the Morocco cell that plotted to sink warships in the Straits of Gibraltar. Citing Dutch and American intelligence sources, the *Sunday Times* of London reported that "the al Qaeda marines may be deployed as squads of divers to attach mines to hulls, bridge supports, dams, or oil rigs."[48]

The paper also noted that the CIA captured "a small non-pressurized submarine from an al Qaeda cell in Southeast Asia" in 2002. The sub can carry up to six scuba divers and descend to 130 feet. Omar al-Faruq, an al Qaeda terrorist captured in 2002, told the CIA that he "planned scuba attacks on U.S. warships in Indonesia."[49] Why would anyone want to learn to be a one-way diver? Intelligence analyst Mansoor Ijaz told me that he thinks the most likely reason is to attack deep-sea oil pumps, which often lie more than five hundred feet below the surface. [50]

Destroying oil pumps and gas pipelines in the shoals of the Caribbean could pinch U.S. energy supplies and cause billions of dollars of environmental cleanup on the shores of Texas, Louisiana, and Mississippi. And those hundreds of miles of pipes, pumps, and equipment are impossible to guard.

PLATIYALI, GREECE—The *Baltic Sky*, a 1,242-ton cargo vessel, steamed out of the Tunisian port of Gabes on May 13, 2003—and promptly disappeared.

Staff at the NATO Intelligence Center, tipped off by an informant in a "southern Mediterranean country," were immediately suspicious.[51] Records showed that the *Baltic Sky* was hauling some seven hundred tons of explosives and detonators. Greek Merchant Marine minister George Anomeritis later crystallized these concerns into a question: "We are investigating who is behind the designated recipient and even if it turns out to be an ordinary company, this is such a huge load, what would they do with it?"[52]

Indeed, the ship was supposedly heading for Port Sudan, a Red Sea anchorage hundreds of miles from commercial mining operations that use such explosives. Most worrying, the ship was supposed to make port in Sudan by May 16—a three-day journey. It still had not arrived by June 1.

Instead, the *Baltic Sky* moved erratically across the eastern Mediterranean, through the Dardanelles, which separate Europe from Asia Minor, and into the Black Sea before retracing its course back into the Mediterranean. The ship seemed to be heading anywhere but its destination.

Meanwhile, intelligence discovered that the ship had been reflagged and renamed in the past year. And where was it registered? The Comoros Islands, a string of Muslim-majority isles off the eastern coast of Africa. These islands are notorious for practicing a severe form of Islam and for registering any ship for a fee.

As soon as the *Baltic Sky* sailed into Greek waters, the Greek navy swung into action. Frogmen and special forces approached the cargo ship in small boats as larger Greek warships watched from the horizon. The operation was over in minutes. The seven-man crew—five Ukrainians and two men from Azerbaijan—was arrested without resistance.

Once in custody, the captain, Anatoly Baltak, told an unbelievable tale. He said he only joined the *Baltic Sky* in Istanbul in early June (the previous captain had disappeared) and that he was told the cargo was to be discharged to another ship in the Ionian Sea, which lies between Greece and Turkey. Given the size and nature of the cargo, that seemed to be impossible.

Investigators were shocked by what they found in the cargo hold: Eight thousand detonators and 680 tons of ANFO, a commercially available explosive used in mining, stacked neatly in boxes. Anomeritis said the cargo's total explosive power was equal to "an atom bomb."

Fortunately, it was a bomb that would never explode.

RIYADH, SAUDI ARABIA—Al-Nashiri's successor did not last long.

Khaled Ali bin Haj was a thirty-year-old Saudi citizen whose family traces its roots to neighboring Yemen. He had been Osama bin Laden's chief bodyguard in Afghanistan in the late 1990s and had been linked to bombings in Riyadh in May and November 2003, which killed fifty-two Saudis and others. He was designated the regional head of al Qaeda for the Persian Gulf and Saudi Arabia.

Then, at a security checkpoint in the Saudi capital on March 15, 2004, he decided to open fire. Police returned fire, riddling his jeep with bullets.

Haj was found dead inside, along with Ibrahim bin Abdul Aziz bin Mohammed al-Muzaini, another suspected terrorist. When police pulled the bodies out, they found two AK-47s, ten magazines of ammunition, six hand grenades, three revolvers, and Saudi currency equal to $137,600.[53]

Al Qaeda threatened to avenge Haj's death. "The mujihideen will teach the enemies of Allah, the mercenaries of Saudi intelligence, a lesson they will never forget."[54] So far, the terror group has proved unable to carry out its threat: One more sign, perhaps, that the strength of al Qaeda is weakening.

Whatever the fate of al Qaeda, the man that the London-based Arabic language paper *Asharq al-Awsat* called "the real chief of al Qaeda in Saudi Arabia" is dead.

WASHINGTON, D.C.—Secretary of the Navy Gordon England knows a lot about developing new weapons systems. He spent more than a decade in the private sector managing the development of products for the Pentagon's arsenal. When I buttonholed him at the National Press Club, he talked briefly about a new craft in development that may prove vital to defeating the terrorists at sea.

Recognizing that the next al Qaeda strike could come from small bomb-packed boats, the Bush administration is rapidly developing a new weapon—the Littoral Combat Ship.

Known as the LCS in military speak, the new craft will move quickly and quietly in shallow waters. Unlike destroyers, frigates, and other large naval vessels, it will be able to engage small craft and cruise very close to the coastline. Its onboard computers will be networked to share images and information with other ships, aircraft, submarines, and even unmanned vehicles, possibly including the Predator and the Global Hawk. Its mission, according to the Pentagon, will be "special operations support, high-speed transit, maritime interdiction operations, intelligence, surveillance and reconnaissance, and anti-terrorism/force protection."[55]

With LCSs, another attack like the one on the USS *Cole* and those attempted since 2000 may prove impossible. That is one reason that Admiral Vern Clark, chief of U.S. naval operations, said, "We need this ship today."[56]

Senate Democrats have also played a key role in securing America from waterborne attacks. Senator Fritz Hollings, a Democrat from South Carolina, saw the danger of attack on the nation's docks and waterways. The Senate adopted Hollings's Port and Maritime Security Act on December 20, 2001. Among other things, the Act requires ships to "electronically transmit their cargo manifests to the port before gaining clearance to enter."[57] The bill compelled ports to take many of the same security measures as airports. "But for some unfathomable reason, we don't take these preventative steps at our seaports—where most of our cargo arrives and where we are most vulnerable," Hollings said before passage of the bill.[58] Now we do.

Even after the Democrats lost control of the Senate, Hollings continued to press for stronger port security measures and propose important new legislation. He is retiring in 2004.

The secret war at sea continues to this day. So far, the tide clearly favors the allies. A major terror operation to sink American and British warships in the Straits of Gibraltar was thwarted. The "al Qaeda admiral" was captured and is revealing the identities of his spidery web of terrorists. Two other key operatives have been killed and others captured. An al Qaeda mole aboard the USS *Benfold* has been discovered. Much of the al Qaeda flotilla has been identified, stopped, and boarded. The threat from the sea remains, but the civilized world is inestimably safer as sailors, airmen, and Marines go about their clandestine, vital work.

CHAPTER SIX

BOMBS AND BALLOTS:

THE MADRID ATTACK AND
THE AMERICAN ELECTION

"Democratic civilization is the first in history to blame itself because another power is trying to destroy it."

— JEAN-FRANCOIS REVEL[1]

"Our readiness to meet the threat is undermined by the legalistic mood that infects judiciary, police, and government. The rhetoric of human rights now predominates over the dictates of defense necessity. We are intellectually disarmed, perhaps the weakest security posture in which it is possible for people to confront danger."

— JOHN KEEGAN[2]

WASHINGTON, D.C.—In July 2004, Homeland Security Secretary Tom Ridge went public with a nightmare scenario that had been plaguing him for months: A terrorist mass murder, in some American metropolis, just before the presidential elections on November 2.

It was a nightmare based on solid intelligence. Captured al Qaeda operatives—some of them newly caught—had been warning that the terror network was planning a dramatic attack on the United States.[3] Additional intelligence, including phone intercepts, led Bush administration officials to conclude that bin Laden might be directly involved in the planning and personnel recruitment phases of the election plot—just as he was in on the early stages of the September 11 attacks.

A big operation seemed to be in the works. U.S. and allied intelligence services were able to intercept some of bin Laden's orders as they filtered down the chain of command. "It sounds like a corporate effort" of the entire al Qaeda apparatus, an unnamed senior administration official told the *New York Times*.[4] My own intelligence sources said a "worldwide collection effort" was under way to "shake the trees" for any information about a possible election bomb plot.

The capture of Mohammed Naeem Noor Khan on July 13, 2004, put American and British intelligence officials on high alert. The twenty-five-year-old computer engineer ran the al Qaeda communication network, which uses the Internet extensively. His testimony, and the documents cached on his hard drive, revealed that al Qaeda was studying the building plans of the New York Stock Exchange as well as banks in Manhattan, Newark, and Washington. These might be the targets selected for an election-eve bombing.[5]

In July, Ridge brought his nightmare out into the light of day. He told reporters that al Qaeda wants to attack the United States during the presidential campaign[6] in order to "disrupt our democratic process."[7]

Intelligence analysts believe that New York's skyscrapers, Washington's public buildings, and Los Angeles's busy airport "all still have symbolic value to al Qaeda,"[8] which might be true, though it assumes that al Qaeda has not significantly changed its target lists since 1998, when the terror organization drew up a wide-ranging hit list for what became the (largely failed) millennium attacks and the September 11 mass murders. Since September 11, however, al Qaeda has sought out "softer" targets, such as synagogues, banks, shopping malls, nightclubs, and train stations.

Ridge insisted the al Qaeda election plot was not simply grim speculation. "These are not conjectures or statements we are making," he said. "These are pieces of information that we can trace comfortably to sources that we deem to be credible."[9]

On August 11, 2004, the *Washington Times*—respected for its intelligence sources—reported that United States intelligence officials expect al Qaeda's next attack to be announced by an assassination and followed by attacks on "multiple targets in multiple venues."

On Mohammed Naeem Noor Khan's laptop computer, intelligence officials found "planning at the screwdriver level" for the plot. "It is very detailed," one official said.[10]

The *Times* reported that "the targets, in addition to the financial institutions in New York, Washington, and Newark, N.J., that have been the subject of public warnings, include such economic-related targets as oil and gas facilities with a view toward disrupting the November election."[11]

Times reporter Bill Gertz quoted an intelligence official: "The goal of the next attack is twofold: to damage the U.S. economy and to undermine the U.S. election. The view of al Qaeda is 'anybody but Bush.'"[12]

An al Qaeda plot to kill thousands on the eve of an election has been tried before—and succeeded. Synchronized railway bombs killed 202 people in the Spanish capital city of Madrid on March 11, 2004. That attack, which became known as 3/11 among analysts, seized the attention of the intelligence community. "Madrid was the wake-up call," one intelligence analyst told me. "It changed the ROE [rules of engagement]."[13]

The Madrid attacks, as columnist Jim Hoagland observed, demonstrated that democracies are "vulnerable politically as well as physically."[14]

Madrid is more than a precedent. It is a harbinger of attacks to come. The method of an election-year attack on the United States might be very different from the train bombs in Spain. Al Qaeda may use trucks laden with explosive fertilizer, chemical bombs hidden in container ships, or even aircraft. But the aftermath might resemble March 11: a government humiliated, as domestic political opponents and the media attempt to turn public opinion against the nation's leaders rather than against the terrorists.

The Madrid attacks cast ominous political portents, especially from the vantage point of the Bush administration. The bombs detonated four days before Spain's national elections. In the last public opinion poll published before the attacks, the center-right Popular Party seemed destined to retain its parliamentary majority. After the attacks, the press and pressure groups pilloried Prime Minister José María Aznar as a "liar" who misstated intelligence reports for political gain, and traumatized voters defeated the center-right government. A similar scenario could happen here.

It is vital, therefore, that Americans learn the lessons of Madrid. At the moment, American understanding of the political fallout of the Madrid attacks is superficial. A more nuanced understanding of what one Spanish official called "the bitter hours" after the Madrid blasts provides a good guide to what America could expect if al Qaeda succeeds in attacking during a campaign season. It should give partisans on both sides pause.

No one should underestimate the shock of a terror attack. The trauma and tragedy is all-consuming. Thanks to aggressive counterterrorism activities at home and abroad and just plain good luck, America has been spared terror strikes since September 11, 2001. In all fairness, the administration has done a heroic job in safeguarding the nation. The Department of Homeland Security and other federal agencies have foiled many terror strikes on American soil. A tenuous feeling of safety has emerged. The nation has recovered just enough that a successful terror strike would be psychologically devastating.

It was a shocking blow to Spain. The Spanish nation had known terrorism, but not on this scale. More than 200 people were killed and another 1,500 injured. The Madrid attacks were the bloodiest events in Spain since its civil war ended more than fifty years earlier. It was the first terror attack in a non-Muslim majority country since President Bush declared war on the bin Laden network in 2001—and in the first hours and days it was terrifying.

At first, the aftermath of this gruesome attack followed the political pattern of the September 11 attacks in the U.S.—the near-unity of public opinion against terrorism, the frantic phone calls and the awful silences, the long lines to give blood, the bodies that could be identified only by DNA, the selfless sacrifice of doctors, nurses, police, and firemen, the ungrudging sympathy of the world.

Even public confidence in the nation's chief executive surged, as it had in America on September 11. In the hours after the bombing, Ana Botella, the wife of Prime Minister Aznar, visited the wounded and the grieving families of the dead. She observed:

> During these visits to the hospitals, I encountered exceptional people. Although they were living through tragedy, all families gave me support and told me to relay to my husband their support, to let him know that they did not know of anyone who had fought against terrorism like him. They were words of affection and gratitude in moments of tragedy for all of us.[15]

Then events departed from the September 11 script. The political opposition waged a careful campaign to undermine the prime minister, constantly questioning his honesty and alleging that he was using the tragedy for partisan advantage. In reality, those charges could be more fairly leveled at the opposition Socialist Party that sought to divide public opinion during the tragedy, trying to eke out an electoral victory. Of course, the prime minister's failure to promptly and forcefully respond to political criticism—in the midst of a national crisis—made the opposition's allegations appear credible. It is not hard to imagine the often tongue-tied Bush White House making the same errors.

To understand the Madrid mass murders and their relevance to America, one must relive them. We will do so partly through the eyes of Ana Botella. While hardly an impartial observer, she provides an insider's minute-by-minute account of the Madrid attacks in her book *Mis Ocho Años en la Moncloa* (*My Eight Years in Moncloa*). Moncloa is Spain's White House. Her account is unique; no other insider has yet written about the attacks in such detail. Since her book is not available in English, I hired a Spanish embassy official to translate it. A Spanish parliamentary inquiry, known informally as the 3-11 Commission, is now under way. New information will surely surface. What follows is based on that translation, as well as news reports, intelligence documents, and interviews.

MADRID—Fortunately, two trains were two minutes late. That small fact meant that hundreds, not thousands, would die.

Atocha Station—with a red brick façade, march of arches, and iron-and-glass dome climbing hundreds of feet skyward—was a glorious remnant of a bygone age. Built in 1892, it sheltered dozens of shops, cafés, and a lush garden of seven thousand tropical plants covering almost two acres under its glass dome. And, at 7:30 on the morning of March 11, 2004, it was crowded with more than three thousand people rushing to work or school.

Two packed trains, coming from the eastern suburb of Alcalá de Henares, were late. Anxious commuters watched their slow progress on electronic monitors. But no one was watching as unbearded boys in Western clothes left their backpacks behind.

Under the train's hard plastic seats, inside the small backpacks preferred by students, were cell phones. Like most cell phones, these could be set like alarm clocks. Silently, as people shuffled in and out of the busy train cars, those alarms were counting down to the zero hour, which investigators believe was 7:34 a.m.

When the alarms sounded, an electric current coursed down a wire from the cell phone to a metal detonator. When the Goma-2 explosive detonated, it sent a spray of nails and screws outward faster than the speed of sound, wounding, maiming, and killing.

The first three bombs would send "body parts through the windows of nearby apartments."[16]

The cheap phones proved to be cruelly efficient. Over the next three minutes, ten separate explosions rocked Atocha and two other train stations.

After the first explosions, a female commuter frantically called a co-worker. She got voicemail. "I'm in Atocha. There's a bomb on the train! We had to. . . ."

Then more explosions.[17]

Cadena Ser, a Madrid radio station, replayed that twelve-second clip repeatedly throughout the day. It said it all.

Fewer than five hundred yards outside of the station, one of the tardy trains exploded, ripping apart the metal train cars and everyone inside.

But the atrocity was not over. El Pozo del Tio Raimundo Station was shaken by explosions. It was three miles from Atocha; no one heard the explosions from the central station. A minute later, at the Santa Eugenia station, a final train car disappeared in an explosion.

By 7:43 a.m., nearly 190 people lay dead or dying and some 1,500 others were wounded, crying for help amid the twisted metal and debris. Within days, as the wounded died, the death toll climbed to 202.

If the four trains had been at their appointed places, the blast waves would not only have pulverized the passengers and commuters, but smashed through the concrete pillars that support Atocha Station's gargantuan roof, bringing down its tons of glass and ironwork, entombing thousands. But one train had tarried at the Tellez Street station, rendering the attack merely the worst al Qaeda strike in European history, not its deadliest ever.

The Spanish public rallied to help. Commuters picked up the wrought iron benches from the rubble of the train station and used them as stretchers to carry out the wounded. Taxi drivers offered their services as ambulances without any thought for fares.

Restaurateurs showed up with free sandwiches and coffee for the rescuers and rescued. At the Gregorio Marañón hospital, the Doce de Octubre hospital, and the Clínico hospital, patients freely gave up their beds for the wounded.

The phone system seized up, just as it had on September 11 in New York and Washington. Everyone was calling loved ones to make sure they were still alive. Telefónica de España, Spain's largest phone company, repeatedly appealed on radio and television, asking people to stay off the lines unless absolutely necessary. It did little good. Who could wait to find out if a sister or brother was still alive?

Not all the frantic calls were answered. In pavilion six of a soccer stadium, beside rows of corpses, Ana Botella saw piles of jackets, briefcases, and backpacks—the property of the dead.[18] As she walked by, a cell phone trilled. "I made a sudden stop and I rushed to pick it up, but they [security personnel] advised me that it could not be touched."[19] In the gray cement makeshift morgue, the phone rang and rang.

Botella felt powerless, just like the families who were phoning the dead line.

Within two hours, reporters gathered to hear the government spokesman, Eduardo Zaplana, explain what little the authorities knew. By 9:30 a.m., little was certain. Even the number of dead and wounded would not be known for hours. Rescuers were still carrying and counting.

Zaplana said that Spanish intelligence believed the atrocity was the work of ETA, an acronym for Euskadi Ta Askatasuna, a local terrorist group that has sought independence for the Basque people since 1959. That group had tried to assassinate Aznar before he became prime minister, with a car bomb on April 19, 1995, and had attempted assassinations of dozens of Spanish politicians and European Union leaders as well. Overall, ETA was responsible for some eight hundred deaths. ETA's campaign of bombings and killings had terrorized the Spanish mainland for decades. Elected after sixteen years of Socialist Party rule, Aznar came to power in 1996 promising to preserve Spain and smash ETA. He proved to be the toughest and most effective leader against the terror group in decades. Aznar refused to negotiate with ETA or work out a political solution with its proxy organizations. He closed its newspapers and banned Batasuna, a political party that was an ETA front group. Corrupt government contracts for ETA supporters were canceled. He tried to choke off even the smallest streams of financial support—even bars in the Basque region had to stop putting out tip jars for ETA. Finally, he adopted a zero tolerance policy for ETA-related crimes, arresting dozens of low-level operatives before they could move up to bombing police stations. Aznar's aggressive use of the police and intelligence services appeared to be on the verge of ending the terrorist threat from ETA. Clearly, ETA wanted Aznar dead and his Popular Party out of power. Calling ETA a "criminal gang of killers," the government spokesman said the terror group was the prime suspect for the Madrid bombing. That simple statement of fact and others like it would later have enormous political ramifications.

The Socialist Party, locked in a closely fought election battle with Aznar's center-right Popular Party, twisted Zaplana's statements, proclaiming them as evidence that the government was lying about ETA to help itself in the upcoming elections. The Socialists were generally seen as more willing to work out a political compromise with ETA; if the public believed ETA was behind the blasts, the Socialists could lose votes. On the other hand, if the bombings were seen as retaliation for Aznar's participation in the liberation of Iraq, his party would suffer. Thus, from the Socialist point of view, all accusations of ETA involvement had to be "lies." (In time, it would turn out that ETA was not behind the bombings—but in the early stages of the investigation no one knew who the culprit was.) Admitting the obvious—that suspecting ETA in

Madrid was as sensible as suspecting the IRA in Belfast—could cost the Socialists votes.

The Socialists might also have had inside knowledge. The prime minister's intelligence reports were filtered through the interior minister. By contrast, many mid-level intelligence officers—some of whom were directly involved in the investigation—regularly phoned Socialist Party leaders, according to a Spanish Socialist I interviewed.[20] The many years of Socialist Party rule had created many friendships, and the intelligence officers knew that the Socialists had a good chance of returning to power. Why not recruit allies when you can? So the opposition usually knew about developments hours before the government itself. This gave the Socialists both the advance warning to plan their "instant responses" and the confidence to challenge the government. It is not hard to imagine "antiwar" officials at the CIA making similar calls to Democratic friends in Congress or the press.

At 10:30 a.m., roughly three hours after the attacks, Arnaldo Otegi, the leader of ETA's political arm, phoned a small radio station.[21] He denied all involvement and blamed the bombings on what he called the "Arab resistance." The Socialists must have been delighted; they couldn't have asked for a better message at the time. And, as it would turn out, Otegi's denial had the added benefit of being true.

At 10:50 a.m., Spanish police found a small white van about the size of a Ford Escort parked at the Alcalá de Henares train station. Under the front passenger seat were seven detonators. In the tape player was an Arabic audiotape. On the floor, a Koran.

The interior minister would not know about it for hours, while the Socialists seemed to know in minutes. The press would not be told for almost twenty-four hours. The Socialists used this delay to charge a "cover up." Of course, it takes time to move information up the chain of command in any bureaucracy and the process of notifying the press is also laborious. Aznar's government did not spur the investigators to quickly pass on information. It did not yet know it was in a battle for the hearts and minds of Spanish voters—it thought it was fighting only terrorists.

At exactly one o'clock, Aznar phoned the editor of *El País*, a Spanish center-left daily that is equivalent in circulation and authority to the *New York Times*. It was an extraordinary call; the prime minister had not called the editor in more than three years. Aznar assured the editor that ETA had carried out the attacks. As information trickled in over the next few days, the *El País* editor felt he had been tricked. He wasn't; Aznar had not known about the van or its suggestive contents when he placed the call. At 1:15 p.m., Interior Minister Angel Acebes, who oversaw Spain's intelligence and police agencies, told the press that he had "no doubt" that ETA was behind the murderous blasts. He did not yet know about the van. At the time, he was probably unaware of Otegi's denial and would not have believed it anyway. The terrorist band is not renowned for its truth-telling. Acebes was simply speaking his mind, but this became one more instance—in the eyes of the opposition and the press—of government spin.

MONCLOA, MADRID—In the late afternoon, inside Moncloa, the meticulously kept palace on the outskirts of Madrid, the prime minister and his senior staff gathered to discuss the investigation and the government's message to the nation.

Before them was a memo drawn up by the counter-terrorism unit of the National Center of Intelligence, a Spanish agency that combines the equivalent of the CIA and the FBI. It arrived by fax at precisely 3:51 p.m. On the day of the attacks, this document was the foundation for the government's belief the ETA was behind the atrocity.

The secret memo has never before appeared in English, as far as I have been able to determine. It was recently declassified and made available to some Spanish reporters. I relied on a Spanish embassy translator and another native Spanish translator to render the document in English.

The intelligence report begins by reminding policymakers that its findings are preliminary: "In following are presented the *first conclusions* about the perpetrator and consequences in the chain of terrorist attacks that occurred in Madrid, *waiting for the police investigation* to extract *conclusive and concrete evidence*" [emphasis added].

It continues: "It is considered *almost certain* that the organization ETA is the perpetrator of these attacks. The following circumstances *guarantee* it [emphasis added]:

- ETA had the intention of getting involved in the electoral campaign by carrying out terrorist attacks in Madrid in order to demonstrate its operating capacity and to benefit from the immediate impact and the propaganda-like publicity they [would] receive. [In other words, Spanish intelligence believed that ETA had a motive for the attacks: publicity and political gain during the elections.]
- In the absence of results from skilled analysis of the composition and characteristics of the remains, the procedure is the same as ETA used in many of the terrorist actions it has carried out or attempted within the last few years. Its plan to blow up the Madrid–Irún train last Christmas with a suitcase packed with explosives is to be kept in mind. Also, the [ETA] terrorists that were detained [by Spanish police] on the morning of 29 February 2004—as they drove to Madrid in a van containing 536 kilograms [roughly 1,180 pounds] of explosives—confessed [to police] that in the same Christmas period they had tried to plant a number of backpack bombs in the ski lodge of Baqueira-Beret. [In

short, ETA has used similar bomb technology in the past, had tried to bomb trains only three months earlier, and even recently used backpack bombs.]

- The magnitude of the attack, the most horrific and bloody committed by ETA, signifies an important change in the execution of their terrorist acts: the indiscriminate nature and absence of prior warning to the FCSE [Spanish police]. [Everyone reading this secret memo knew that ETA was on the ropes due to Aznar's aggressive counter-terror measures. The intelligence community believed that this unprecedented attack was a response to ETA's defeats and signaled a new aggressiveness. This was a plausible theory, just wrong.]

- With this tremendous terrorist attack, ETA would like to repeat the plan it used in 1997 with the kidnapping and later assassination of Miguel Angel Blanco [a local Spanish politician]. At that time, the terrorist gang [ETA] was going through a difficult situation, although less grave than the current situation. It wanted to find an escape by generating a great convulsion with a terrorist attack against the government. With the social impact that the [1997] execution made, ETA believed that it had succeeded. [Following the murder of Blanco,] Basque nationalist leaders began to meet a few weeks later with representatives of Herri Batasuna, [a once legal, now banned political party friendly to Basque independence]. That meeting led to the Pact of Lizarra in 1998. [Whenever threatened in the past, ETA has gained politically through an unprecedented attack, such as the kidnapping and killing of local leaders. The Madrid railway bombs seemed to fit that pattern.]

- The precarious situation of the ETA and its web of support can explain why they opted for a terrorist attack of this magnitude. If not for the massive public opposition [to earlier ETA attacks] and for the difficult situation in which it placed the organization, the ETA leadership would not have decided to perform this criminal action. It was persuaded that it had little time before the majority of the voices [public opinion] would be in favor of a solution through dialogue of the "Basque conflict," so that they [the Basques] will be able to attain their traditional claims. [Spanish public opinion was gradually forming a consensus that would not be favorable to Basque regional autonomy. ETA knew this. So it struck in order to prevent its defeat at the hands of Spanish voters—a peaceful solution granting some measure of local autonomy that would forestall full independence.]

■ Finally, ETA pretends to show publicly, and in every manner, that it continues as a player in the political future of the Comunidad Autonóma Vasca y Navarra, in comparison to the anti-terrorist policy that during the last two legislatures has been led by the government of Spain. ETA has special interest in both being perceived by the responsible political nationalist [organizations] and by its own membership as a political player. [ETA has to appear to be a player in its political region or else a political resolution will emerge without its consent, threatening both its power and its goals.]

On the other hand, with all the data available at the moment, it cannot be confirmed that an organization linked to Jihad International could be responsible for the carrying out of these terrorist attacks. Despite the existence of certain similarities in regards to the process used and the attack of a generic objective—means of public transportation—

with those carried out by the radical Islamic terrorist groups, the coincidences are to be expected in a terrorist attack of this magnitude. ["Jihad International" is how Spanish and other intelligence services refer to al Qaeda and other militant Muslim groups. Intelligence dismissed the similarities as coincidental. Significantly, the senior Spanish intelligence officers who prepared this memo did not know about the white van and therefore did not mention it. If they had known, their analysis might have been very different.]

One of the most significant footprints [clues] of this type of attack is also missing: the suicide bomber. [This was not a suicide attack like September 11 or other recent al Qaeda strikes. ETA never uses suicide attacks, bin Laden often does.]

That it [the bombings] happened exactly three and a half years after 9/11 in the United States does not have any relevance or significance to Islamic groups. [Again, the timing of the attack is written off as a coincidence. One former CIA official once told me, "If you believe in coincidences, you don't belong in intelligence." It appears that the Spanish service was making an elemental, but honest, analytic mistake.]

Here the document ends. It does not mention the one point that the press would hammer away at for weeks—the lack of a warning call. Supposedly, ETA always issues a warning before an attack. But this is a canard, intelligences sources told me. Sometimes ETA warns, sometimes it does not. Regardless, my sources say that the warnings are often minutes before the attack—too late to spare anyone. The secret memo did nothing to challenge the prevailing views in the executive mansion, reinforcing them instead.

Still, it is reasonable to take the position that the Aznar government did: When you hear hoof beats in Manhattan, you don't look for zebra. Spain had been at war with ETA for decades. The prime minister was nearly killed and other politicians had been murdered by ETA. Most of Spain's 150 counter-terrorist analysts were deployed against ETA—it was the main enemy. By contrast, fewer than thirty analysts tracked al Qaeda full-time. Al Qaeda was a distant threat, one that sometimes operated out of Spain but did not kill there. What's more, the intelligence seemed certain that ETA had carried out the attacks.

Ana Botella maintains:

> It was impossible to think of any other perpetrators. We have been suffering their murders for the last thirty years. When they informed us about the attack in Atocha we remember about their last two attempts to provoke a massacre in Madrid. . . . I thought: "What they could not do on Christmas, they have done now."

STRASBOURG, FRANCE—Outside of Aznar's cabinet, many Spanish and European politicians also suspected ETA. Later, it would be alleged that Aznar "lied" about suspecting ETA in order to boost his party's chances in upcoming elections. Yet many Spanish leaders—of different parties—told me that at the time they too had suspected ETA, not al Qaeda.

When the backpack bombs detonated in the commuter trains in Madrid, Inigo Méndez de Vigo y Montojo, a member of the European Parliament and a leading figure in Aznar's political party, was in a legislative meeting in Strasbourg, France. "I immediately suspected ETA," he told me.

De Vigo had been living with ETA threats for more than a decade. Even though his wife is Basque and the couple has a home in the Basque region, they dare not visit it because of longstanding death threats by ETA.

De Vigo later talked to Patrick Cox, an Irish lawmaker who was serving as president of the European Parliament. Like de Vigo, he was shocked by the attack—and immediately suspected ETA. These two European leaders were not simply bystanders. A few months earlier, ETA had sent a letter to the European Parliament threatening to kill Cox.

Cox took the terrorist assassination plot with a characteristic bit of Irish swagger. He responded by saying that he had been receiving death threats from ETA for months and that Irish politicians already knew they had to deal with such threats. He was not going to give in to terror by changing his lifestyle. Nonetheless, European Parliament security was put on high alert. The threat was deemed "highly credible."

The day after the Madrid mass murders, de Vigo spoke with Spanish intelligence. He said he was told that ETA was behind the blasts, suggesting "perhaps" it had partnered with an Arab terror network.

Joan Colom i Naval is a longtime activist in the Spanish Socialist Party. The regional Catalan government (which has long been controlled by the Socialist Party) recently named him president of the Catalan Court of Auditors. Colom i Naval told me that he, too, had suspected ETA initially. He strongly disagreed with Aznar's policies—especially with regard to the Iraq War, the privatization of Spanish industries (which, he alleged, always seemed to benefit Aznar's friends), and the cleanup efforts of the November 2002 wreck of the oil tanker *Prestige* that coated the Spanish coast in oil—but said he had little doubt, immediately after the attacks, that it was the work of ETA.[22] Later, he would change his mind, and so would the world.

MADRID, SPAIN—At 1:00 p.m.—almost six hours after the bombings— Prime Minister Aznar spoke to the nation. He pledged to track down and capture those behind the attacks. "We will not back down in the face of terrorist killings. The perpetrators will be tried and convicted."

Importantly, he did not name ETA. Aznar was trying to accurately convey both the uncertainty in the intelligence as well as the consensus of the intelligence community that ETA was the mastermind. Given the possibility that the bombings could be the work of what the intelligence memo called "Jihad International," Aznar wisely kept silent about the identity of the perpetrators. This restraint on his part did not seem to catch the attention of the media. Aznar encouraged his fellow Spaniards to join marches against terrorism to be held the following night, March 12.

In a televised speech that evening, King Juan Carlos called on the nation to stand strong and united in the face of "terrorist barbarity." Following Aznar's line, the king did not speculate as to which terror group was behind the attacks. After the king's address, and fewer than fourteen hours after the attacks, Interior Minister Acebes made a dramatic announcement. Police had found a van. Inside were seven detonators similar to what was used in the Atocha attack. Most telling, the police patrol found an audiotape with an Arabic chant, believed to be a recording of the *Suras* of the Koran. It was a tape designed to teach classical Arabic, but some members of the press treated it as an important al Qaeda message.

Some Popular Party officials discounted the importance of the van and the tape. Gustavo de Arístegui, a former diplomat posted to Arab capitals who was once the target of a failed ETA attack, told the *New York Times* that the "Koranic teaching tape may have been the work of the Popular Party's political enemies."[23] In other words, planted evidence. It was election season, after all, and Spanish politics can be a rough sport.

He was also unsure of the value of the tape. "I cannot picture a radical Islamist with a beginner's tape," he said. "Normally it would be someone with more sophisticated material. Anybody could have planted a tape there."[24]

A Spanish intelligence official also speculated that the van, detonators, and tape could be red herrings—false clues meant to disguise ETA's involvement.

Inside Moncloa, the Arabic tape had little impact on official opinion, as Botella notes:

> At that moment, we still believed that ETA had perpetrated the attack. We believed that the massacre had ETA's trademark. The official information was persistent in its indications towards ETA, even though the second line of investigation had been already opened. In its majority, ETA was the main suspect because of the time when the massacre occurred, because they had tried many times, and because they had used a van [as they had in an earlier attempted attack]. Logically, we thought ETA was responsible, in spite of the existence of a tape with verses from the Koran.

A herd mentality was settling in, and soon it would lead the Spanish government over a cliff. Once they develop a theory about a crime, investigators tend to discount evidence that does not fit their thesis until such evidence accumulates that the old theory is discredited. Although this is simply human nature and applies to nearly every investigation, it would later be cited by the opposition party as evidence of a "cover up."

Later that night, *Al-Quds al-Arabi*, an Arabic newspaper based in London, reported that it had received an e-mail from a group calling itself "Abu Hafs al-Masri Brigade/Al-Qaeda." The group took credit for the Madrid bombs, saying they were retribution for Spain's role in the Iraq war. (Politically, this was a gift to the Socialist Party. First ETA had denied responsibility and now al Qaeda had claimed it. The news only made Aznar's position appear more foolish. This is not to imply that al Qaeda and the Socialists were coordinating, far from it, but al Qaeda's statement was the political equivalent of found money.)

Spanish intelligence quickly discounted al Qaeda's claim, noting that the same group had falsely claimed credit for the New York blackout in the summer of 2003. The al Qaeda claim was not ignored by investigators, but few people in the intelligence community saw it as a red warning light. British intelligence also doubted al Qaeda's claim of responsibility.[25]

On the morning of Friday, March 12, Spanish foreign minister Ana Palacio sent a cable to all Spanish embassies worldwide about the Madrid attacks. She wrote that "everything appears to indicate" that ETA was behind the atrocity. She instructed embassy personnel to tell the foreign press that the government believed ETA had carried out the attacks.

This was an honest statement of what the government believed at the time. But opposition political leaders and the center-left press would portray it as part of a conspiracy to mislead the Spanish nation and the world.

A few hours later, Prime Minister Aznar emphatically told reporters that "no lead will be ignored" and insisted the government was not spinning intelligence information. He seemed defensive and angry. A hostile line was developing in the press.

Around 6 p.m., only thirty-five hours after the attacks, Interior Minister Acebes revealed to the press that a young policeman had found an unexploded bomb with a cell phone timer in a discarded backpack taken from one of the wrecked trains.

It was a dud, a bomb meant to be part of the strike. The timer was set for "p.m." instead of "a.m." and the police were able to disarm it in time. This was a real coup. Bomb designs are like fingerprints; they reveal either the identity of the bomb maker or the identity of those who trained him. The bomb design was similar (but not identical) to previous ETA bombs, but the metal Goma-2 ECO detonator was different. Had ETA developed a new bomb?

Or was it the work of another group? It was too soon to tell. Still, Acebes added, the government has "opened new lines of investigation" about possible perpetrators.

Later, police would examine the cell phone itself. In its memory chip was a record of recent calls and details showing that it had been purchased at a shop run by Jamal Zougam, a Moroccan immigrant who had been watched by Spanish intelligence following the Casablanca bombings the year before. In its second denial, at 6:30 Friday night, an anonymous ETA spokesman phoned *Gara*, a pro-separatist Basque newspaper routinely used by ETA to air its views. The second ETA denial was widely cited by Socialist Party leaders as further evidence that the conservative government was lying about ETA's involvement in the Madrid blasts.

Ten minutes later, Acebes responded curtly: "I don't believe them."[26] That night, March 12, the people answered Aznar's call to march in solidarity "with the victims, with the constitution, for the defeat of terrorism." They came out in the millions.

Across Spain, more than eleven million people (out of a nation of forty-two million) joined in peaceful marches to condemn terrorism. Whole towns emptied into the street. People thronged the wide boulevards of Madrid despite the pounding rain. They thumped drums and waved candles. In Madrid's Colon Square, they shouted, "No to terrorism!" One sign in the demonstration summed up the public mood: "We were all on that train."[27]

It was a mighty display of unity, solidarity, and determination. But the Socialist Party activists saw it as an opportunity to divide the public against the government.

At the head of the demonstration, Prime Minister Aznar marched with French prime minister Jean-Pierre Raffarin, Italian premier Silvio Berlusconi, and European Commission president Romano Prodi. And, for the first time in Spanish history, members of the royal family joined a street demonstration: Prince Felipe and the princesses, Cristina and Elena, were marching along with their subjects. The nation was seemingly unified against the terrorists. But, as Botella writes, for the government, the "bitter hours" were just beginning.

Once again, Spaniards' answer to terrorism went on display. We are a great nation.

But for some people, that evening was already dark. The investigation about the perpetration of the attack began to be more important for them than the attack itself. And that started to be noticeable.

When we arrived at the head of the demonstration, I immediately realized that it was going to be an ordeal. There was a group of people who screamed during the whole event. Although they were not representative of what was going on inside the multitude of millions, they yelled at us; they seemed to be well organized.

I had my cell phone on just in case the City Hall had to get in touch with me. No one called me. But they called my children, who were with me, from other points of the demonstration to tell them that everything was amazing, that there were a lot of people who were protesting either in silence or yelling against the terrorists. . . .

However, what we perceived at the head of the demonstration was something totally different: organized groups yelling constantly against the head of the demonstration. The same groups who demonstrated against the war.

As soon as the demonstration was over, I started to perceive that some people wanted to transform the massive peaceful act into something else: They had transformed the information received to the minute into concealment of facts and the investigation carried out conscientiously into manipulation.

The disruption at the anti-terror march was no accident or spontaneous reaction. It was part of a plan coordinated by José Blanco, the campaign manager of the Socialist Party. "They [the government] are going to try to avoid making all the information known until after Sunday," which was election day, he told reporters on Friday.[28] This dark conspiratorial insinuation flew in the face of the constant announcements the government had made during the investigation—all of which the Socialists had cited as evidence of manipulation. Meanwhile, the candidate and party leader, José Luis Rodríguez Zapatero, stayed above the fray. "Now is not the time to establish political consequences regarding the authorship of the attacks," he said at a news conference. "There will be time for that."[29] A classic two-sided political strategy. It would work brilliantly. Breaking news seemed to confirm the opposition's line of argument. After 8 p.m., Interior Minister Acebes announced a string of arrests: three Moroccan Arabs and two Indian Muslims. The recovered cell phone from the dud bomb had connected them to the bombings.

Acebes also announced the discovery of an Arabic videotape in a trash can near a popular mosque. On the tape, a masked figure calling himself Abu Dujan al-Afghani said he was "the military spokesman for al Qaeda in Europe." He took credit for the murderous attacks: "We declare our responsibility for what has occurred in Madrid, exactly two and half years after the attacks in New York and Washington."

Every new development pointed to al Qaeda. Despite Aznar's tepid attempts to be vague about the perpetrators, his government's early statements about ETA had been repeated and reinforced by the press and the Socialist Party. There was no graceful way to climb down now.

Meanwhile, Socialist Party activists—perhaps whipped into a frenzy by party leaders—mounted angry demonstrations across Spain. Their hate was directed not at the terrorists, but at the government. Sometimes these demonstrations turned violent. The Popular Party headquarters in La Coruña was burned. Party activists were beaten.[30]

On Saturday, March 13, the Socialists staged mass rallies across Spain. These were technically illegal. Under Spanish law, the day before an election is supposed to be a "day of reflection" during which all campaigning ceases. When conservative candidate Mariano Rajoy pointed out that the increasingly violent demonstrations were illegal, he was criticized for campaigning during the mandated quiet period.

The Socialist strategy worked. By nine o'clock Sunday night, the election results were final. The Socialist Party triumphed with 43 percent of the vote; the conservative Popular Party carried 38 percent. The balance went to smaller parties.

Almost immediately, the world press—especially the American and British media that *opposed* the war in Iraq—announced that it was Aznar's Iraq policy that had pushed his party out of power. The British and American press that *favored* the liberation of Iraq came to the conclusion that Spain had capitulated to terrorism, that al Qaeda had won this battle.

This was the view taken by Botella and, by all accounts, by her husband, the prime minister.

> What more can terrorists ask than being capable to intervene in the politics of democratic countries through their terror attacks? If we accept this, we are dead. . . . [W]e are serving their influence on a silver tray: terrorists will set up dates to bomb all democratic countries and change their governments and politics.[31]

This is true, but beside the point. It was the Socialist Party's Michael Moore-style campaign, not the terrorists per se, that determined the election. The world press missed the "big story."

First, the media ignored the way the bombings emboldened the Socialist Party to attack the government's credibility. The Socialists' campaign was calculated and clever: a constant barrage of attacks on every government announcement about the bomb investigation while constantly accusing the government of lying and covering up. No aspect of the investigation was spared.

Next, the media overlooked that the attacks on March 11 and the massive anti-terror demonstration on March 12—which brought more than one-quarter of the electorate out into the streets—significantly boosted voter turnout. And higher turnout wasn't good for the ruling party. Indeed, days before the election, some Spanish political observers predicted that higher than usual turnout would topple the center-right Popular Party government. Two days before the attacks, University of Madrid professor Belen Barreiro wrote an article in *El País*, the Spanish daily, noting that (at best) the conservatives had a 3 percent advantage over the Socialists, and adding that a higher turnout would erase this margin and result in a Socialist Party victory.[32] This is what happened.

Third, while media accounts consistently stressed the conservatives were ahead in the polls, they rarely mentioned that under Spanish law, polls cannot be published in the last five days of a campaign. The last polls made public were conducted more than three days before the bombings. So the publicly available polls were meaningless—they did not measure the Spanish reaction to the biggest terrorist attack in Iberian history.

What's more, even the publicly available polls showed the race tightening. More than a week before the election, some polls put the conservative Popular Party nine points ahead of its rival. Yet one of the last polls published revealed that the Socialists had cut the lead to only 4.5 percent. So Aznar's party was losing momentum even before the attacks.

What about more recent *internal* party polls? Joan Colom i Naval told me that internal polls taken the day before the Madrid bombings showed the Socialists ahead by 1 percent. So Aznar's party was in trouble before the bombs went off.

Fourth, consider "tactical voting." That's when a voter who favors a minority party candidate (like Ralph Nader) decides to vote for a majority party candidate (like John Kerry) to change an election result. In Spain, minority left-wing parties lost votes—compared to previous local and national elections—to the center-left Socialists.

Why the tactical voting? Colom i Naval thinks Aznar's handling of the Madrid attacks sickened left-wing voters and drove them to support the Socialists. It is a plausible hypothesis. More likely, the Socialists' barrage of attacks on Aznar made his party look weak and encouraged the voters to switch from fringe left-wing parties to the establishment left. That tipped a close election to the Socialists.

Fifth, Aznar himself was not up for reelection, as he was keeping a political promise to serve only two terms. His successor, Mariano Rajoy, was on the ballot. Rajoy was less known and less popular. And, significantly, Aznar's handling of the crisis did not boost Rajoy in the polls—the credit went to Aznar while the blame went to the Popular Party as a whole.

Finally, Aznar did not respond forcefully to his critics or exude much public emotion about the victims. He was his formal, polite self—and therefore out of sync with the raw and traumatized public mood.

Perhaps Aznar's crowning mistake was not visiting the ruins of the Atocha train station. Try to imagine Bush declining to go to the Pentagon or to the World Trade Center in the days after September 11 and you get a sense of the magnitude of Aznar's blunder.

Now let's sort out what is unique about the Spanish experience from what might parallel an American election.

It is at least plausible that a terror attack would energize the president's political opponents to attack him for failing to prevent it. They would demand an investigation and criticize any apparent lapses. This is essentially the way the Democratic Party handled the Iraq War: as a series of mistakes to be microscopically examined.

Second, it is reasonable to assume that an attack would boost voter turnout. But it is difficult to say whether higher voter turnout would help or hurt a president like George W. Bush. Certainly registered Democrats outnumber registered Republicans nationwide. But presidential elections are not national elections; they are the sum of fifty separate state elections. And Democratic voters, as numerous as they are, tend to be concentrated in a handful of states like New York, Illinois, and California, which Bush would expect to lose anyway.

Third, the polls show that the U.S. presidential race is neck-and-neck, just as the Spanish polls showed prior to the bombing. And as with Spanish elections, American elections tend to tighten as the election approaches.

Fourth: tactical voting. Would an election-year bomb encourage Green Party and other left-wing "third party" voters to support the Democrats? It seems likely. Nader voters were excoriated for costing Gore the election in 2000, and editors of *The Nation* and other left-wing opinion leaders virtually begged Nader not to run again. In the wake of an attack, those same leaders would press Nader voters to "come home."

Some of Aznar's mistakes President Bush could not afford to repeat. He must not speculate or allow anyone in his administration to ruminate on possible attackers until all the evidence is in. He must prevent leaks from the FBI and CIA, or, failing that, make certain that information is sent to him directly and quickly. Most important, he must do what Aznar did not: visit the scene of the attacks and commiserate with the wounded and the grieving.

So, on the whole, there are many similarities between what happened in Spain and what could happen here. The differences are minor: Unlike Aznar, few would expect President Bush to avoid all emotion in the wake of a terrorist attack on the heartland. The War on Terror is something that Bush has always been passionate about, as the world saw when he grabbed a bullhorn in the rubble of the World Trade Center.

Perhaps the most interesting aspect of the Madrid mass murders was the opposition's calculated campaign to undermine the government. The mechanics and arguments of this effort can easily be exported from Spain to the rest of the democratic world and almost certainly will be.

If there is another terrorist attack in the United States before election day, it won't be another September 11; it will be another Madrid. The opposition will mobilize rapidly and use the same techniques and arguments.

Let's consider the elements of what we could call "the Madrid strategy:" mass demonstrations led by radicals; constant allegations of government "lies;" intense skepticism of "slow" release of information from the government; an increasingly hostile media (which gives more credit and air to opposition leaders than to government officials); a razor-thin election margin that fuels extremist rhetoric; a continuous barrage of personal attacks on the leader; persistent questions about "intelligence failures;" and a cynical attempt to hijack the grief of victims and survivors.

All of these elements are reminiscent of the "antiwar" movements that emerged simultaneously in all Western countries following the liberation of Iraq. Much of the multifaceted "antiwar movement" is dominated by avowed left-wing organizations. Now it appears that these groups and their battle-proven tactics are shifting from opposing the occupation of Iraq to opposing the War on Terror.

By itself, an al Qaeda attack almost certainly will not change the tide of public opinion, which will almost certainly flow in sympathy with the victims—at least initially. But the underlying current can change, if the Democrats want to change it by implementing the Madrid strategy. The hours after an attack will be a character-revealing test.

The Democrats may well see the benefit in standing with Bush in a united front against terror. This would be statesman-like—and it would discourage bin Laden from carrying out similar strikes on America's allies during their elections. It would also reassure the nation that it is in safe hands with both parties.

Or other voices may prevail. The strategy of Spain's Socialist Party may prove tempting. After a ritualistic denunciation of terrorists, the opposition party could fire a barrage of tiny criticisms against Bush: We should have known sooner. Why was this particular report ignored? And so on. Perhaps a political victory can be eked out. What have we got to lose?

It is impossible to know where the Democratic Party's instincts will lead it until after the bombs go off. But a terrible suspicion lingers that Kerry will take the course laid out by the Spanish Socialists. After all, the opposition's relentless attacks brought them electoral victory.

Some Bush administration officials comfort themselves that their incredible record of success at killing or capturing scores of major al Qaeda figures will buy them some goodwill with the public, perhaps even enough to blunt the force of post-attack Democratic Party criticism. That's not what happened in Spain. Aznar was perhaps Europe's most effective counter-terrorism leader. His government had arrested dozens of al Qaeda operatives. His political base remembered that and voted for him. But the swing voters did not.

Should the elections be postponed in the wake of an attack? Again, this issue was first debated in Spain. Ultimately, Spanish authorities decided that the elections should not be moved. American leaders seem to have already reached the same conclusion.

In a letter to Homeland Security chief Tom Ridge, as well as to congressional leaders of both parties, DeForest Blake Soaries, chairman of the U.S. Election Assistance Commission, called attention to the lack of national election contingency plans. In that letter, he noted that New York City primary elections slated for September 11, 2001, were postponed. By contrast, he wrote, "the federal government has no agency that has the statutory authority to cancel and reschedule an election."

Soaries was making a serious point. As New Jersey's secretary of state, he oversaw elections in the Garden State; he later ran for Congress as a Republican in 2002. "I'm absolutely opposed to postponing elections in November," he said. "But we should be able to communicate what procedure, process, and protocols are in place in the event of a disruption."[33]

The Bush administration publicly disavowed any thought of postponing the elections. "We've had elections in this country when we were at war, even when we were in civil war. And we should have the elections on time. That's the view of the president, that's the view of the administration," National Security Advisor Condoleezza Rice told CNN.[34]

And, as in the Spanish case, the simple discussion of a "what-if?" scenario was played by some elements of the media and the opposition party as a dark plot to use the threat of terrorism for political advantage, alleging that Bush had a secret plan to move the election.

The Bush administration and its supporters should consider a sad warning from Ana Botella, who writes, "It is part of my eight years of life in La Moncloa: Sometimes, the truth is less credible than the manipulation of fanaticism."[35]

For the foreseeable future, the War on Terror will be fought by soldiers and spies abroad and by politicians and the press at home. From all the evidence, the Bush administration is winning the War on Terror. Still, as Machiavelli counsels, the appearance of winning might be more important.

After the Spanish elections, American policymakers will have to seriously ponder the growing political opposition to waging the War on Terror. A significant minority in America and in all democracies—in Europe, Japan, Australia, the Philippines, and elsewhere—is now opposed to almost all serious measures to fight terror. It is against more than simply the war in Iraq. It opposes domestic counter-terror measures like the Patriot Act and the detention of al Qaeda combatants without charge or trial. It has many principled objections, and these should not be lightly tossed aside, but the sum of its objections could make victory all but impossible.

The Bush administration, and its successors and counterparts abroad, will have to learn from the sophisticated and disciplined tactics of its opposition. Merely preventing attacks and arresting scores of al Qaeda masterminds is not enough. The administration and its allies will have to develop and articulate a coherent set of principles and arguments for fighting terrorism. The smoldering memory of September 11 is no longer enough. Ideological warfare—not just against the terrorists, but also against the "antiwar" crowd at home—is now required, as in the Cold War.

After September 11, America opened a front against al Qaeda. After March 11, America has to admit it is fighting a two-front war.

EPILOGUE

"We have the terrorists on the run. We're keeping them on the run. One by one, the terrorists are learning the meaning of American justice."
— PRESIDENT GEORGE W. BUSH[1]

WHY DO THE INSIDERS—the National Security Council, the CIA, the FBI, other intelligence services, and the Defense Department— think the War on Terror is going well, while the press and public wonder darkly if the terrorists are winning?

Of course, insiders always believe things are going about as well as can be reasonably expected; they know the internal compromises and trade-offs that they made. To think otherwise would call their leadership into question. So there is always a degree of self-confidence among insiders.

But that factor alone cannot explain the gulf between the view from within the national security apparatus and the view from without.

Extensive interviews with American officials and others leading the War on Terror paint a more detailed picture. A few officials are complacent and confident. Many more, while still being anxious about al Qaeda's next deadly surprise, see a record of hard-won successes. These victories are real and measurable (the terrorists are either in custody or dead). This seems to confirm their belief that America is slowly winning.

And, most of the time, these achievements are no secret. The Taliban, who provided a safe harbor for bin Laden, are vanquished. Saddam Hussein, whose regime provided arms, training, and money to bin Laden, no longer rules Iraq (see Appendix D, which details the many links between the Iraqi dictatorship and the bin Laden network). The head of Pakistan's nuclear arms program, A. Q. Khan, has apparently ceased helping nations and terrorists gain weapons of mass destruction. Libya, which murdered scores of Americans aboard Pan Am Flight 103 and funded terror groups that joined bin Laden, has renounced terrorism and atomic weapons. Yet the press, the people's intelligence service, has not focused on these victories. It focused on the Abu Ghraib prisoner abuse scandal, the failure to find weapons of mass destruction in Iraq, and the validity of intelligence about Iraqi efforts to buy uranium from Niger. Why? Some suggest ideological bias or institutional incentives to sell newspapers. While there is some merit to both of these suspicions, the root cause is something more subtle: a failure of imagination. The media does not understand the workings of the intelligence community or the military and, therefore, does not understand the war. And the War on Terror is unlike all previous wars, except one.

Let's examine the differences between the War on Terror and other wars. The War on Terror is seemingly infinite; it is not limited by time, terrain, uniformed combatants, established alliances, or economic considerations. Its sheer scope defies easy understanding.

Time

The war is not limited by time: It has a beginning (September 11, 2001) but no foreseeable end. In most wars, the troops and the public know that particular victories will end the fighting. During World War II, for example, Americans understood that winning in Berlin and Tokyo would mean the end of the war. What capital can the U.S. take to stop terrorism?

Unlike earlier conflicts, the enemy is not a nation or a specific list of nations. Even the "Axis of Evil" (Saddam Hussein's Iraq, Iran, and North Korea) is not an exhaustive list. Any country harboring terrorists is a potential foe.

Even the death of bin Laden will not end the war. This is one of the aspects of the War on Terror that the president has been quite chillingly clear about: It is not limited to the end of bin Laden or even of al Qaeda, but of all terrorists "with global reach."

This seems to mean endless war. Bush's vision shocks his critics. They ask, "When will it end?"

Ask President Harry Truman. He did not know when the Cold War would end, but he waged it nonetheless. And so did eight more presidents. And, in 1989, the Berlin Wall fell.

Wars against ideological foes (like Communists or Islamists) are different from those against territorial powers; they can drag on for decades and end suddenly.

The War on Terror is more akin to the Cold War than to any other conflict in American history. I will return to this point.

Terrain

Before 2001, al Qaeda was known to be active in at least fifty-five countries—stretching from the archipelago of the Philippines to the peaks of Central Asia to the neighborhoods of East London.

As a result, American and allied forces and intelligence services are active in more than seventy countries. These are not calm police actions. In many of these countries, America or its allies have engaged in shootouts with al Qaeda terrorists. In the Philippines, Filipino special forces have destroyed terrorist training camps in bloody jungle battles. In Thailand, India, Indonesia, and Pakistan, police have shot their way into bin Laden's safe houses and remote camps. In Pakistan, Afghanistan, and Iraq, American and allied forces have fought in kill-or-be-killed battles involving mortars, artillery, rockets, and aerial bombardment against entrenched foes, who relentlessly pour down machine-gun fire and rocket-propelled grenades.

The global battlefield puts U.S. troops in East Africa, the Middle East, and Central Asia and intelligence operations in Micronesia, Southeast Asia, Australia, South America (including recent operations in Uruguay and Brazil), Europe, and North America. The only place where one is unlikely to find America's anti-terror brigades is Antarctica.

The "home front" is not a metaphor anymore. A "shoe bomber" was taken into custody at an American airport, and a man who planned to detonate a radioactive "dirty bomb" was seized in another one. In July 2000, federal law enforcement agents raided a farm near the small town of Bly, Oregon—and found a terrorist training camp. One of the suspects later arrested, James Ujaama, had fought alongside al Qaeda in Afghanistan and had been treated by bin Laden's personal physician. In the prosperous northern Virginia suburbs, investigators learned that the "Virginia Jihad Network" was using paintball games to train for martyrdom operations—less than an hour's drive from the U.S. Capitol. In August 2004, two leaders from a mosque in Albany, New York, were arrested for allegedly plotting to acquire a shoulder-fired missile. The mosque leaders were linked to Ansar al-Islam, an Iraq-based al Qaeda affiliate. The arrests were based on intelligence found in Iraq. Hundreds of men believed to be terrorists have been captured in tranquil, tree-lined American suburbs. There is no "front" and no "safe zone."

Some, including the *Wall Street Journal*'s James Taranto, have dubbed the conflict "World War IV." (World War III was the Cold War, Taranto says.) Even this is something of a misnomer. The world has seen global conflicts long before the Europeans began numbering their world wars. The eighteenth-century wars between the French and the British empires were waged on a world scale, fought in the backwoods of North America, the subcontinent of India, the islands of Asia, and the fields of Europe, as well as on any patch of sea where two opposing men o' war met. Even the nineteenth century's Napoleonic Wars were global if one includes naval battles and island raids. The War on Terror is simply the latest world war.

And the lessons of history—the harsh experiences of past world wars and the Cold War—are likely to help America and its allies prevail. After all, the terrorists do not have a reservoir of comparable combat experiences to draw on—while the free world does.

The United States and its allies have fought insurgencies— sometimes fomenting them, other times combating them—for more than a century in places as diverse as the Philippines and Nicaragua. So the American military has institutional knowledge and established doctrine. It also has a vast military training apparatus, which absorbs and disseminates new developments from battles in Afghanistan and Iraq as well as covert operations in Southeast Asia and East Africa.

Al Qaeda, in contrast, has only the experience of the anti-Soviet jihad and terror campaigns against Arab dictatorships to draw on. The Arab armies have rigid, unchanging doctrines that often fail to adapt to new tactics (in this they resemble the Soviet army of the past). Bin Laden's fighters have been adept at capitalizing on their enemies' tendency to repeat past mistakes. But much of the terror network's institutional knowledge—contained in training manuals and computer hard drives—is now in allied hands; its training camps have been destroyed; its trainers have been scattered or slain; and its leaders and operatives are being hunted down.

Some critics fret that the global scale of the War on Terror makes victory, or even resolution, impossible. They forget that world wars have been won before. Again, the best parallel is the

Cold War against Soviet Communism. Each side deployed soldiers and secret agents around the world. Sometimes there were battles and even wars. But much of the fighting was done in shadows, in settings far from active war zones. And the free world won. There is no reason history cannot repeat itself.

Uniformed armies

The War on Terror is not limited to uniformed armies. The enemy, a motley collection of terrorist groups affiliated with radical Islam, wears no uniform and carries no flag.

America and its allies are fielding an army of plainclothes civilians alongside its soldiers, sailors, airmen, and Marines. Some work in intelligence. In a secret executive order, Bush reinvigorated the CIA's paramilitary force while New York still smoldered and ordered it into Afghanistan within days of September 11, 2001.[2] Uniformed troops followed a month later, when war was declared against the Taliban.

The civilian employees of virtually every federal agency are now fighting the War on Terror. The Treasury Department and the Internal Revenue Service have deployed regulators to cut off funds supporting global terror. More than $136 million in terrorist-related assets have been seized and more than 315 individuals and entities (mostly bogus charities) have been closed down.[3] The U.S. Immigration and Customs Enforcement Bureau (ICE) now provides constant air surveillance over Washington, D.C., and boasts its own Office of Intelligence to collect and analyze terrorist threats. Using that intelligence, ICE and the FBI arrested Hemant Lakhani, a shadowy arms dealer, on August 12, 2003. Lakhani was at the center of a plot to shoot down commercial aircraft inside America using shoulder-fired missiles. Another tragedy averted.

Even state and local officials are now front-line troops. One example: In January 2004, the California Highway Patrol raced to track a missing truck laden with hazardous materials. It was found. Even now, they're not sure if they prevented a major terrorist attack.

Since 2001, some $13 billion has been spent to train and equip local officials to respond to emergencies, including terror strikes. State and local police and firefighting offices are now littered with faxes and piled high with reports on emerging terrorist threats. Most of these will remain unknown to the public, unless the worst happens.

Old alliances are dead

The War on Terror binds America both to its traditional "Anglo-Saxon" allies and to its old ideological foes.

Troops from the UK, New Zealand, and Australia fight alongside the United States in Afghanistan, Iraq, and other places. Canadian troops are in Afghanistan. And indeed, the intelligence cooperation between America, Australia, and Britain has become so close that Australian and British officials are now free to wander around the cubicles of the State and Defense departments without a minder. "They're considered virtual Americans," one State Department official told me.

Many new alliances are also being forged. A global intelligence-sharing arrangement now incorporates more than one hundred nations. A senior official in Singapore's intelligence service said it is now routine to exchange leads with intelligence agencies as far flung as Norway, Israel, and Uzbekistan. "And when we ask the U.S. for satellite photos, we receive them in hours, not days."

Even the traditional ideological division that split the world between "pro-American" and "anti-American" nations has faded. America's old nemesis, Russia, is now a key ally in the bloody battle against global terror. Russian president Vladimir Putin recently revealed that he warned President Bush about Saddam Hussein's terrorist ambitions against the United States in the week after September 11, 2001. Russian intelligence has trained its sights on Islamic radicals across Russia and the former Soviet republics. Russia even had a September 11 moment of its own when Muslim terrorists seized a Moscow theater with some three hundred people inside. Fighting terrorism is as much a matter of homeland security for Moscow as it is for Washington. And, despite the rhetoric of its beleaguered politicians, French intelligence has supplied the U.S. with reams of vital information and French troops are in Afghanistan.

Authorities in Saudi Arabia have killed or captured hundreds of al Qaeda terrorists. Even Yemen, the traditional home of the bin Laden family and the sole Arab nation to oppose U.S. efforts to liberate Kuwait from Saddam's grip in 1991, has arrested scores of al Qaeda members.[4]

Nations that reside on America's dreaded "terrorist sponsors" list have also covertly come to Washington's aid. Libya, Syria, and especially Sudan have arrested, interrogated, or executed hundreds of al Qaeda members.

President Bush has built a global alliance as unconventional as the foe arrayed against us.

Economic limits

In most wars, the enemy is limited economically. Bomb its factories and enflame its farms, and its ability to make war diminishes. Terrorists, traditionally, are even more limited by money. Taking hostages and robbing banks are their usual means of finance, if they cannot find a rogue state to underwrite their deadly efforts.

In the War on Terror, there is no infrastructure to bomb, aside from terrorist training camps, which are easily rebuilt. And damming the flow of cash to bin Laden has proved difficult, despite dozens of arrests and hundreds of frozen bank accounts.

Still, al Qaeda may be starting to feel the pinch. Bin Laden's personal wealth is often imagined to be enormous—sometimes estimated as high as $300 million. But most intelligence officials who study bin Laden's finances agree that his personal wealth is probably a small fraction of that, perhaps as little as $3 million. Indeed, detainees who knew bin Laden in Afghanistan say he often complained of "cash crunches."

Al Qaeda's funds seem to come from places that cannot easily be bombed. Bin Laden's money apparently comes from drug sales (mostly heroin) that the United States has been all but powerless to stop, and from terror states, like Iran, which the U.S. has failed to influence over the last two decades.

■ ■ ■

Neither the president nor the press has managed to make the War on Terror into a comprehensible narrative. Instead, it is presented to the public as a string of shootouts and arrests, with no sense of the big picture. Why?

For national security and political reasons, there are things that the president cannot tell the public. The president might be winning the war, but to tell us where and how would expose spies and allies, thereby endangering some allied efforts.

Besides, the Bush administration—especially the president himself—prizes secrecy. The administration's Republican friends in Congress may rue this fact, but they cannot change it. This means that the administration routinely receives rounds of critical coverage, sometimes based on incomplete information.

The next political casualty of the war might be the president himself. President Bush faces a dilemma in 2004: If he reveals some of the war's surprising successes, he might gain votes but impede the war's progress, while he risks his electoral future by leaving the "shadow war" in the shadows. So far, Bush has kept his silence. That is a revealing and risky choice, putting the nation's security ahead of political gain in an election with razor-thin margins.

By and large, the press has failed to use a wide-angle lens in their war coverage; some of the biggest developments in the War on Terror have gone unnoticed. Instead, reporters have offered us shards of information, fragments about terrorists with strange names from faraway lands, or brief clips of politicians and generals. We get only headlines, sound bites, and snapshots. No record of victories, defeats, or draws. It is, as one critic wrote on another subject, "the context of no context." No big picture.

If the press had covered World War II the way they cover the War on Terror, we would have seen exhaustive coverage of the carnage of the Pearl Harbor attack but missed entirely Doolittle's raid on Tokyo, the heroic defeat on Wake Island, the desperate defense of Guadalcanal, and the come-from-behind victory in the Battle of Midway. With a press like this, at the end of 1942 America would have no idea whether World War II was a hopeless cataclysm or a purposeful march to victory.

The unreported story of the War on Terror is that we can win it, and that the victories are being won now.

APPENDIX A

SUDANESE INTELLIGENCE DOCUMENTS

A secret memo from Sudanese intelligence detailing al Qaeda's movements in Africa.

ـ معلومات مهمان الواردة في مارس تفيد بعبور قافلة من ثلاثة سيارات مدنية تحت ساتر رحلة صيد تحمل خمسة من اعضاء جماعة الجهاد التابعة للتنظيم المحظور في طريقهم الي معسكرات تتبع للحرس الجمهوري التشادي .

ـ معلومات رجلنا في الجيريا تفيد بان الخمسة المذكورين هم ثمرة اولي لاتفاق تم بين التنظيم المحظور وجماعة الشيخ في فبراير عقب زيارة قام بها (م / ع) من مساعدي الشيخ الي تلك الدولة تمخض عن اتفاق بين الطرفين بغرض تقديم مساعدات لهم في حربهم المقدسة في غرب السودان مقابل توفير بعض الدعم لهم والملازات الامنة لبعض المطارين من اعضاءهم خاصة لما يتوفر لتنظيم الشيخ من علاقات عالمية .

ـ معلومات الجيريا تفيد بان الخمسة ثلاثة منهم مختصين في اعمال الارهاب ومهاجمة القري ولهم باع وخبرة طويلة في ذلك وان اثنان منهم من ذوي الدراية التامة باعمال الامداد الفني خاصة في المناطق الصحراوية والجبلية التي تشابه طبيعة الاقليم المشتعل في غرب السودان .

ـ معلومات ابشي المؤرخة في ابريل تفيد بوصول خبراء تدريب ستة تم توزيعهم علي ثلاثة معسكرات ثلاثة منهم تخصص عمل ارهاب قروي والاخرون حرب مدن .

ـ افادات انجمينا تؤكد وصول ثلاثة من التنظيم المحظور من اصول وسحنات افريقية الي العاصمة التشادية تحت غطاء انهم مستثمرين في الصمغ العربي وعلي اتصال بشقيق الرئيس وجري تحركهم الي شرق البلاد ليلتحقوا بعد ايام بسابقيهم القادمين من الشمال .

ـ معلومات متوفرة من باكستان عن طريق اصدقاءنا هناك ترجح ان تكون اسلام اباد هي المحطة التي تحركوا منها بتطابق الملامح المذكورة مع شخصيات مطلوبة من التنظيم المحظور.

ـ افادة رجلنا في انجمينا تؤكد وصول شخصين قامين من نيروبي تم استقبالهم وترحيلهم بطريقه مريبة توحي بان لهما علاقة بالاحداث المشتعلة في الاقليم الغربي , حيث تم تمريرهما الي داخل العاصمة دون اجراءات جوازات او غيره وذلك عند تطابق وصولهما مع طائرة تقل بعض السودانيين قادمة من اديس . اكدت بعد ذلك مصادر رجلنا في المحطة ذاتها وصول الشخصين الي معسكرات المتمرد في شرق تلك الدولة .

1. Important information, conveyed in March, speaks of a convoy of three civilian cars, carrying five members of the Jihad, an affiliate of the banned organization [al Qaeda], cross [into Chad] under cover of a hunting trip and join military camps belonging to the Chadian Republican guards.

2. Our man's information in Algeria says that these five men are the first result of the agreement reached between the banned group [al Qaeda] and the Sheikh's [Hassan al-Turabi] organization in February [2003] following a visit by M.A., an aide of the Sheikh, Algeria, which resulted in an agreement between the two which aims at providing assistance in their sacred war in the west of Sudan in return for certain support and security arrangements for them and to those members on the run, in particular seeing as the sheikh enjoys international connections.

3. Algerian information says that of the five, three are specialists in terrorist activities and the art of attacking villages and have long experiences in that domain and that the other two are specialists in organizing logistical support, especially in desert and mountainous areas similar to the territory of western Sudan.

4. The latest information from Abache in April talks of the arrival of six training specialists who have been distributed across three military camps specializing in village terrorism and two in urban warfare.

5. From N'Djamena statements speak of the arrival of three of the banned organization [al Qaeda]. They are of African origin and visited the capital of Chad under the cover of being interested in the Arab glue business and [claimed to be] friends of the president's brother. They were moved to the east of the country to join other members [of al Qaeda] arriving from the north.

6. Information received from our friends in Pakistan [the Inter-Services Institute] suggest that Islamabad is the origin from which they embarked, and this is based on certain physical characteristics that tally with some wanted members of the Tanzeem who disappeared last year.

7. Our man in N'Djamena says two people arrived from Nairobi who were welcomed in a manner which suggests that they are linked with the incidents in the western region [Darfur, in Sudan], as they were whisked to the city without going through passport controls and the like. Their plane arrived at the exact time of another flight bringing some Sudanese from Addis Ababa. Our men confirmed the arrival of the two men to the rebel camps east of that city [N'Djamena].

APPENDIX B

CIA INTERROGATION MEMO

Transcript of the CIA polygraph interrogation of Bilal Sulayman, the Sudanese military captain who lied to the CIA for years. His lies about the "Mekki plot" were discovered in this polygraph test.

---

1. THE FOLLOWING IS A BRIEF SUMMARY OF THE POLYGRAPH THAT WAS ADMINISTERED TO BILAL 'IWAD SULAYMAN ((NASIR)), DPOB; 1973 DURING THE EVENING OF 16 MARCH 2003. THE BOTTOM LINE IS THAT BILAL HAD NO KNOWLEDGE THAT MEKKI WAS PART OF A PLOT TO FLY AN AIRCRAFT INTO THE WHITE HOUSE.

2. DURING THE INTERVIEW SESSION BILAL ADVISED THAT HE HAD NEVER HEARD OF A THREAT AGAINST THE WHITE HOUSE OR AMERICAN INTERESTS IN AFRICA. HE STATED THAT THE STORY OF MEKKI MOHAMMED ((MEKKI)) TRAVELING TO THE US WITH ORDERS TO FLY AN AIRCRAFT INTO THE WHITE HOUSE WAS A STORY HE PUT TOGETHER (ON HIS OWN) AND PART OF AN ASSUMPTION HE MADE OF MEKKI BEING IN THE U.S.. HE EXPLAINED THAT THE ASSUMPTION WAS BASED ON MEKKI'S PAST ASSOCIATION WITH FUNDAMENTALIST ISLAMIC ELEMENTS AND MEKKI RECEIVING PILOT TRAINING IN PAKISTAN THAT WAS POSSIBLY PAID FOR BY AL-QA'IDA.

WHEN ASKED THE FOLLOWING RELEVANT QUESTION DURING THE POLYGRAPH "DO YOU HAVE ANY DIRECT KNOWLEDGE OF A PLAN TO ATTACK THE WHITE HOUSE IN AMERICA"?

ANSWER, "NO".

THERE WAS NO DECEPTION INDICATED WHEN HE ANSWERED THIS QUESTION.

3. SUBJECT ADVISED THAT HE VOLUNTARILY WENT TO THE US EMBASSY IN KHARTOUM DURING AUGUST 2002 SEEKING A VISA.

1. THE FOLLOWING IS THE COMPLETE REPORT ON THE POLYGRAPH EXAMINATION ADMINISTERED TO THE BILAL 'IWAD SULAYMAN NASIR (SUBJE(WHO PROVIDED INFORMATION ON A THREAT AGAINST THE WHITE HOUSE.

2. BACKGROUND: SUBJECT IS A 30-YEAR-OLD SINGLE MALE WHO IS A CITIZEN OF SUDAN AND A MEMBER OF THE SUDAN AIR FORCE. HE CAME INT(THE EMBASSY SEVERAL TIMES BETWEEN 2001 AND 2003. WHEN SUBJECT CA INTO THE EMBASSY IN AUGUST 2002 HE PROVIDED THE NAMES OF NINE SUDANESE PILOTS WHO, ACCORDING TO SUBJECT, WERE TRAINED IN PAKIST AND RECRUITED TO CONDUCT TERRORIST ACTS AGAINST THE UNITED STATE INCLUDING THE WHITE HOUSE. SUBJECT ALSO ADVISED THAT ONE OF THE PILOTS WAS IN THE UNITED STATES AND PLANNED TO UNDERTAKE AN ATTA(AGAINST THE WHITE HOUSE. SUBJECT HAD NOT PREVIOUSLY RECEIVED A POLYGRAPH EXAMINATION. HE WAS AWARE OF U.S. GOVERNMENT INVOLVEMENT IN THE POLYGRAPH EXAMINATION.

3. PURPOSE: WE REQUESTED A POLYGRAPH EXAMINATION OF SUBJECT T(DETERMINE IF SUBJECT (A) HAD VALID INFORMATION ABOUT A PLANNED ATTACK AGAINST THE WHITE HOUSE AND IF SUBJECT WAS (B) DIRECTED BY ANYONE, TO COME INTO THE EMBASSY

4. PROCEDURE: THE POLYGRAPH EXAMINATION WAS ADMINISTERED TO SUBJECT DURING THE EVENING OF 16 MARCH 2003 IN KHARTOUM BETWEEN 2100 HRS AND 0200 HRS. THE POLYGRAPH EXAMINATION WAS CONDUCTED I ARABIC WITH AN ARABIC LINGUIST ACTING AS AN INTERPRETER. ALL POLYGRAPH EXAMINATION QUESTIONS WERE REVIEWED IN ADVANCE WITH SUBJECT AND HE CLAIMED COMPLETE UNDERSTANDING. SUBJECT ALSO CLAIMED TO BE IN GOOD HEALTH AND FREE FROM THE INFLUENCE OF DRUGS

5. RESULTS: NO DECEPTION WAS INDICATED WHEN SUBJECT DENIED HAVING DIRECT KNOWLEDGE OF A PLAN TO ATTACK THE WHITE HOUSE.

6. THE POLYGRAPH EXAMINATION RESULT WAS INCONCLUSIVE AND REMAINS INCOMPLETE REGARDING SUBJECT BEING DIRECTED BY A PERSON OF AUTHORITY TO COME TO THE U.S. EMBASSY IN KHARTOUM DURING AUGUST 2002. THE INCONCLUSIVE RESULT WAS CAUSED BY IRREGULAR AND INCONSISTENT REACTIONS WHEN THE QUESTION WAS ASKED DURING THE POLYGRAPH EXAMINATION. THE INCONCLUSIVE RESULT NEITHER SUPPORTS NOR REFUTES SUBJECT'S CLAIM THAT HE WAS NOT DIRECTED TO MAKE CONTACT WITH THE EMBASSY.

7. DURING THE COURSE OF THE INTERVIEW WITH SUBJECT HE ADVISED THAT HE NEVER HEARD A STATEMENT INVOLVING A THREAT AGAINST THE WHITE HOUSE OR AGAINST ANY U.S. INTERESTS IN AFRICA, INCLUDING NAIROBI. SUBJECT SAID THAT THE WHITE HOUSE THREAT INFORMATION INVOLVING ANOTHER SUDANESE NATIONAL IN THE U.S. (MEKKI) WAS A FABRICATION OR ASSUMPTION ON HIS PART BASED ON MEKKI BEING ASSOCIATED WITH THE PEOPLE'S POLICE, HIS PILOT TRAINING IN PAKISTAN THAT WAS REPORTED TO HAVE BEEN PAID FOR BY AL-QA'IDA, AND THE REPORTED ISLAMIC JIHAD INDOCTRINATION DURING THE PILOT TRAINING.

8. SUBJECT ALSO ADVISED THAT HE DOES NOT KNOW IF MEKKI WENT TO THE UNITED STATES AT THE DIRECTION OF AL-QA'IDA OR IF HE WENT TO ESCAPE AL-QA'IDA.

9. THE RELEVANT QUESTIONS ASKED DURING THE POLYGRAPH EXAMINATION AND THE ANSWERS GIVEN ARE AS FOLLOWS:

   A. DO YOU NOW HAVE DIRECT KNOWLEDGE OF A PLAN TO ATTACK THE WHITE HOUSE IN AMERICA? ANSWER: NO. IN OTHERWORDS, INFORMATION THAT SUBJECT HAD CONCERNING AN ATTACK ON THE WHITE HOUSE WAS A FABRICATION.

   B. WERE YOU TOLD BY A PERSON OF AUTHORITY TO GO TO THE AMERICAN EMBASSY LAST AUGUST (2002)? ANSWER: NO.

NO DECEPTION WAS INDICATED WHEN SUBJECT DENIED HAVING ANY DIRECT KNOWLEDGE OF A PLAN TO ATTACK THE WHITE HOUSE IN AMERICA (QUESTION "A").

10. THE POLYGRAPH EXAMINATION RESULTS WERE INCONCLUSIVE AND ARE INCOMPLETE REGARDING SUBJECT BEING DIRECTED TO MAKE CONTACT WITH THE U.S. EMBASSY DURING AUGUST (QUESTION "B"). THE RESULTS WERE INCONCLUSIVE BECAUSE OF IRREGULAR AND INCONSISTENT REACTIONS WHEN THE QUESTION WAS ASKED DURING THE POLYGRAPH EXAMINATION. THE ISSUE WAS NOT PURSUED IN MORE DETAIL DUE TO TIME CONSTRAINTS AND REMAINS INCOMPLETE. AT 0200 HRS (LOCAL) THE SESSION WAS AMICABLY TERMINATED.

APPENDIX C

STATUS OF TOP AL QAEDA OFFICERS

OSAMA BIN LADEN, Saudi, supreme leader: **At large**, on FBI most wanted terrorists list.

AYMAN AL-ZAWAHRI, Egyptian, bin Laden's doctor, spiritual advisor: **At large**, on FBI most wanted terrorist list.

MOHAMMED ATEF, Egyptian, military chief: **Killed in U.S. airstrike.**

KHALID SHAIKH MOHAMMED, Kuwaiti, suspected mastermind of September 11 attacks: **Captured.**

ABU ZUBAYDAH, Palestinian-Saudi, terrorist coordinator: **Captured.**

SAIF AL-ADEL, Egyptian, bin Laden security chief: **At large**, on FBI most wanted terrorist list.

SHAIKH SAEED AL-MASRI, Egyptian, bin Laden chief financier: **At large.**

ABDUL RAHIM AL-NASHIRI, Saudi, Persian Gulf operations chief: **Captured.**

TAWFIQ ATTASH KHALLAD, Yemeni, operational leader, suspected mastermind of USS *Cole* bombing in October 2000: **At large.**

QAED SALEM SINAN AL-HARETHI, Yemeni, Yemen operations chief: **Killed in U.S. airstrike.**

OMAR AL-FARUQ, Kuwaiti, Southeast Asia operations chief: **Captured.**

IBN AL-SHAYKH AL-LIBI, Libyan, training camp commander: **Captured.**

SAAD BIN LADEN, Saudi, bin Laden's son: **At large.**

ABU MOHAMMAD AL-MASRI, Egyptian, training camp commander: **At large**, on FBI most wanted terrorist list as **ABDULLAH AHMED ABDULLAH.**

TARIQ ANWAR AL-SAYYID AHMAD, Egyptian, operational planner: **Killed in U.S. airstrike.**

MOHAMMED SALEH, Egyptian, operational planner: **Killed in U.S. airstrike.**

ABD AL-HADI AL-IRAQI, training camp commander: **Captured.**

ABU MUSAB AL-ZARQAWI, Jordanian, operational planner: **At large.**

ABU ZUBAIR AL-HAILI, Saudi, operational planner: **Captured.**

ABU HAFS THE MAURITANIAN, operational and spiritual leader: **At large.**

SULAIMAN ABU GHAITH, Kuwaiti, al Qaeda spokesman: **At large.**

MOHAMMED OMAR ABDEL-RAHMAN, Egyptian, operational planner and trainer: **At large.**

MIDHAT MURSI, Egyptian, chemical and bioweapons researcher: **At large.**

MOHAMMED JAMAL KHALIFA, Saudi, financier: **At large.**

SAAD AL-SHARIF, Saudi, financer: **At large.**

MUSTAFA AHMED AL-HASAWI: September 11 financer: **Captured.**

HAMZA AL-QATARI, financier: **Killed.**

AHMAD SAID AL-KADR, Egyptian-Canadian, financier: **Killed.**

ZAID KHAYR, operational leader: **At large.**

ABU SALAH AL-YEMENI: logistics, **Killed.**

ABU JAFAR AL-JAZIRI, aide to Abu Zubaydah: **Killed.**

ABU BASIR AL-YEMENI, Yemeni, aide to Osama bin Laden: **At large.**

ABD AL-AZIZ AL-JAMAL, aide to al-Zawahiri: **At large.**

RAMZI BINALSHIBH, Yemeni, planner and organizer of September 11 attacks: **Captured.**

ZACARIAS MOUSSAOUI, Moroccan, charged as conspirator with September 11 hijackers: **Captured.**

ZAKARIYA ESSABAR, member of cell with chief September 11 hijacker Mohamed Atta: **At large.**

SAID BAHAJI, German, member of cell with chief September 11 hijacker Mohamed Atta: **At large.**

THE IRAQ—AL QAEDA CONNECTION

EVERY DAY IT SEEMS ANOTHER AMERICAN soldier is killed in Iraq. These grim statistics have become a favorite of network news anchors and political chat show hosts. Never mind that they mix deaths from accidents with actual battlefield casualties; or that the average is actually closer to one American death for every two days; or that enemy deaths far outnumber ours. What matters is the overall impression of mounting, pointless deaths.

That is why is important to remember why we fight in Iraq— and who we fight. Indeed, many of those sniping at U.S. troops are al Qaeda terrorists operating inside Iraq. And many of bin Laden's men were in Iraq prior to the liberation. A wealth of evidence on the public record—from government reports and congressional testimony to news accounts from major newspapers—attests to long-standing ties between bin Laden and Saddam going back to 1994.

Those who try to whitewash Saddam's record don't dispute this evidence; they just ignore it. So let's review the evidence, all of it on the public record for months or years:

- Abdul Rahman Yasin was the only member of the al Qaeda cell that detonated the 1993 World Trade Center bomb to remain at large in the Clinton years. He fled to Iraq. U.S. forces recently discovered a cache of documents in Tikrit, Saddam's hometown, that show that Iraq gave Yasin both a house and monthly salary.
- Bin Laden met at least eight times with officers of Iraq's Special Security Organization, a secret police agency run by Saddam's son Qusay, and met with officials from Saddam's mukhabarat, its external intelligence service, according to intelligence made public by Secretary of State Colin Powell, who was speaking before the United Nations Security Council on February 6, 2003.
- Sudanese intelligence officials told me that their agents had observed meetings between Iraqi intelligence agents and bin Laden starting in 1994, when bin Laden lived in Khartoum.
- Bin Laden met the director of the Iraqi mukhabarat in 1996 in Khartoum, according to Secretary Powell.
- An al Qaeda operative now held by the U.S. confessed that in the mid-1990s, bin Laden had forged an agreement with Saddam's men to cease all terrorist activities against the Iraqi dictator, Secretary Powell told the United Nations.
- In 1999, the *Guardian*, a British newspaper, reported that Farouk Hijazi, a senior officer in Iraq's mukhabarat, had journeyed deep into the icy mountains near Kandahar, Afghanistan, in December 1998 to meet with al Qaeda men. Hijazi is "thought to have offered bin Laden asylum in Iraq," the *Guardian* reported.

■ In October 2000, another Iraqi intelligence operative, Salah Suleiman, was arrested near the Afghan border by Pakistani authorities, according to Jane's Foreign Report, a respected international newsletter. Jane's reported that Suleiman was shuttling between Iraqi intelligence and Ayman al-Zawahiri, now al Qaeda's number two man.

(Why are all of those meetings significant? The London *Observer* reports that FBI investigators cite a captured al Qaeda field manual in Afghanistan, which "emphasizes the value of conducting discussions about pending terrorist attacks face to face, rather than by electronic means.")

■ As recently as 2001, Iraq's embassy in Pakistan was used as a "liaison" between the Iraqi dictator and al Qaeda, Secretary Powell told the United Nations.
■ Spanish investigators have uncovered documents seized from Yusuf Galan—who is charged by a Spanish court with being "directly involved with the preparation and planning" of the September 11 attacks—that show the terrorist was invited to a party at the Iraqi embassy in Madrid. The invitation used his "al Qaeda nom de guerre," London's *Independent* reports.
■ An Iraqi defector to Turkey, known by his cover name as "Abu Mohammed," told Gwynne Roberts of the *Sunday Times* of London that he saw bin Laden's fighters in camps in Iraq in 1997. At the time, Mohammed was a colonel in Saddam's fedayeen. He described an encounter at Salman Pak, the training facility southeast of Baghdad. At that vast compound run by Iraqi intelligence, Muslim militants trained to hijack planes with knives—on a full-size Boeing 707. Col. Mohammed recalls his first visit to Salman Pak this way: "We were met by Colonel Jamil Kamil, the camp

manager, and Major Ali Hawas. I noticed that a lot of people were queuing for food. (The major) said to me: 'You'll have nothing to do with these people. They are Osama bin Laden's group and the PKK and Mojahedin-e Khalq.'"

■ In 1998, Abbas al-Janabi, a longtime aide to Saddam's son Uday, defected to the West. At the time, he repeatedly told reporters that there was a direct connection between Iraq and al Qaeda.

■ The *Sunday Times* found a Saddam loyalist in a Kurdish prison who claims to have been al-Zawahiri's bodyguard during his 1992 visit with Saddam in Baghdad. Al-Zawahiri was a close associate of bin Laden at the time and was present at the founding of al Qaeda in 1989.

■ Following the defeat of the Taliban, almost two dozen bin Laden associates "converged on Baghdad and established a base of operations there," Secretary Powell told the United Nations in February 2003. From their Baghdad base, the secretary said, they supervised the movement of men, materiel, and money for al Qaeda's global network.

■ In 2001, an al Qaeda member "bragged that the situation in Iraq was 'good,'" according to intelligence made public by Secretary Powell.

■ That same year, Saudi Arabian border guards arrested two al Qaeda members entering the kingdom from Iraq.

■ Abu Musaab al-Zarqawi oversaw an al Qaeda training camp in Afghanistan, Secretary Powell told the United Nations. His specialty was poisons. Wounded in fighting with U.S. forces, he sought medical treatment in Baghdad in May 2002. When al-Zarqawi recovered, he restarted a training camp in northern Iraq. Al-Zarqawi's Iraq cell was later tied to the October 2002 murder of Lawrence Foley, an official of the U.S. Agency for International Development, in Amman, Jordan. The captured assassin confessed that he received orders and funds from Zarqawi's cell in Iraq, Secretary Powell said. His accomplice escaped to Iraq.

- Al-Zarqawi met with the military chief of al Qaeda, Mohammed Ibrahim Makwai (aka Saif al-Adel) in Iran in February 2003, according to intelligence sources cited by the *Washington Post*.

- Mohammad Atef, the head of al Qaeda's military wing until the U.S. killed him in Afghanistan in November 2001, told a senior al Qaeda member now in U.S. custody that the terror network needed labs outside of Afghanistan to manufacture chemical weapons, Secretary Powell said. "Where did they go, where did they look?" said the secretary. "They went to Iraq."

- Abu Abdullah al-Iraqi was sent to Iraq by bin Laden to purchase poison gases several times between 1997 and 2000. He called his relationship with Saddam's regime "successful," Secretary Powell told the United Nations.

- Mohamed Mansour Shahab, a smuggler hired by Iraq to transport weapons to bin Laden in Afghanistan, was arrested by anti-Hussein Kurdish forces in May 2000. He later told his story to American intelligence and a reporter for the *New Yorker* magazine.

- Documents found among the debris of the Iraqi Intelligence Center show that Baghdad funded the Allied Democratic Forces, a Ugandan terror group led by an Islamist cleric linked to bin Laden. According to a London's *Daily Telegraph*, the organization offered to recruit "youth to train for the jihad" at a "headquarters for international holy warrior network" to be established in Baghdad.

- Mullah Melan Krekar, ran a terror group (Ansar al-Islam) linked to both bin Laden and Saddam Hussein. Krekar admitted to a Kurdish newspaper that he met bin Laden in Afghanistan with other senior al Qaeda officials. His acknowledged meetings with bin Laden go back to 1988. When he organized Ansar al Islam in 2001 to conduct suicide attacks on Americans, "three bin Laden operatives showed up with a gift of $300,000 'to undertake jihad,'" *Newsday* reported. Krekar is now in custody in the Netherlands. His group operated in a portion of northern Iraq loyal to Saddam Hussein—and attacked independent Kurdish groups hostile to Saddam. A spokesman for the Patriotic Union of Kurdistan told a United Press International correspondent that Krekar's group was funded by "Saddam Hussein's regime in Baghdad."

■ After October 2001, hundreds of al Qaeda fighters are believed to have holed up in Ansar al-Islam's strongholds inside northern Iraq.

Some skeptics dismiss the emerging evidence of a longstanding link between Iraq and al Qaeda by contending that Saddam ran a secular dictatorship hated by Islamists like bin Laden.

In fact, there are plenty of "Stalin-Roosevelt" partnerships between international terrorists and Muslim dictators. Saddam and bin Laden had common enemies, common purposes and interlocking needs. They shared a powerful hate for America and the Saudi royal family. They both saw the Gulf War as a turning point. Saddam suffered a crushing defeat which he had repeatedly vowed to avenge. Bin Laden regards the U.S. as guilty of war crimes against Iraqis and believes that non-Muslims shouldn't have military bases on the holy sands of Arabia. Al Qaeda's avowed goal for the past ten years has been the removal of American forces from Saudi Arabia, where they stood in harm's way solely to contain Saddam.

The most compelling reason for bin Laden to work with Saddam is money. Al Qaeda operatives have testified in federal courts that the terror network was always desperate for cash. Senior employees fought bitterly about the $100 difference in pay between Egyptians and Saudis (the Egyptians made more). One al Qaeda member, who was connected to the 1998 embassy bombings, told a U.S. federal court how bitter he was that bin Laden could not pay for his pregnant wife to see a doctor.

Bin Laden's personal wealth alone simply is not enough to support a profligate global organization. Besides, bin Laden's fortune is probably not as large as some imagine. Informed estimates put bin Laden's pre–September 11, 2001, wealth at perhaps $30 million. $30 million is the budget of a small school district, not a global terror conglomerate. Meanwhile, *Forbes* estimated Saddam's personal fortune at $2 million.

So a common enemy, a shared goal, and powerful need for cash seem to have forged an alliance between Saddam and bin Laden. Former CIA director George Tenet recently told the Senate Intelligence Committee: "Iraq has in the past provided training in document forgery and bomb making to al Qaeda. It also provided training in poisons and gasses to two al Qaeda associates; one of these [al Qaeda] associates characterized the relationship as successful. Mr. Chairman, this information is based on a solid foundation of intelligence. It comes to us from credible and reliable sources. Much of it is corroborated by multiple sources."

The Iraqis, who had the Third World's largest poison-gas operations prior to the Gulf War I, have perfected the technique of making hydrogen-cyanide gas, which the Nazis called Zyklon-B. In the hands of al Qaeda, this would be a fearsome weapon in an enclosed space—like a suburban mall or subway station.

First published on September 25, 2003,
at www.techcentralstation.com

APPENDIX E

OFFICIAL WARNING FROM THE U.S. STATE DEPARTMENT

PUBLIC ANNOUNCEMENT - WORLDWIDE CAUTION

Terrorist threat information released by the Department of State on May 12, 2001.

Dear American:

The U.S. Government has learned that American citizens abroad may be the target of a terrorist threat from extremist groups with links to Usama Bin Ladin's Al-Qaida organization. In the past, such individuals have not distinguished between official and civilian targets.

As always, we take this information seriously. U.S. Government facilities worldwide remain at a heightened state of alert. In addition, U.S. Government facilities have and will continue to temporarily close or suspend public services as necessary to review their security posture and ensure its adequacy.

In light of the above, U.S. citizens are urged to maintain a high level of vigilance and to take appropriate steps to increase their security awareness to reduce their vulnerability. Americans should maintain a low profile, vary routes and times for all required travel, and treat mail and packages from unfamiliar sources with suspicion.

In addition, American citizens are also urged to avoid contact with any suspicious, unfamiliar objects, and to report the presence of the objects to local authorities. Vehicles should not be left unattended, if at all possible, and should be kept locked at all times. U.S. Government personnel overseas have been advised to take the same precautions.

U.S. citizens planning to travel abroad should consult the Department of State's Public Announcements, Travel Warnings, Consular Information Sheets, and regional travel brochures, all of which are available at the Consular Affairs Internet website at http://travel.state.gov. We will continue to provide updated information should it become available.

Department of State travel information and publications are available at Internet address: www.travel.state.gov. U.S. travelers may hear recorded information by calling the Department of State in Washington, D.C. at 202-647-5225 from their touchtone telephone, or receive information by automated telefax by dialing 202-647-3000 from their fax machine.

This Public Announcement replaces the Public Announcement - Worldwide Caution of January 5, 2001 to alert Americans that they may be the target of a terrorist threat. This Public Announcement expires on August 11, 2001.

The State Department issued this warning about bin Laden *before* the September 11 attacks.

PRESIDENT BUSH'S ADDRESS

TO A JOINT SESSION OF CONGRESS AND THE AMERICAN PEOPLE

SEPTEMBER 20, 2001

THE PRESIDENT: Mr. Speaker, Mr. President Pro Tempore, members of Congress, and fellow Americans:

In the normal course of events, Presidents come to this chamber to report on the state of the Union. Tonight, no such report is needed. It has already been delivered by the American people.

We have seen it in the courage of passengers, who rushed terrorists to save others on the ground—passengers like an exceptional man named Todd Beamer. And would you please help me to welcome his wife, Lisa Beamer, here tonight.

We have seen the state of our Union in the endurance of rescuers, working past exhaustion. We have seen the unfurling of flags, the lighting of candles, the giving of blood, the saying of prayers—in English, Hebrew, and Arabic. We have seen the decency of a loving and giving people who have made the grief of strangers their own.

My fellow citizens, for the last nine days, the entire world has seen for itself the state of our Union—and it is strong.

Tonight we are a country awakened to danger and called to defend freedom. Our grief has turned to anger, and anger to resolution. Whether we bring our enemies to justice, or bring justice to our enemies, justice will be done.

I thank the Congress for its leadership at such an important time. All of America was touched on the evening of the tragedy to see Republicans and Democrats joined together on the steps of this Capitol, singing "God Bless America." And you did more than sing; you acted, by delivering $40 billion to rebuild our communities and meet the needs of our military.

Speaker Hastert, Minority Leader Gephardt, Majority Leader Daschle and Senator Lott, I thank you for your friendship, for your leadership and for your service to our country.

And on behalf of the American people, I thank the world for its outpouring of support. America will never forget the sounds of our National Anthem playing at Buckingham Palace, on the streets of Paris, and at Berlin's Brandenburg Gate.

We will not forget South Korean children gathering to pray outside our embassy in Seoul, or the prayers of sympathy offered at a mosque in Cairo. We will not forget moments of silence and days of mourning in Australia and Africa and Latin America.

Nor will we forget the citizens of 80 other nations who died with our own: dozens of Pakistanis; more than 130 Israelis; more than 250 citizens of India; men and women from El Salvador, Iran, Mexico and Japan; and hundreds of British citizens. America has no truer friend than Great Britain. Once again, we are joined together in a great cause—so honored the British Prime Minister has crossed an ocean to show his unity of purpose with America. Thank you for coming, friend.

On September 11, enemies of freedom committed an act of war against our country. Americans have known wars—but for the past 136 years, they have been wars on foreign soil, except for one Sunday in 1941. Americans have known the casualties of war—but not at the center of a great city on a peaceful morning. Americans have known surprise attacks—but never before on thousands of civilians. All of this was brought upon us in a single day—and night fell on a different world, a world where freedom itself is under attack.

Americans have many questions tonight. Americans are asking: Who attacked our country? The evidence we have gathered all points to a collection of loosely affiliated terrorist organizations known as al Qaeda. They are the same murderers indicted for bombing American embassies in Tanzania and Kenya, and responsible for bombing the USS *Cole*.

Al Qaeda is to terror what the mafia is to crime. But its goal is not making money; its goal is remaking the world—and imposing its radical beliefs on people everywhere.

The terrorists practice a fringe form of Islamic extremism that has been rejected by Muslim scholars and the vast majority of Muslim clerics—a fringe movement that perverts the peaceful teachings of Islam. The terrorists' directive commands them to kill Christians and Jews, to kill all Americans, and make no distinction among military and civilians, including women and children.

This group and its leader—a person named Osama bin Laden—are linked to many other organizations in different countries, including the Egyptian Islamic Jihad and the Islamic Movement of Uzbekistan. There are thousands of these terrorists in more than sixty countries. They are recruited from their own nations and neighborhoods and brought to camps in places like Afghanistan, where they are trained in the tactics of terror. They are sent back to their homes or sent to hide in countries around the world to plot evil and destruction.

The leadership of al Qaeda has great influence in Afghanistan and supports the Taliban regime in controlling most of that country. In Afghanistan, we see al Qaeda's vision for the world.

Afghanistan's people have been brutalized—many are starving and many have fled. Women are not allowed to attend school. You can be jailed for owning a television. Religion can be practiced only as their leaders dictate. A man can be jailed in Afghanistan if his beard is not long enough.

The United States respects the people of Afghanistan—after all, we are currently its largest source of humanitarian aid—but we condemn the Taliban regime. It is not only repressing its own people, it is threatening people everywhere by sponsoring and sheltering and supplying terrorists. By aiding and abetting murder, the Taliban regime is committing murder.

And tonight, the United States of America makes the following demands on the Taliban: Deliver to United States authorities all the leaders of al Qaeda who hide in your land. Release all foreign nationals, including American citizens, you have unjustly imprisoned. Protect foreign journalists, diplomats and aid workers in your country. Close immediately and permanently every terrorist training camp in Afghanistan, and hand over every terrorist, and every person in their support structure, to appropriate authorities. Give the United States full access to terrorist training camps, so we can make sure they are no longer operating.

These demands are not open to negotiation or discussion. The Taliban must act, and act immediately. They will hand over the terrorists, or they will share in their fate.

I also want to speak tonight directly to Muslims throughout the world. We respect your faith. It's practiced freely by many millions of Americans, and by millions more in countries that America counts as friends. Its teachings are good and peaceful, and those who commit evil in the name of Allah blaspheme the name of Allah. The terrorists are traitors to their own faith, trying, in effect, to hijack Islam itself. The enemy of America is not our many Muslim friends; it is not our many Arab friends. Our enemy is a radical network of terrorists, and every government that supports them.

Our War on Terror begins with al Qaeda, but it does not end there. It will not end until every terrorist group of global reach has been found, stopped and defeated.

Americans are asking, why do they hate us? They hate what we see right here in this chamber—a democratically elected government. Their leaders are self-appointed. They hate our freedoms—our freedom of religion, our freedom of speech, our freedom to vote and assemble and disagree with each other.

They want to overthrow existing governments in many Muslim countries, such as Egypt, Saudi Arabia, and Jordan. They want to drive Israel out of the Middle East. They want to drive Christians and Jews out of vast regions of Asia and Africa.

These terrorists kill not merely to end lives, but to disrupt and end a way of life. With every atrocity, they hope that America grows fearful, retreating from the world and forsaking our friends. They stand against us, because we stand in their way.

We are not deceived by their pretenses to piety. We have seen their kind before. They are the heirs of all the murderous ideologies of the twentieth century. By sacrificing human life to serve their radical visions—by abandoning every value except the will to power—they follow in the path of fascism, and Nazism, and totalitarianism. And they will follow that path all the way, to where it ends: in history's unmarked grave of discarded lies.

Americans are asking: How will we fight and win this war? We will direct every resource at our command—every means of diplomacy, every tool of intelligence, every instrument of law enforcement, every financial influence, and every necessary weapon of war—to the disruption and to the defeat of the global terror network.

This war will not be like the war against Iraq a decade ago, with a decisive liberation of territory and a swift conclusion. It will not look like the air war above Kosovo two years ago, where no ground troops were used and not a single American was lost in combat.

Our response involves far more than instant retaliation and isolated strikes. Americans should not expect one battle, but a lengthy campaign, unlike any other we have ever seen. It may include dramatic strikes, visible on TV, and covert operations, secret even in success. We will starve terrorists of funding, turn them one against another, drive them from place to place, until there is no refuge or no rest. And we will pursue nations that provide aid or safe haven to terrorism. Every nation, in every region, now has a decision to make. Either you are with us, or you are with the terrorists. From this day forward, any nation that continues to harbor or support terrorism will be regarded by the United States as a hostile regime.

Our nation has been put on notice: We are not immune from attack. We will take defensive measures against terrorism to protect Americans. Today, dozens of federal departments and agencies, as well as state and local governments, have responsibilities affecting homeland security. These efforts must be coordinated at the highest level. So tonight I announce the creation of a Cabinet-level position reporting directly to me—the Office of Homeland Security.

And tonight I also announce a distinguished American to lead this effort, to strengthen American security: a military veteran, an effective governor, a true patriot, a trusted friend—Pennsylvania's Tom Ridge. He will lead, oversee and coordinate a comprehensive national strategy to safeguard our country against terrorism, and respond to any attacks that may come.

These measures are essential. But the only way to defeat terrorism as a threat to our way of life is to stop it, eliminate it, and destroy it where it grows.

Many will be involved in this effort, from FBI agents to intelligence operatives to the reservists we have called to active duty. All deserve our thanks, and all have our prayers. And tonight, a few miles from the damaged Pentagon, I have a message for our military: Be ready. I've called the Armed Forces to alert, and there is a reason. The hour is coming when America will act, and you will make us proud.

This is not, however, just America's fight. And what is at stake is not just America's freedom. This is the world's fight. This is civilization's fight. This is the fight of all who believe in progress and pluralism, tolerance and freedom.

We ask every nation to join us. We will ask, and we will need, the help of police forces, intelligence services, and banking systems around the world. The United States is grateful that many nations and many international organizations have already responded— with sympathy and with support. Nations from Latin America, to Asia, to Africa, to Europe, to the Islamic world. Perhaps the NATO Charter reflects best the attitude of the world: An attack on one is an attack on all.

The civilized world is rallying to America's side. They understand that if this terror goes unpunished, their own cities, their own citizens may be next. Terror, unanswered, can not only bring down buildings, it can threaten the stability of legitimate governments. And you know what—we're not going to allow it.

Americans are asking: What is expected of us? I ask you to live your lives, and hug your children. I know many citizens have fears tonight, and I ask you to be calm and resolute, even in the face of a continuing threat.

I ask you to uphold the values of America, and remember why so many have come here. We are in a fight for our principles, and our first responsibility is to live by them. No one should be singled out for unfair treatment or unkind words because of their ethnic background or religious faith.

I ask you to continue to support the victims of this tragedy with your contributions. Those who want to give can go to a central source of information, libertyunites.org, to find the names of groups providing direct help in New York, Pennsylvania, and Virginia.

The thousands of FBI agents who are now at work in this investigation may need your cooperation, and I ask you to give it.

I ask for your patience, with the delays and inconveniences that may accompany tighter security; and for your patience in what will be a long struggle.

I ask your continued participation and confidence in the American economy. Terrorists attacked a symbol of American prosperity. They did not touch its source. America is successful because of the hard work, and creativity, and enterprise of our people. These were the true strengths of our economy before September 11, and they are our strengths today.

And, finally, please continue praying for the victims of terror and their families, for those in uniform, and for our great country. Prayer has comforted us in sorrow, and will help strengthen us for the journey ahead.

Tonight I thank my fellow Americans for what you have already done and for what you will do. And ladies and gentlemen of the Congress, I thank you, their representatives, for what you have already done and for what we will do together.

Tonight, we face new and sudden national challenges. We will come together to improve air safety, to dramatically expand the number of air marshals on domestic flights, and take new measures to prevent hijacking. We will come together to promote stability and keep our airlines flying, with direct assistance during this emergency.

We will come together to give law enforcement the additional tools it needs to track down terror here at home. We will come together to strengthen our intelligence capabilities to know the plans of terrorists before they act, and find them before they strike.

We will come together to take active steps that strengthen America's economy, and put our people back to work.

Tonight we welcome two leaders who embody the extraordinary spirit of all New Yorkers: Governor George Pataki, and Mayor Rudolph Giuliani. As a symbol of America's resolve, my administration will work with Congress, and these two leaders, to show the world that we will rebuild New York City.

After all that has just passed—all the lives taken, and all the possibilities and hopes that died with them—it is natural to wonder if America's future is one of fear. Some speak of an age of terror. I know there are struggles ahead, and dangers to face. But this country will define our times, not be defined by them. As long as the United States of America is determined and strong, this will not be an age of terror; this will be an age of liberty, here and across the world.

Great harm has been done to us. We have suffered great loss. And in our grief and anger we have found our mission and our moment. Freedom and fear are at war. The advance of human freedom—the great achievement of our time, and the great hope of every time—now depends on us. Our nation—this generation—will lift a dark threat of violence from our people and our future. We will rally the world to this cause by our efforts, by our courage. We will not tire, we will not falter, and we will not fail.

It is my hope that in the months and years ahead, life will return almost to normal. We'll go back to our lives and routines, and that is good. Even grief recedes with time and grace. But our resolve must not pass. Each of us will remember what happened that day, and to whom it happened. We'll remember the moment the news came—where we were and what we were doing. Some will remember an image of a fire, or a story of rescue. Some will carry memories of a face and a voice gone forever.

And I will carry this: It is the police shield of a man named George Howard, who died at the World Trade Center trying to save others. It was given to me by his mom, Arlene, as a proud memorial to her son. This is my reminder of lives that ended, and a task that does not end.

I will not forget this wound to our country or those who inflicted it. I will not yield; I will not rest; I will not relent in waging this struggle for freedom and security for the American people.

The course of this conflict is not known, yet its outcome is certain. Freedom and fear, justice and cruelty, have always been at war, and we know that God is not neutral between them.

Fellow citizens, we'll meet violence with patient justice—assured of the rightness of our cause, and confident of the victories to come. In all that lies before us, may God grant us wisdom, and may He watch over the United States of America.

NOTES

PROLOGUE

1. Rohan Gunaratna, "Inside Al Qaeda: Network of Terror," *San Jose Mercury News*, September 1, 2002. Note: This is a summary of a speech to the Commonwealth Club that appeared in an "advertorial" in the *Mercury News*.

2. Author interviews, spring 2004.

3. Niles Lathem, "Elite unit sets sights on Osama," *New York Post*, February 24, 2004.

4. Author interview.

5. President Bush, "Address to a Joint Session of Congress and the American People," September 20, 2001.

6. Paul Martin, "Chicago, L.A. Towers were next targets," *Washington Times*, March 30, 2004.

7. Mohammed and Ramzi Yousef, the terror master behind the 1993 World Trade Center bombing, had initially planned the September 11 attacks in the early 1990s by flipping though picture books of American skyscrapers. Later, the plan changed. They plotted a second wave of attacks to follow September 11.

8. Martin, "Chicago, L.A. Towers were next targets."

9. Martin, "Chicago, L.A. Towers were next targets."

10. Martin, "Chicago, L.A. Towers were next targets."

11. Mattea Battaglia, "Carte en Main: Planète Terroriste," *Le Monde 2*, April 18, 2004.

12. "Recent terror attacks at a glance," Associated Press, March 13, 2004.

13. "Recent terror attacks at a glance," Associated Press, March 13, 2004.

14. Mark Huband, "Madrid bombers met in Turkey to plan attack," Financial Times, April 9, 2004.

15. Crispin Black, "Never say inevitable," *The Guardian*, March 7, 2004.

16. Murray Weiss, *The Man Who Warned America* (New York: Regan Books, 2003), 393–94.

17. Roger Hardy, "Analysis: 'Hard Slog' against al-Qaeda," BBC News, December 24, 2003.

18. "Remarks by the president on the one-year anniversary of the U.S. Department of Homeland Security," March 2, 2004.

19. Of course, bin Laden's war on America began much earlier: on December 29, 1992, with an attack on two towers housing U.S. Marines in Aden, Yemen. Fifty-nine Americans died from bin Laden's attacks from 1992 to 2000. For a more detailed account of the first phase of bin Laden's campaign, the secret war between President Clinton and bin Laden, please see *Losing bin Laden: How Bill Clinton's Failures Unleashed Global Terror* by Richard Miniter [Washington, D.C.: Regnery, 2003]. Bin Laden's war on the West arguably began earlier still, with the Iranian Revolution in 1979, a war that included assassinations inside America, massive terror strikes, and a murderous attack on U.S. Marines in Beirut in 1983. Time is a limitation in another sense, too. After a war is won or at least concluded, historians can identify the decisive moments and therefore what was critical to the story.

20. This includes the deaths in the 1993 World Trade Center attack, the assault on U.S. Army Rangers in Somalia in 1993, the bombing of a U.S. company in Saudi Arabia in 1995, the two simultaneous explosions at U.S. embassies in East Africa and the waterborne terror strike on the USS *Cole* in 2000. The 1996 attack on the U.S. Air Force barracks known as the Khobar Towers is not counted because it is believed to be the work of Iran using Saudi "cut-outs."

21. Michael Moore, "George of Arabia; what are the president's ties to the bin Laden family and the Saudi royals? Two years after the towers fell on September 11, Bush still hasn't come clean," *Rolling Stone*, October 30, 2003.

22. While such reconstructions have become a staple of journalism, they are unavoidably limited by the recollections and biases of witnesses, the thoroughness of secondary sources, and the author's interpretations.

Chapter One: BIN LADEN'S SECRET REFUGE

1. Neil MacFarquhar, "Al Qaeda Says Bin Laden Is Well, and It Was Behind Tunis Blast," *New York Times*, June 23, 2002.

2. This was fairly widely reported at the time. See, for example, Tom Fennell's "The Invisible Man; Where is Osama bin Laden—and why can't the United States catch its public enemy number 1," *Maclean's* (Toronto edition), December 2, 2002.

3. Peter Finn, "Arrests Reveal al Qaeda Plans; three Saudis seized by Morocco outline post-Afghanistan strategy," *Washington Post*, June 16, 2002.

4. Philip Smucker, *Al Qaeda's Great Escape: The Military and Media on Terror's Trail* (Washington, D.C.: Brassey's, 2004), 55.

5. Author interview.

6. Author interview.

7. Interview with Norberto Gonzalez, national security advisor of the Philippines, Manila, March 2004.

8. Author interview, June 2004.

9. According to a transcript of Deputy Secretary of Defense Paul Wolfowitz's meeting with the *King County Journal* editorial board in Tacoma, Washington, on Saturday, July 24, 2004.

10. Author interview.

11. According to an Iranian intelligence officer interviewed by the author.

12. According to an Iranian intelligence officer interviewed by the author.

13. According to an Iranian intelligence officer interviewed by the author.

14. Author interview, June 2004.

15. *Al Hayat*, December 14, 2003. Translated by FBIS.

16. Nimrod Raphaeli, "Ayman Muhammad Rabi' Al-Zawahiri: The Making of an Arch-terrorist," *Terrorism and Political Violence*, Vol. 14, No. 4 (winter 2002), 9. Published by Frank Cass, London.

17. Author interview with an Arab intelligence official.

18. Another interview with a former leader in the Moro Islamic Liberation Front included a Filipino congressman, Hussin U. Amin, from the Muslim-majority island of Sulu. He also said that he met Iraqi dictator Saddam Hussein several times, including most recently a few weeks before the start of the Iraq War.

19. Author interview, March 2004.

20. Lebanese Broadcasting Corporation, Beirut, Lebanon. Translated by FBIS.

21. Richard Sale, "Al Qaeda Strikes at the Kingdom," United Press International, May 13, 2003.

Chapter Two: UNHEARD THUNDER

1. This comment comes from a transcript compiled from an Italian police eavesdropping operation. It was first reported by the Canadian Broadcasting Corporation's CBC News program "The National," by reporter Terence McKenna, in a segment called "The Recruiters." (June 2002) See http://www.cbc.ca/national/news/recruiters/network.html.

2. Speech to Federal Emergency Management Agency, October 1, 2001.

3. The 9-11 Commission essentially agrees with this timing, as it outlines in Staff Statement No. 16. However, in an interview with staff director Philip Zelikow, I was told they believe the war council occurred in another camp, which he did not name.

4. "Outline of the 9-11 Plot," Staff Statement No. 16, 9-11 Commission.

5. "Outline of the 9-11 Plot," Staff Statement No. 16, 9-11 Commission.

6. "Outline of the 9-11 Plot," Staff Statement No. 16, 9-11 Commission.

7. "Outline of the 9-11 Plot," Staff Statement No. 16, 9-11 Commission.

8. Counting the unborn son of Monica Smith.

9. Staff Statement No. 16, 9-11 Commission, June 2004.

10. "Outline of the 9-11 Plot," Staff Statement No. 16, 9-11 Commission.

11. See, for example, an article the author wrote for *The Australian*, that nation's largest daily, in October 2001.

12. This quote is widely cited. See, for example, "Markaz Dawa al Irshad: Talibanisation of nuclear Pakistan," by B. Raman, South Asia Analysis Group.

13. Author interview with Ambassador Kenneth Adelman. The comments of Baker, Rumsfeld, and others are all according to Adelman's recollection.

14. Interview with the author.

15. Though this was denied by some former Clinton administration officials, a General Services Administration investigation later found that the computer keyboards were indeed vandalized.

16. Of course, after Senator Jim Jeffords became an independent and the Democrats assumed control of the Senate, the approval process for presidential nominees slowed sharply. Most of the key officials below the deputy secretary level at the Defense and State Departments were not approved by the Senate until after September 11, 2001.

17. Richard Clarke, *Against All Enemies: Inside America's War on Terror* (New York: Free Press, 2004), 229.

18. Clarke, 229.

19. Clarke, 229.

20. Clarke, 229.

21. Clarke, 230.

22. Author interview, June 2004. Crowley is now a senior fellow at the Center for American Progress in Washington, D.C.

23. See pages 187–96 in Richard Miniter's *Losing Bin Laden: How Bill Clinton's Failures Unleashed Global Terror* (Washington, D.C.: Regnery, 2003).

24. Clarke, 230.

25. Clarke, 230.

26. Clarke, 231.

27. Clarke, 231.

28. General Downing announced that he was leaving the Bush administration in June 2002. See Thomas E. Ricks, "Downing Resigns as Bush Aide; Anti-terror advisor was Hawk on Iraq," *Washington Post*, June 28, 2002. He was replaced by another retired general, John A. Gordon, who had been a deputy director of the CIA.

29. Clarke, 234.

30. For a brief overview of Goss and his views, see Michael Barone and Richard E. Cohen, *The Almanac of American Politics 2002* (Washington, D.C.: National Journal Group, 2002), 402–03.

31. Barone and Cohen, *The Almanac of American Politics 2004* (Washington D.C.: National Journal Group, 2004), 421.

32. "The Road to Ground Zero," *Sunday Times*, January 14, 2002.

33. Author interview with James Woolsey.

34. Miniter, 92.

35. Investigative reporter Joel Mowbray has done a very good job in breaking this story for *National Review*, the *New York Post*, and other publications.

36. Steven A. Camarota, "The Open Door: How Militant Islamic Terrorists Entered and Remained in the United States, 1993–2001," Center for Immigration Studies, Center Paper 21, Washington, D.C. Available at www.cis.org. The Center estimates that forty-one of the forty-eight terrorists admitted to the U.S. from 1993 to 2001 received visas from U.S. embassies or consulates. If one subtracts the nineteen September 11 hijackers, all of whom received visas abroad, from the forty-one admitted, the result is twenty-two.

37. Camarota, 23.

38. Joel Mowbray, *Dangerous Diplomacy* (Washington, D.C.: Regnery, 2003), 178.

39. As cited by Joel Mowbray in "State of Deception," *National Review Online*, July 18, 2002.

40. Author interview with Joel Mowbray.

41. Audrey Hudson, "Saudis get easy access to visas," *Washington Times*, July 10, 2002.

42. Hudson, "Saudis get easy access to visas."

43. Some 800,000 Yemeni men were expelled from Saudi Arabia and the Gulf States in the run-up to the Gulf War. At the time, Yemen had opposed U.S. action against Iraq. For a good account of Yemen generally, see Paul Dresch, *A History of Modern Yemen* (Cambridge: Cambridge University Press, 2000).

44. "The Road to Ground Zero."

45. "The man who knew," Frontline, Public Broadcasting Service, aired in December, 2002.

46. *Washington Post*, citing an unnamed "senior administration official."

47. Released by the White House on April 1, 2004. This passage was also cited by National Security Advisor Condoleezza Rice in her testimony before the 9-11 Commission.

Chapter Three: THE 2002 PLOT TO KILL BUSH

1. Some suggest that it was the arrest of the "Lackawana six," a group of immigrants who were arrested near Buffalo, New York, and had trained in Afghanistan with al Qaeda, which had triggered the uptick in alert status. Certainly that was one reason. Yet another was what was later known as the "Mekki plot," which is outlined in this chapter for the first time in full anywhere.

2. This pattern would continue. The bombings in Bali, Indonesia, on October 12, 2002, were on the second anniversary of the attack on the USS *Cole* in Aden harbor in 2000. Seventeen sailors were killed and another thirty-eight wounded in that attack. Jordan's embassy in Baghdad was bombed on August 7, 2003—the fifth anniversary of the U.S. embassy attack.

3. While the American and allied forces had come to liberate Kuwait from Iraqi subjugation in 1990, they had stayed on in the oil-rich kingdom to patrol the "no-fly" zones over northern and southern Iraq. Though they were there to protect Saudi Arabia and Kuwait, Osama bin Laden and other Islamic radicals considered the mere presence of infidel troops to be a violation of the traditions of the prophet Mohammed, who said on his deathbed, "Let there not be two religions in Arabia." And, as a purely religious matter, bin Laden's interpretation may well be correct. In 641 A.D, year 20 in the Muslim era, the caliph Umar, one of the prophet's successors, had expelled all Christians and Jews from the Hijaz, the Muslim holy land that includes the pilgrimage cities of Mecca and Medina. Thus they are ancient words used by terrorists to kill modern men.

4. In the novel, a Japanese pilot uses a Boeing 747. See Tom Clancy, *Debt of Honor* (New York: Berkeley Books, 1994), 985–87 in the paperback edition.

5. For more information, see chapter five of Richard Miniter's *Losing bin Laden: How Bill Clinton's Failures Unleashed Global Terror* (Washington, D.C.: Regnery, 2003).

6. Kansteiner left the U.S. government in 2003 and works at the Scowcroft Group.

7. As told to the author.

8. Phoebe Zerwick, "Custody: Taxi Driver in Jail After Agent's Visit," *Winston-Salem Journal*, September 24, 2002. The reporter has a great eye for detail, but the date of Mekki's arrest is wrong.

9. I was unable to locate Knapp and this account is based on news reports.

10. "Unidentified Rolling Objects" by Richard Miniter, in his column "The Visible Hand" which appeared on September 10, 2001, on the *Wall Street Journal's* www.OpinionJournal.com web site. The other two states that do not ask driver's license applicants for a social security number are Utah and Tennessee.

11. "Sudanese Detained In Terror Inquiry; U.S. trying to determine link to plane-attack plot," *Winston-Salem Journal*, September 21, 2002.

12. Mike Phelan, "Sudanese pilot ordered held without bond," CNN, September 23, 2002.

13. Zerwick, "Custody: Taxi Driver in Jail After Agents' Visit."

14. "Sudan contacting U.S. official regarding pilot's case," Associated Press, September 22, 2002.

15. Interestingly, he had a foolish cover, claiming to be an "international investor." The man's accent identified him as an American and everyone in Khartoum knew that a U.S. embargo made such investment impossible.

16. Author interview.

17. *CIA World Fact Book*: Sudan, http://www.odci.gov/cia/publications/factbook/print/su.html, 9.

18. Author interview.

19. Miniter, *Losing bin Laden*, 113–14.

20. "Decision to Strike Factory in Sudan Based Partly on Surmise", *Washington Post*, September 21, 1998. Also see "Sudan Attack Blamed on US Blunders," *The Times* (London), September 22, 1998.

21. The report, which does not appear on CIA letterhead, says the polygraph occurred on May 16, 2003. It is unclear if this is a second polygraph after the September 2002 polygraph. Multiple sources put the date of Bilal's polygraph as September 2002, but it is possible that they are wrong and the CIA is correct. Aside from the dates, the CIA report and the accounts of my sources match perfectly.

22. The name al-Khobar is a corrupted Arabic version of Cooper, after a British governor who had the prison built in the 1880s.

23. Author interview.

24. Amy Goldstein et al., "A Deliberate Strategy of Disruption; massive, secretive detention effort aimed mainly at preventing more terror," *Washington Post*, November 4, 2001.

25. Goldstein et al., "A Deliberate Strategy of Disruption; massive, secretive detention effort aimed mainly at preventing more terror."

26. "No Bail for Sudanese Pilot," www.Foxnews.com, September 23, 2002.

27. Tim Whitmire, "Sudanese Pilot Ordered Held," Associated Press, September 24, 2002.

28. Whitmire, "Sudanese Pilot Ordered Held."

29. The intelligence liaison who provided documents attesting to these figures asked me to round them to the nearest number wholly divisible by ten. I have done so.

30. Princeton N. Lyman and J. Stephen Morrison, "The Terrorist Threat in Africa," *Foreign Affairs*, January/February 2004, 77.

Chapter Four: THE NEW AFGHANISTAN AND THE NEXT BATTLEFIELD?

1. Webster's New Geographical Dictionary (Springfield, Massachusetts: Merriam-Webster, Inc.).

2. Citing Moroccan intelligence, the Moroccan newspaper *Al-Ahdath al-Maghribia* reported this in March 2004.

3. Damien McElroy, "U.S. forces hunt down al-Qaeda in Sudan," *Telegraph* (UK), August 1, 2004.

4. McElroy, "U.S. forces hunt down al-Qaeda in Sudan."

5. Citing Moroccan intelligence, the Moroccan newspaper *Al-Ahdath al-Maghribia* reported this in March 2004.

6. This quote first appeared in "We fight on, says demon of Darfur," by Richard Miniter, *Sunday Times* (London) July 28, 2004.

7. Cherif Ouazani, "Algerian GSPC's number two leader, 'el para,' killed in accident in Chad," *Jeune Afrique—l'intelligent*, April 25, 2004. Translated by FBIS.

8. Alexis Debat, "Truck bomb plot targeted U.S. embassy," ABC News, June 5, 2004.

9. "Dakar Rally 'Kidnap Plot' Foiled," by BBC News, January 29, 2004.

10. For more information, see Richard Miniter's *Losing bin Laden: How Bill Clinton's Failures Unleashed Global Terror* (Washington, D.C.: Regnery, 2003).

11. Author interview, July 2004.

Chapter Five: TERROR AT SEA

1. As quoted in Charles Glass, "Piracy in the 21st Century," *The Independent* (London), January 11, 2004.

2. "Is terrorism heading for the high seas?" *Yomiuri Shimbun* (Japan), October 7, 2003.

3. Tim Weiner, "U.S. law puts world ports on notice," *New York Times*, March 24, 2004. The article relies on an article in *Defense Horizons* written by Admiral James M. Loy, deputy secretary of Homeland Security, in 2002.

4. Author interview.

5. Peter Finn, "Arrests reveal al Qaeda plans; three Saudis seized by Morocco outline post-Afghanistan strategy," *Washington Post*, June 16, 2002.

6. Douglas Frantz, "U.S. enlists Morocco's help to counter terrorist plots," *New York Times*, June 24, 2002.

7. Finn, "Arrests reveal al Qaeda plans; three Saudis seized by Morocco outline post-Afghanistan strategy."

8. Finn, "Arrests reveal al Qaeda plans; three Saudis seized by Morocco outline post-Afghanistan strategy."

9. Andrew Miga, "Captured al Qaeda leader now aiding CIA," *Boston Herald*, November 22, 2002.

10. "Western agents provided tip for arrest of top al Qaeda suspect in UAE," Agence France Presse, December 24, 2002.

11. John Mintz, "15 freighters believed to be linked to al Qaeda; U.S. fears terrorists at sea; Tracking ships is difficult," *Washington Post*, December 31, 2002.

12. The foiled attack was based on a real insight: Airport metal detectors stopped at a passenger's ankles.

13. Michael Richardson, "Terror at sea: The world's lifelines are at risk," *The Straits Times* (Singapore).

14. Richardson, "Terror at sea: The world's lifelines are at risk."

15. Mansoor Ijaz, "The maritime threat from al Qaeda," *Financial Times*, October 20, 2003.

16. Weiner, "U.S. law puts world ports on notice."

17. Mintz, "15 freighters believed to be linked to al Qaeda; U.S. fears terrorists at sea; Tracking ships is difficult."

18. Mintz, "15 freighters believed to be linked to al Qaeda; U.S. fears terrorists at sea; Tracking ships is difficult."

19. "U.S. Navy searches suspect ship, finds no al Qaeda link," Agence France Presse, October 24, 2002. The ship cited in the headline is not the *Twillinger* but the *Tara*.

20. "Massive multi-national naval hunt for al Qaeda ship," Debkafile, October 26, 2002.

21. "Massive multi-national naval hunt for al Qaeda ship," Debkafile.

22. Chris Varcoe, "Oil producers adapt to reality of terrorism," *Financial Post* (Canada), March 11, 2003.

23. Yonah Alexander and Tyler Richardson, "Maritime terrorism phase next?" *Washington Times*, October 20, 2002.

24. Hammoud Mounassar, "Yemen finally admits deadly French tanker blast was terror attack," Agence France Presse, October 17, 2002.

25. "Newsweek: U.S. intelligence had warning of imminent attack against ships in Persian Gulf, Yemen, days before French tanker was bombed," News release, PR Newswire, October 20, 2002.

26. "Yemen says tanker blast was terrorist attack," *Edmonton Journal* (Canada), October 18, 2002.

27. Peter Goodspeed, "New attacks target world's fuel supply," *National Post* (Canada), October 18, 2002.

28. "Yemeni forces hunt al Qaeda gunmen after deadly firefight," Agence France Presse, December 21, 2002.

29. Jack Fairweather, "Al Qaeda hunt turns to Yemen as man admits attack on tanker," *The Scotsman*, November 18, 2002.

30. "Attack on French Oil tanker to cost Yemen $3.8 million per month: US," Agence France Presse, November 9, 2002.

31. "U.S. Navy searches ship, finds no al Qaeda link," Agence France Presse.

32. Author interview.

33. Miga, "Captured al Qaeda leader now aiding CIA."

34. "UAE admits it handed over to CIA al Qaeda operations manager," *Al-Bawaba*, December 24, 2002.

35. Author interview.

36. Miga, "Captured al Qaeda leader now aiding CIA."

37. Sometimes known as "Abu Ali."

38. Author interview, March 2004.

39. David Rennie and David Millward, "Briton had Gulf battle plans and links to U.S. Navy role," *Daily Telegraph*, August 7, 2004.

40. Rennie and Millward, "The Imperial College Student accused of waging jihad in South Kensington," *Daily Telegraph*, August 7, 2004.

41. Rennie and Millward, "The Imperial College Student accused of waging jihad in South Kensington."

42. Adam Fresco and Elaine Monaghan, "I don't want to go, says man the US wants to extradite," *The Times*, August 7, 2004.

43. "Pirate attack raises fear of terrorism," *Energy Compass*, April 3, 2003.

44. "Concerns mount about shipping security in key Asian choke point," International Oil Daily, April 2003. His name is misspelled "Neil" in this article.

45. "Singapore reiterates call for multilateral approach to protecting Straits," AFX-Asia, May 20, 2004.

46. Ijaz, "The maritime threat from al Qaeda."

47. "Missing tugs raise fears of planned terror attack, says Aegis," *Lloyd's List*, November 4, 2003.

48. Justin Sparks and Tom Walker, "Al Qaeda trail to diving school," *Sunday Times*, September 7, 2003.

49. Mintz, "U.S. tracking 15 mystery ships," *Toronto Star*, January 2, 2003. Mintz cites as his source Tanner Campbell, vice president of the Marine Intelligence Group, a private consulting firm for the shipping industry.

50. Author interview.

51. "Mystery explosives-laden ship was illegally registered," Agence France Presse, June 25, 2003.

52. Catherine Boitard, "Greece probes explosives ship amid Sudan, Tunisia anger," Agence France Presse, June 24, 2003.

53. Suleiman Nimr, "Yemeni militant killed in Riyadh was al Qaeda leader for Gulf operations," Agence France Presse, March 16, 2004.

54. Nimr, "Yemeni militant killed in Riyadh was al Qaeda leader for Gulf operations." The wire story cites the following website: http://groups.yahoo.com/group/Islamic_Media/.

55. "Navy announces Flight Littoral Combat Ship (LCS) contract option awards," news release no. 516-04, May 27, 2004.

56. "Navy announces Flight Littoral Combat Ship (LCS) contract option awards."

57. "Senate unanimously approves Hollings' port security legislation," news release, December 20, 2001.

58. "Senate unanimously approves Hollings' port security legislation."

Chapter Six: BOMBS AND BALLOTS:
THE MADRID ATTACK AND THE AMERICAN ELECTION

1. As cited by Roger Kimball in "Institutionalizing Our Demise: America vs. Multiculturalism," *The New Criterion*, June 2004. The magazine puts the date of Revel's quote as 1970. Revel was perhaps the leading anti-Communist voice in France for more than thirty years. Like many prophets, he suffered before many knew he was right and suffered even more when he was proved right.

2. John Keegan, "Imitate the Army—don't butcher it," *Daily Telegraph*, July 7, 2004. Keegan, a former instructor at the British military academy and the author of several well-regarded books on military history, is the defense editor at the *Telegraph*.

3. David Johnston and David Stout, "Bin Laden Is Said to Be Organizing for a U.S. Attack," *New York Times*, July 8, 2004.
4. Johnston and Stout, "Bin Laden Is Said to Be Organizing for a U.S. Attack."
5. Michael Evans, Stewart Tendler, and Daniel McGrory, "Plan to attack London found in al Qaeda raid," *The Times* (London), August 3, 2004.
6. Katherine Pfleger Shrader, "Warnings on pre-election attack not political: Ridge," *Chicago Sun-Times*, July 15, 2004.
7. "Senior al-Qaida leaders behind terror threat: Ridge: 'How high up remains to be seen,'" NBC, MSNBC, and news services, July 09, 2004.
8. Johnston and Stout, "Bin Laden Is Said to Be Organizing for a U.S. Attack."
9. Johnston and Stout, "Bin Laden Is Said to Be Organizing for a U.S. Attack."
10. Bill Gertz, "Bin Laden hints major assassination," *Washington Times*, August 11, 2004.
11. Gertz, "Bin Laden hints major assassination."
12. Gertz, "Bin Laden hints major assassination."
13. Author interview.
14. Jim Hoagland, "Fight back and vote," *Washington Post*, March 16, 2004.
15. Ana Botella, *Mis Ocho Años en la Moncloa* (Madrid, 2004). Translation by Yolanda Rodriguez, Spanish embassy, Washington, D.C. I have not supplied page numbers because the translation page numbers do not correspond easily to the book's page numbers.
16. Lawrence Wright, "The Terror Web," *New Yorker*, August 2, 2004.
17. Elaine Sciolino, "Grieving crowds in Spain seethe at train attacks," *New York Times*, March 12, 2004.
18.　The body bags were color-coordinated (black, white, and orange), indicating which train had become their tomb. In pavilion eight of a soccer stadium turned morgue, Botella went to comfort the grieving families. According to her, "They were coming into this pavilion after going through all hospitals, after going through all lists of wounded and not being able to locate their own. They went there to receive the worst of the news. Many of them would remain there for several hours. Some dead bodies could not even be identified."
19. Botella, *Mis Ocho Años en la Moncloa*.
20. According to a high-level staffer in the Socialist Party of Spain, who spoke to me on the condition of anonymity.
21. Here I am relying on a timeline published in *El País* on July 29, 2004.
22. He does believe that Aznar later hyped the ETA line for political purposes—which is the Socialist party line.

23. Sciolino, "Grieving crowds in Spain seethe at train attacks."

24. Sciolino, "Grieving crowds in Spain seethe at train attacks."

25. Sciolino, "Grieving crowds in Spain seethe at train attacks."

26. His words in Spanish were: *"No nos lo creemos."*

27. Sciolino, "Grieving crowds in Spain seethe at train attacks."

28. Sciolino, "Grieving crowds in Spain seethe at train attacks."

29. Sciolino, "Grieving crowds in Spain seethe at train attacks."

30. Botella, *Mis Ocho Años en la Moncloa.*

31. Botella, *Mis Ocho Años en la Moncloa.*

32. As noted in "The Spanish elections," letter to the editor, Peter Burbidge, School of Law, University of Westminster, *The Times* (London), March 30, 2004.

33. Ken Serrano, "Soaries urges U.S. to establish election plan; Wants protocol if terrorists disrupt vote," *Home News Tribune* (New Jersey), July 13, 2004.

34. This quote has been widely cited. See, for example: "Rice: No Vote Delay Plan Eyed," CBS News, CBSNews.com, July 13, 2004.

35. Botella, *Mis Ocho Años en la Moncloa.*

EPILOGUE

1. Daniel Byman, "Scoring the War on Terrorism," The National Interest, National Affairs, Inc., summer 2003.

2. "'All Necessary Means'—Employing CIA Operatives in a Warfighting Role Alongside Special Operations Forces," by Colonel Kathryn Stone, U.S. Army, U.S. Army War College, April 7, 2003.

3. Frank Gardner, "Choking off al-Qaeda's cash lifeline," BBC News, February 10, 2003.

4. "Yemen arrests 'al Qaeda members'," BBC News, March 4, 2004. Among the captured was Sayyed Imam Sherif, who founded Egyptian Islamic Jihad. This terror group supplied most of the leadership of al Qaeda, including Ayman al-Zawahiri, bin Laden's personal doctor and al Qaeda's second in command.

ACKNOWLEDGMENTS

TO THE MANY SOURCES in the intelligence services and foreign services of the United States and other nations whom I cannot publicly name, especially those who supplied me with documents and eye-witness accounts, thank you.

Perhaps the most valuable sources of information—outside of the intelligence community—were the high-ranking Bush administration officials who agreed to be interviewed, either on or off the record. This book would not have been possible without them.

There are also many sources from outside the United States who were willing to talk to me, either on or off the record.

Overseas

Afghanistan: Haroun Amin, former Washington representative of the Northern Alliance; Ottilie English, onetime lobbyist for the Northern Alliance, who knows more about Afghanistan than the State Department; Sayed Rahin Makhdoom; Nabeel Miskinyar; Amrullah Saleh, head of Afghan intelligence.

Italy: Defense Minister Antonio Martino and his wife, Carol; Guiseppe Moles, his aide; Alberto Mingardi, an indispensable source and the most prolific journalist in two languages that I know; Lorenzo Vidino of "The Investigative Project;" and journalist Renato Farina, who broke the story of the Vatican plot in the Italian press.

The Philippines: President Gloria Macapagal-Arroyo, who graciously gave me an hour of time while on the campaign trail on the island of Occidental Negros; former *Asian Wall Street Journal* editorial page writer Brett M. Decker, who has the best rolodex in Southeast Asia; Norberto B. Gonzales, national security advisor; Rigoberto D. Tiglao, presidential chief of staff; Hussin V. Amin, a Filipino congressman from the majority-Muslim island of Sulu; Milton A. Alingod, press secretary for the president of the Philippines; Dr. Parouk S. Hussin, regional governor of Mindanao; Ignacio R. Bunye, presidential spokesman; Jose de Venecia, speaker of the House of Representatives, a visionary who was always ready to help and served wonderful fish for lunch; Defense Secretary Eduardo Ermita, who talked for hours and supplied some unpublished photos of President George W. Bush; and Orlando Mercado, former defense secretary who gave me a lot of his time while running for a congressional seat and, despite what critics say, has a strong singing voice.

Singapore: U.S. ambassador Franklin Lavin and his staff, who provided on-the-spot observations; FBI special agent Chris Reiman, who helps fight al Qaeda in the city-state, and members of Singapore's ISD, whom I can not name, who provided a detailed briefing and other assistance.

Thailand: General Anu, who met me for a long lunch in Chiang Mai when he didn't really have the time and literally handed over his voluminous rolodex; Christian Freedom International President Jim Jacobson, who is one of the most well-connected Americans living in Thailand; and Lt. Gen. Krit, a member of the Thai National Security Council who liaises with the CIA and MI-6.

Hong Kong: Jimmy Li, owner of the *Apple Daily*, the largest Chinese language daily in the Special Administrative Region, the Beijing colony formerly known as "Hong Kong;" Kin Ming and the *Apple Daily's* editorial page editor, Mark Simon, who provided many contacts, insights, drinks, and cigars; Teon of the *Far Eastern Economic Review*, who helped with understanding Malay politics; Mike Gonzalez, editorial page editor of the *Asian Wall Street Journal*; and C. P. Ho, the head of the Hong Kong Foreign Correspondents Club, who graciously invited me to give a luncheon address at the famous clubhouse on Lower Albert Road.

Sudan: Gutbi al-Mahdi, Sudan's former intelligence chief, who spent hours with me in Khartoum; Mahdi Ibrahim, Sudan's former ambassador to the United States, who met with me several times; Sudan's peace and development minister Ghazi and El-Mahdi Habib-Alla, who described to me his meeting with Abdullah Azzam in Jordan; Also, Abdul Ali Hodari, Abdel Mahmoud al-Koronky, at Sudan's embassy in London; Janet McElligott, onetime lobbyist for Sudan, who gave me an endless stream of phone numbers in Sudan; David Hoile, who arranged a trip to the front lines in Sudan's battle with al Qaeda; Fatih Erwa, Sudan's ambassador to the United Nations; Peter Stapel, manager of the Khartoum Hilton, who discovered that

I am a poor shot with a pistol, and his wife, Rose; Dr. Mustafa Osman Ismail, the foreign minister of Sudan, who welcomed me into his home on the banks of the Nile and provided many insights; Anis Haggar, perhaps the richest man in Sudan and the most charming—a Christian Arab who has been quietly working for peace between the Muslim North and Christian South since 1995, for his insights, sense of history, his frank assessments—and for the Cohibo Lacero; the editors of *Sudan Vision*, that country's largest English daily, for providing a valuable perspective; Sudan's head of mission and ambassador to the U.S., Khidir H. Ahmed; and Abubaker Y. Ahmed al-Shingieti, vice president for Islamic programs at the International Center for Religion and Diplomacy.

Saudi Arabia: David Bass, for introducing me to Saudi sources and always staying for one more at the Palm; and Adel al-Jubeir.

France: Christian de Fouloy and several sources in French intelligence.

Spain: Judge Joan Colom i Naval; Artur Munoz-Baizan; member of European Parliament Inigo Méndez de Vigo y Montojo; Yolanda Rodriguez of Spain's embassy in Washington; and photographer Santiago A. Portillo.

Belgium: Charles Tannock, a member of the European Parliament who is the British Conservative Party spokesman for foreign affairs.

United Kingdom: Stephen Pollard, for insights into Home Secretary David Blunkett. I look forward to reading his biography of the most interesting man in Tony Blair's cabinet. Stephen Grey, whose calls from Iraq were expensive but always welcome; and Mary Winchester, an airport security expert who tells frightening and frank stories, among others who shall not be named.

General

Authors: I'd also like to thank several authors and reporters whom I've never met, but whose work was vital to my understanding al Qaeda, intelligence, or military operations: Peter Bergen, Youssef Bodansky, Rohan Gunaratna, Simon Reeve, Robert Baer, Bruce Hoffman, the *Washington Times*'s Bill Gertz, the *Washington Post*'s Barton Gellman, Rick Atkinson, Matthew Brzezinski, the BBC's Jane Corbin, and CNN's Phil Hirschkorn. And the *Financial Times*'s Mark Huband, whose long articles were invaluable.

Staff

I'd also like to thank my researcher, the indefatigable Martin Morse Wooster, my Brussels assistants Victoria "Tory" Vidler (check out her new blog at http://toryvidler.blogspot.com/), and Aoife White, my excellent transcriber in Hong Kong, Carol Hopkins, and my Arabic-language translator, Robert Kirk of Houston, Texas. James Rogers, who designed my personal web site, **www.richard-miniter.com**; and Winfred J. "Skip" Keats II of nextstrategy.com, who is developing a new version of the site.

Inspirational people

I'd like to thank the owners and staff of Portner's in Alexandria, Virginia, and Rendez-Vous Des Artistes and Havana Corner in Brussels. They let me work for hours in their fine establishments while ordering only coffee and water and they never complained about the cigars or the dog, Boxer. I'd also like to thank Tommy Jocamo for letting me turn the front room of the Palm into a salon for interviewing cigar-smoking foreign intelligence officers and as an impromptu studio for a PBS television crew; and Laurent Menoud of Café Milano, who always found me a last-minute table to entertain a source. And yes, Laurent, they were all ambassadors.

Most of all, I would like to thank Monica Morrill. She did a wonderful job translating Italian documents, finding important stories in the European press, and setting up interviews with everyone from sea captains to members of the European Parliament. She was dedicated and so hardworking as to be a one-woman threat to the European work ethic.

Hats off to Mel Berger, my agent at William Morris; Harry Crocker, a great book editor; my friend Bill Schulz, who has finally kicked *Reader's Digest* to the curb, so as not to shorten our lunches at the Palm or give up valuable time at the track; law professor Eugene Kontorovich (any man who wears a hat as well as Seth Lipsky and smokes cigars like H. L. Mencken should junk the law and return to journalism); journalist Sam Dealey (thanks for asking no questions about that mysterious Italian visitor); James Taranto (sorry about Barcelona, dude); Brett Decker (who is so well connected in the Philippines that he should be made U.S. ambassador there); the always ebullient Horace Cooper, who should learn someday to swing from chandeliers like a proper libertarian; Doug Heye, who is right about New York wine (okay, I admit it); and Kevin Washington, a true gentleman whose impeccable taste should rub off on me someday. And Gene J. Koprowski, a helpful Chicago-based journalist who supplied a great unnamed source.

Several people were just plain encouraging, which counts for a lot when writing a book. Cecilia Kindstand; Kalle Isaksson; Per Heister (who reviewed *Losing bin Laden* for a Swedish newspaper); Jeremy Slater, who is the most classic British journalist abroad that I know; Ulrike Dennerborg; Jenny Persson, who is right about art noveau and a whole lot more; Alexis Ulbrich, who lives as large as a man can who is half French, half German, and working for a Japanese company; Annette Godart-van der Kroon, the president of the Ludwig von Mises Institute-Europe, who brought me as her guest to the Mont Perelin Society in Hamburg; Joshua Livestro, who writes well and knows the secret lives of European commissioners; and Claudia Rosett, who runs the best smoke-easy in New York and who broke the UN Oil-for-Food scandal. She deserves a statue at Turtle Bay. Maybe the UN could chip in, what with all of the money they save on parking tickets.

BIBLIOGRAPHY

Abate, Frank R., ed. *The Oxford Essential Geographical Dictionary (American Edition)*. New York: Berkley Books, 1999. Perhaps the best reference book of its kind.

Abu Khalil, As'ad. *Bin Laden, Islam and America's New "War on Terrorism."* New York: Seven Stories Press, 2002. A harshly critical account of the War on Terror.

Abuza, Zachary. *Militant Islam in Southeast Asia: Crucible of Terror*. Boulder: Lynne Rienner Publishers, 2003. An excellent resource on terrorism in Southeast Asia. The author has regional intelligence sources, a good grasp of history, and writes with authority. Simply indispensable.

Alexander, Yonah. *Combating Terrorism: Strategies of Ten Countries*. Ann Arbor, University of Michigan Press, 2002. A strong, scholarly study.

Alexander, Yonah, and Michael S. Swetnam. *Usama bin Laden's al-Qaida: Profile of a Terrorist Network*. New York: Transnational Publishers, Inc., 2001. A good primer.

Al-Rasheed, Madawi. *A History of Saudi Arabia*. Cambridge, Cambridge University Press, 2002. A good introduction to the history of Arabia.

Anonymous. *Through Our Enemies' Eyes: Osama bin Laden, Radical Islam, and the Future of America*. Washington, D.C.: Brassey's, Inc., 2002. A former intelligence agent asks and answers "why they hate us." Worth reading closely.

Anonymous. *Terrorist Hunter: The Extraordinary Story of a Woman Who Went Undercover to Infiltrate the Radical Islamic Groups Operating in America*. New York: HarperCollins Publishers, 2003. The true story of a housewife who penetrates several domestic Islamic terror groups. This should be required reading at the CIA, FBI, and DIA.

Armstrong, Karen. *Islam: A Short History*. New York: Random House, 2000. A good overview from a liberal scholar. Her discussion of the Arab pre-Islamic roots of Islam (especially Islam's pilgrimage to Mecca pre-dating the prophet Mohammed by hundreds of years), is invaluable.

Avni, Zeev. *False Flag: The Soviet Spy Who Penetrated the Israeli Secret Intelligence Service*. London: St. Ermin's Press, 1999. The story of a Swiss Jewish Communist who became a double agent—against the legendary Mossad. Most interesting, especially given that the author is now a psychiatrist, is the mental states of terrorists and traitors. That self-loathing could cause anti-state violence is a theme that should be further investigated.

Aznar, José María. *Ocho Años de Gobierno: Una Visión Personal de España*. Barcelona: Planeta, 2004. Available only in Spanish. I had portions translated—revealing that the Madrid bombing was more complicated than the American media acknowledged.

Bamford, James. *Body of Secrets: Anatomy of the Ultra-Secret National Security Agency*. New York: Anchor Books/Random House, 2002. Bamford is the best kind of critic—one with inside sources. A must read.

Barkey, Henri J., and Graham E. Fuller. *Turkey's Kurdish Question*. New York: Carnegie Corporation, 1998. A dry, thorough treatment of the Kurds inside Turkey. Particularly good on the ideology of the PKK.

Barnett, Thomas P. M. *The Pentagon's New Map: War and Peace in the Twenty-First Century*. New York: G. P. Putnam's Sons, 2004. A fascinating 30,000-foot perspective on America's new strategic landscape. It should bury lingering Cold War notions.

Barone, Michael, and Grant Ujifusa. *The Almanac of American Politics 2000*. Washington, D.C.: National Journal Group, 1999. The bible of Washington. Its pithy profiles of senators and congressmen are indispensable and well written.

Barone, Michael, Richard E. Cohen, and Grant Ujifusa. *The Almanac of American Politics 2002*. Washington, D.C.: National Journal Group, 2001. The section on Representative Porter Goss is essential background.

———. *The Almanac of American Politics 2004*. Washington, D.C.: National Journal Group, 2003.

Baer, Robert. *See No Evil: The True Story of a Ground Soldier in the CIA's War on Terrorism*. New York: Three Rivers Press, 2002. A very readable account by a CIA officer operating in Lebanon in the 1980s and Iraq in the 1990s.

————. *Sleeping With the Devil: How Washington Sold Our Soul for Saudi Crude*. New York: Crown Publishers, 2003. Baer's criticism of U.S. policy toward Saudi Arabia.

Bearden, Milt. *The Black Tulip*. New York: Random House, 1998. This is a novel written by a former CIA officer responsible for working with the Afghan mujihideen and conveys a good sense of what the U.S. hoped to gain with its Faustian bargain with the anti-Soviet guerrillas.

Bearden, Milt, and James Risen. *The Main Enemy: The Inside Story of the CIA's Final Showdown with the KGB*. New York: Random House, 2003. A masterful account of Cold War intelligence operations against the Soviets. Some of those mentioned here are now directing operations against al Qaeda.

Benjamin, Daniel, and Steven Simon. *The Age of Sacred Terror*. New York: Random House, 2002. One of the very few inside accounts of the Clinton years. The authors were directors on the National Security Council. Though unduly defensive in certain areas, this is an important book.

Bennett, William J. *Why We Fight: Moral Clarity and the War on Terrorism*. Washington, D.C.: Regnery Publishing, Inc., 2003. A call to arms, with interesting arguments.

Bergen, Peter L. *Holy War, Inc.: Inside the Secret World of Osama bin Laden*. New York: Simon & Schuster, 2002. An excellent early account of bin Laden by a veteran CNN producer.

Berman, Paul. *Terror and Liberalism*. New York: W. W. Norton & Company, 2003. Academic but interesting.

Bodansky, Yossef. *Target America—Terrorism in the U.S. Today*. New York: S.P.I. Books, 1993. Unlike his later works, this was not a bestselling book, but a serious student of terrorism should read it; among other things, it describes terrorist sleeper cells in the

United States and an interesting account of the terrorist attack out-side CIA headquarters in 1993. It also mentions Iran's plans to fly planes into buildings in the 1980s.

————. *The High Cost of Peace: How Washington's Middle East Policy Left America Vulnerable to Terrorism*. Roseville: Prima Publishing, 2002. Primarily concerned with the Israeli–Palestinian peace process, it reveals why peace must come from outside the West Bank.

————. *Bin Laden: The Man Who Declared War on America*. Roseville: Prima Publishing, 2001. At a meeting in his hideaway office, a senator on the Intelligence Committee summed it up best: "great book, no footnotes." A treasure trove of information and analysis. Given the nature of his sources, it can be hard to verify some items. The ones that the author has been able to check through intelligence sources have all checked out.

Boot, Max. *The Savage Wars of Peace: Small Wars and the Rise of American Power*. New York: Basic Books, 2002. An interesting book by an engaging writer and former *Wall Street Journal* editorial page features editor. For policymakers and citizens, it provides a good primer for how the U.S. once fought and won small-unit wars. This is probably how the War on Terror will be won. Useful for evaluating U.S. operations in the Philippines, Iraq, Afghanistan, and elsewhere.

Botella, Ana. *Mis Ocho Años en La Moncloa*. Spain: Random House, 2004. Spain's former first lady lays out the intelligence documents that her husband, Prime Minister Aznar, saw in the hours following the March 11, 2004, Madrid bombing in "Chapter Zero." I had that vital chapter translated by a member of the Spanish embassy in Washington, D.C.

Bush, George W. *We Will Prevail: On War, Terrorism, and Freedom*. New York: The Continuum International Publishing Group

Ltd., 2003. A collection of Bush speeches and documents. A handy reference.

Carew, Tom. *Jihad! The Secret War in Afghanistan*. Edinburgh: Main Stream Publishing, 2000. While unreliable in certain details, it is an interesting early account of the Taliban. Misses the Pakistan connection to the Taliban, though.

Carr, Caleb. *The Lessons of Terror: A History of Warfare Against Civilians—Why It Has Always Failed and Why It Will Fail Again*. New York: Random House, 2002. Really an extended essay, but worth a read.

Casey, Ethan. *09/11 8:48am: Documenting America's Greatest Tragedy*. Booksurge.com, 2001. A poorly produced book that nonetheless helps convey the shock of September 11. It brings you back to that terrible day.

Child, Greg. *Over the Edge: A True Story of Kidnap and Escape in the Mountains of Central Asia*. London: Judy Piatkus, Ltd., 2002. Documents an early hostage-taking effort by an al Qaeda–affiliated group.

Clancy, Tom. *Debt of Honor*. New York: Berkley Books, 1994. A fictional account of a Japanese pilot flying a commercial jetliner into the U.S. Capitol—written long before September 11, 2001.

Clarke, Richard A. *Against All Enemies: Inside America's War on Terror*. New York: Simon & Schuster/Free Press, 2004. The first chapter and the last few chapters are worth reading, even though he gets many checkable small facts wrong.

Cole, Steve. *Ghost Wars: A Secret History of the CIA, Afghanistan, and Bin Laden from the Soviet Invasion to September 10, 2001*. New York: The Penguin Press, 2004. An excellent piece of reporting about Central Asia's cauldron of terror.

Cooley, John K. *Unholy Wars: Afghanistan, America, and International Terrorism*. London: Pluto Press, 2000. An energetic critic.

Coughlin, Con. *Saddam*. London: Macmillan, 2002. An excellent and readable account of the rise and rule of Saddam Hussein. Saddam's early esteem for the Nazis is especially interesting.

Corbin, Jane. *The Base: Al-Qaeda and the Changing Face of Global Terror*. London: Pocket Books/Simon & Schuster, 2003. A veteran BBC reporter writes a serious, detailed account. A must read.

Crile, George. *Charlie Wilson's War: The Extraordinary Story of the Largest Covert Operation in History*. New York: Atlantic Monthly Press, 2003. A very lively book that explores U.S. endeavors to drive the Soviets from Afghanistan through the efforts of a colorful, self-destructive congressman.

De Blij, H. J., and Peter O. Muller. *Geography: Realms, Regions, and Concepts 2000*. 9th ed. New York: John Wiley & Sons, Inc., 2000.

DeLong, Candice. *Special Agent—My Life on the Front Lines as a Woman in the FBI*. New York: Hyperion, 2001. Too long on feminist complaints and a bit dated, but a solid account of what's wrong with the FBI.

Douglas, John, and Mark Olshaker. *Mind Hunter: Inside the FBI's Elite Serial Crime Unit*. New York: Pocket Books, 1995. How the FBI catches serial killers. The same methodology could be applied to counter-terror operations—but so far it hasn't been.

Drell, Sidney D., Abraham D. Sofaer, and George D. Wilson, eds. *The New Terror: Facing the Threat of Biological and Chemical Weapons*. Stanford: Hoover Institution Press, 1999. An early warning of what terrorists could do with WMD.

Dresch, Paul. *A History of Modern Yemen*. Cambridge: Cambridge University Press, 2000. Good, recent books on Yemen are hard to find. This is one.

Elshtain, Jean Bethke. *Just War Against Terror: The Burden of American Power in a Violent World*. New York: Basic Books, 2003. A rare pro-interventionist argument.

Emerson, Steven. *American Jihad: The Terrorists Living Among Us*. New York: The Free Press, 2002. An excellent account of sleeper cells within America and the blindness of the American establishment in the 1990s.

Esposito, John L. *Unholy War: Terror in the Name of Islam*. New York: Oxford University Press, 2002. The consensus, establishment view on radical Islam.

Farah, Douglas. *Blood from Stones: The Secret Financial Network of Terror*. New York: Broadway Books, 2004. Good reporting from West Africa.

Frum, David, and Richard Perle. *An End to Evil: How to Win the War on Terror*. New York: Random House, 2003. The reviewers wasted their time worrying if evil exists or if it could be ended. They should have actually read this fascinating book.

Geraghty, Tony. *Who Dares Wins: The Special Air Service—1950 to the Gulf War*. London: Time Warner Paperbacks, 1992. A classic account of British special forces.

Gertz, Bill. *Breakdown: How America's Intelligence Failures Led to September 11*. Washington, D.C.: Regnery Publishing, Inc., 2002. By the dogged *Washington Times* investigative reporter with excellent intelligence sources. The section about "Project Bojinka" in the Philippines is especially good.

Gold, Dore. *Hatred's Kingdom: How Saudi Arabia Supports the New Global Terrorism*. Washington, D.C.: Regnery Publishing,

Inc., 2003. While academic in tone, it provides many fresh details linking the oil kingdom to terrorism. The history chapters are particularly strong.

Griffin, Michael. *Reaping the Whirlwind: Afghanistan, Al Qa'ida and the Holy War*. London: Pluto Press, 2003. Good, fresh details on the Taliban.

Gudjonsson, Gisli H. *The Psychology of Interrogations and Confessions: A Handbook*. West Sussex: John Wiley & Sons, Ltd, 2003. The definitive book on how intelligence operatives get information from prisoners. Recommended to me by David Rose of *Vanity Fair*.

Gunaratna, Rohan. *Inside Al Qaeda*. New York: Columbia University Press, 2002. Thorough and academic, but a must-read. Gunaratna is widely respected in the field, often consulted by intelligence services, and carefully parses his facts. One small example: We learn that bin Laden never got a degree in engineering, as was widely reported.

Halberstam, David. *War in the Time of Peace: Bush, Clinton, and the Generals*. New York: Touchstone/Simon & Schuster, 2002. A good account of the major players during the Clinton years.

Hoffman, Bruce. *Inside Terrorism*. New York: Columbia University Press, 1998. Hoffman is a giant in this field. This book shows why.

Hoge, James F. Jr., and Gideon Rose. *How Did This Happen? Terrorism and the New War*. New York: Council on Foreign Relations, Inc., 2001. Authoritative and thorough.

Hoile, David. *The Search for Peace in the Sudan: A Chronology of the Sudanese Peace Process 1989–2001*. London: European–Sudanese Public Affairs Council, 2002. A pro-Sudan look at the political situation in Africa's largest country.

———. *Images of Sudan: Case Studies in Propaganda and Misrepresentation*. London: European–Sudanese Public Affairs

Council, 2003. A pro-Sudan activist makes his case, with many footnotes.

Holt, P. M, and M. W. Daly. *A History of the Sudan: From the Coming of Islam to the Present Day*. Essex, UK: Pearson Education Limited, 2000. A good history of post-1956 Sudan. Important for understanding the various deep currents in Sudanese politics.

Huntington, Samuel P. *The Clash of Civilizations and the Remaking of World Order*. New York: Simon & Schuster Inc., 1996. Essential for understanding the background of the current debate.

Ismail, Dr. Mustafa Osman. *The New World Order: Law of Might or the Power of Law*. Khartoum, Sudan: Dar Alassalah Publishing House, 2004. The Sudanese foreign minister weighs in with his views of the 1998 strike on the "aspirin factory" in Khartoum.

Jordan, Eric. *Operation Hebron*. London: International Media Group Ltd., 2000. By a former CIA station chief. And fun. Like the Bearden novel, it is not a source for facts. But it helps one enter the mind of an intelligence operative.

Kaplan, Robert D. *The Coming Anarchy: Shattering the Dreams of the Post Cold War*. New York: Vintage Books, 2000. A good tour through many failed states that may yet become cauldrons of terror.

Kessler, Ronald. *The Bureau*. New York: St. Martin's Press, 2002. A good, critical history of the FBI. Excellent sources. Note the website where agents and retirees grumble.

Kessler, Ronald. *The CIA at War: Inside the Secret Campaign Against Terror*. New York: St. Martin's Press, 2003. A good read that is obviously the product of many interviews.

Lance, Peter. *1000 Years for Revenge: International Terrorism and the FBI, the Untold Story*. New York: HarperCollins/ReganBooks, 2003. Lance's account of the O'Neill-Bodine dispute is valuable.

Laqueur, Walter. *The New Terrorism: Fanaticism and the Arms of Mass Destruction*. New York: Oxford University Press, 1999. An unblinking look at the root causes of terror.

Laqueur, Walter, ed. *Voices of Terror: Manifestos, Writings and Manuals of Al Qaeda, Hamas, and Other Terrorists from Around the World and Throughout the Ages*. New York: Reed Press, 2004. A good collection of primary source documents from a variety of terror groups.

Lesser, Ian O., Bruce Hoffman, John Arquilla, David Ronfeldt, and Michele Zanini. *Countering the New Terrorism*. Santa Monica: RAND (Project Air Force), 1999. A collection of essays, some of which are penetrating.

Lewis, Bernard. *The Middle East: A Brief History of the Last 2,000 Years*. New York: Touchstone, 1995. Probably the best single-volume history of the Middle East accessible to the layman.

——. *What Went Wrong?: Western Impact and Middle Eastern Response*. Oxford: Oxford University Press, 2002. A masterful essay about Islam and the West, from one of the premier scholars in the field. A must read.

——. *The Crisis of Islam: Holy War and Unholy Terror*. London: Weidenfeld & Nicolson, 2003. Clear-eyed and well-written, especially chapter three, "From Crusaders to Imperialists."

Lewis, Jon E. *The Mammoth Book of SAS & Elite Forces: Graphic Accounts of Military Exploits by the World's Special Forces*. London: Constable and Robinson, Ltd, 2001. More information on the equipment and technologies of the British special forces.

Mackey, Sandra. *The Iranians: Persia, Islam and the Soul of a Nation*. New York: Plume Books, by the Penguin Group, 1998. A good history of Iran.

Maley, William, ed. *Fundamentalism Reborn?: Afghanistan and the Taliban*. New York: New York University Press, 2001. An interesting pre–September 11 assessment.

Mead, Walter Russel. *Power, Terror, Peace, and War: America's Grand Strategy in a World at Risk*. New York: Borzi by Random House, 2004. A Council on Foreign Relations fellow offers a "Jacksonian" view on foreign policy. Very interesting.

Miller, John, and Michael Stone. *The Cell: Inside the 9/11 Plot, and Why the FBI and CIA Failed to Stop It*. New York: Hyperion, 2003. Probably the single best account so far. Well documented.

Miniter, Richard. *Losing bin Laden: How Bill Clinton's Failures Unleashed Global Terror*. Washington, D.C.: Regnery Publishing, Inc., 2003. My first book on terrorism, with accounts from many Clinton insiders, including counter-terrorism czar Richard Clarke, Secretary of State Madeleine Albright, CIA Director James Woolsey, and others. Includes intelligence documents received from Sudanese intelligence on al Qaeda and rare photos of bin Laden's house, office, and plane.

Moore, Robin. *The Hunt for bin Laden: Task Force Dagger—On the Ground with the Special Forces in Afghanistan*. New York: Random House, 2003. A solid account that deserves more attention than it got.

Moussaoui, Abd Samad. *Zacarias, My Brother: The Making of a Terrorist*. New York: Seven Stories Press, 2003. Originally published in French. An intimate portrait of an ordinary man who became seduced by terror and why.

Mylroie, Laurie. *The War Against America: Saddam Hussein and the World Trade Center Attacks*. Washington D.C.: AEI Press, 2001. The book argues that Iraq was behind the 1993 World Trade Center bombing.

Nojumi, Neanatollah. *The Rise of the Taliban in Afghanistan: Mass Mobilization, Civil War, and the Future of the Region*. New York: Palgrave, 2002. It was first written as a dissertation and still reads that way. But there are many valuable facts and insights.

Oren, Michael B. *Six Days of War: June 1967 and the Making of the Modern Middle East*. New York: Oxford University Press, Inc., 2002. Essential reading.

Parfrey, Adam, ed. *Extreme Islam: Anti-American Propaganda of Muslim Fundamentalism*. Los Angeles: Feral House, 2001. An examination of the messages of radical Islam. Some interesting details.

Patterson, Bradley H., Jr. *The White House Staff*. Washington, D.C.: The Brookings Institution, 2000. Good reference guide to the internal workings of the world's most important residence.

Peters, Rudolph. *Jihad in Classical and Modern Islam: A Reader*. Princeton: Markus Wiener Publishers, 1996. An interesting collection of primary sources.

Pope, Nicole and Hugh. *Turkey Unveiled: A History of Modern Turkey*. London: John Murray, 1997. A reliable, readable history of modern Turkey by a veteran *Wall Street Journal* reporter.

Prados, John. *America Confronts Terrorism: Understanding the Danger and How to Think About It; A Documentary Record*. Chicago: Ivan R. Dee, 2002. A good collection of primary sources.

Qutb, Seyyid. *Milestones*. Damascus: Dar Al-Ilm, undated. By the author of *In the Shade of the Koran*. Qutb is one of the founding philosophers of radical Islam.

Rashid, Ahmed. *The Taliban: The Story of the Afghan Warlords*. London: Pan Books, 2001. Well written, with a reporter's eye for telling detail.

———. *Jihad: The Rise of Militant Islam in Central Asia*. New Haven: Yale University Press, 2002. An essential guide to the region.

Reeve, Simon. *The New Jackals: Ramzi Yousef, Osama bin Laden, and the Future of Terrorism*. Boston: Northeastern University Press, 1999. A very readable reporter's account of the 1993 World Trade Center bombing and its subsequent investigation.

Ressa, Maria A. *Seeds of Terror: An Eyewitness Account of Al-Qaeda's Newest Center of Operations in Southeast Asia*. New York: Free Press/Simon & Schuster, 2003. By a CNN reporter with excellent sources. Especially good on the Philippines and Indonesia.

Reich, Walter. *Origins of Terrorism: Psychologies, Ideologies, Theologies, States of Mind*. Washington, D.C.: Woodrow Wilson Center Press, 1998. A good, general text that pays little direct attention to bin Laden.

Robins, Christopher. *Air America: From World War II to Vietnam*. Bangkok: Asia Books, 2002. The history of the CIA-operated airline. A good contrast with today's CIA. Very readable.

Robinson, Adam. *Bin Laden: Behind the Mask of the Terrorist*. New York: Arcade Publishing, 2001. Hard to verify, especially with respect to bin Laden's teenage years. But interesting.

Sageman, Marc. *Understanding Terror Networks*. Philadelphia: University of Pennsylvania Press, 2004.

Sammon, Bill. *Fighting Back: The War on Terrorism from Inside the Bush White House*. Washington, D.C.: Regnery Publishing, Inc., 2002. The *Washington Times* White House correspondent chronicles the early days of Bush's war.

Scarborough, Rowan. *Rumsfeld's War: The Untold Story of America's Anti-Terrorist Commander*. Washington, D.C.: Regnery Publishing, Inc., 2004. A *Washington Times* reporter takes a fresh look at Rumsfeld.

Sciolino, Elaine. *Persian Mirrors: The Elusive Face of Iran*. New York: Touchstone/Simon & Schuster, 2000. A well-written history.

Sifaoui, Mohamed. *Inside Al Qaeda: How I Infiltrated the World's Deadliest Terrorist Organization*. New York: Thunder's Mouth Press, 2003. A Luxembourg journalist, born in Algeria, worms his way inside an al Qaeda cell. An interesting perspective that reveals how terrorists are drawn in and how tawdry their lives truly are.

Silvers, Robert B., and Barbara Epstein, eds. *Striking Terror: America's New War*. New York: The New York Review of Books, 2001. A good anthology of writing from the Left.

Smucker, Philip. *Al Qaeda's Great Escape: The Military and the Media on Terror's Trail*. Washington, D.C.: Brassey's, Inc., 2004. A *Christian Science Monitor* reporter tells an engaging story.

Stern, Jessica. *Terror in the Name of God: Why Religious Militants Kill*. New York: HarperCollins Publishers, 2003. A Harvard professor takes a steely-eyed look at radical Islam. Well documented.

Verton, Dan. *Black Ice: The Invisible Threat of Cyber-Terrorism*. Emeryville: McGraw-Hill/Osborne, 2003. The definitive book on the subject. To those who say cyber-terror will never be a threat, I say read "Black Ice."

Walker, Martin. *The Iraq War: As Witnessed by the Correspondents and Photographers of United Press International*. Washington, D.C.: Brassey's Inc., 2004. A good collection of UPI articles on the war.

Weaver, Mary Anne. *A Portrait of Egypt: A Journey Through the World of Militant Islam*. New York: Farrar, Straus and Giroux, 2000. Beautifully written and penetrating, by a writer who lived in Egypt during the pivotal late 1970s.

————. *Pakistan: In the Shadow of Jihad and Afghanistan.* New York: Farrar, Straus and Giroux, 2002. A well reported account. The bits about Bhutto and Musharif are very interesting.

Weiss, Murray. *The Man Who Warned America: The Life and Death of John O'Neill, the FBI's Embattled Counterterror Warrior.* New York: HarperCollins/ReganBooks, 2003. By a distinguished police reporter who knew O'Neill well. Very readable with many fresh facts.

West, Bing, and Major General Ray L. Smith. *The March Up: Taking Baghdad with the 1st Marine Division.* New York: Bantam Dell, 2003. Two Vietnam-era commanders ride along with the troops. Incidentally demolishes the comparisons between the Iraq and Vietnam Wars.

Williams, Paul, L. *Al Qaeda: Brotherhood of Terror.* New York: Alpha, 2002. An early account. The description of bin Laden rejoicing at the 1993 World Trade Center bombing is a first.

Woodward, Bob. *Bush at War.* New York: Simon & Schuster, 2002. The Pulitzer Prize winner spent three hours with Bush and interviewed all of the other principals. A must read.

————. *Plan of Attack.* New York: Simon & Schuster, 2004. As always, excellent fly-on-the-wall material from inside the White House.

INDEX